MARKETING
FUNDAMENTALS
FOR FUTURE PROFESSIONALS

D1571438

MARKETING
FUNDAMENTALS
FOR FUTURE PROFESSIONALS

VERSION 1.1

By Bruce Robertson

San Francisco State University

Bassim Hamadeh, CEO and Publisher
Jennifer Allen, Senior Acquisitions Editor
Carrie Montoya, Revisions and Author Care
Sean Adams, Project Editor
Emely Villavicencio, Senior Graphic Designer
Luiz Ferreira, Senior Licensing Specialist
Natalie Piccotti, Director of Marketing
Kassie Graves, Vice President of Editorial
Jamie Giganti, Director of Academic Publishing

First published in the United States of America in 2019 by Cognella, Inc.

Printed in the United States of America

ISBN: 978-1-5165-3847-8 (pbk) / 978-1-5165-9349-1 (al) 978-1-5165-3848-5 (br)

www.cognella.com   800-200-3908

CONTENTS

WHAT IS THE DEAL WITH THIS BOOK?

INTRODUCTION

This is a textbook for a college-level Principles of Marketing course. The typical marketing textbook is around 600 pages long and loaded with colorful examples illustrating the many concepts associated with the discipline. Such a textbook has to be revised every couple of years because the examples go out of date even when the principles they illustrate are essentially the same. So what is the deal with this book? It's about half that long and doesn't have any color at all.

There are three reasons why I wrote this book. The first reason is that I've been teaching Principles of Marketing for 18 years and have seen more than 30,000 students in various incarnations of the class. All that time, I've been looking for a bare-bones text that covers the language and theories associated with marketing without all of the bells and whistles. The reality is that very few students actually read a "Principles of Marketing" textbook cover to cover. A significant number choose not to buy the text in the first place. I didn't want my students to have to pay for a lot of examples they weren't going to use. So I wrote a shorter, concise marketing text that covers all of the topics you would expect to find in a Principles of Marketing Course. Hopefully, this will be easier for students to read and easier for students to buy.

The second reason is that I ended up working in sales and marketing for a number of years before being able to go back to school to pick up an MBA degree. During that time, I had to rely on the marketing I learned as part of my undergraduate program. I found that a lot of what I learned in school had application in the "real world" and having a Bachelor's degree in Marketing helped me in my career. There were other topics that came up on the job that I wish had been covered in school, or, at least, I wish I had been paying attention when the subject came up in class.

As part of the development process for this book, I conducted a series of focus interviews with marketing professionals at various stages of their careers. The purpose of these interviews was to help ensure that the content in this book is relevant to what is happening in the field for people beginning their professional careers. Topics covered in these interviews included career paths, skills and competencies expected of Marketing graduates, and the role of college in developing these competencies.

In this book, I've emphasized the practical side of marketing principles. In appearance, the book looks more like a marketing handbook than a marketing textbook. It is designed that way to encourage graduates to hang on to it and use it as a resource as they begin their careers. Many times, I have former students contact me asking for lecture notes or videos from class. They remember a topic being covered in class and find that they are being asked to use the topic on the job.

The third reason is that there are areas in the field of marketing where things are rapidly changing, and there are other areas in the field of marketing that have remained essentially unchanged since their discovery. Students using Maynard and Beckman's *Principles of Marketing* 5th Edition[1] in 1952 would find that many of the principles they learned 60 years ago are still valid. On the other hand, they would be clueless about search engine optimization or sales force automation.

With that in mind, I've taken a flexible, modular approach when writing this book. The book consists of 100 individual topics organized into 23 chapters. Each topic is more or less self-contained. This allows us to update the topics that need updating without having to revise the entire book. This allows for cost-effective, frequent, partial revisions.

I hope you will find this to be an informative and affordable resource to help you discover and understand marketing principles and to help you apply those principles over a long and successful career.

(ENDNOTES)

1. Maynard, Harold H., and Theodore N. Beckman, 1952, *Principles of Marketing*, New York: The Ronald Press Company, revised by Theodore N. Beckman with William R. Davidson.

THE PROFESSIONALS' PERSPECTIVE

A special thank you to the Marketing professionals who participated in focus interviews in support of this book. They were generous in sharing their time and experience in order to help you succeed as you launch your career. Throughout the book, you will find excerpts from these interviews relating to career development, skills and competencies needed to be successful in marketing, and using the college experience to prepare for a successful career.

Ted Church
Principal and Founder
Anthem Branding

Julie Clarke
Senior Manager, Integrated
Marketing
Xilinx

Lauren Nguyen Cohen
Director, Marketing
Sapient

Neil Cohen
Adjunct Professor, Marketing
San Francisco State University

Beverly Connelly
Marketing Executive
Entrepreneur

Grant Doster
CEO
Doster Training and
Consulting, LLC

Anadelia Fadeev
Demand Generation Manager
ToutApp

Justin Garrett
Vice President, Brand
Marketing
JPMorgan Chase & Co.

Todd Harvey
Senior Vice President,
Consumer Marketing
Activision

Kevin Heung
Senior Manager, Paid Social
Marketing
Uber

Justin Keller
Senior Marketing Director
Whil Concepts

Kathryn Pellegrini Inglin
Presidio Trust

Marian Kwon
Co-founder
Epic Sky

Greg Macchia
Founder/CEO
Clean Conscience, LLC

Lauren Messmer
Co-owner
Director of Business Strategy
MeetGeraldine, LLC

Steven H. Pollyea
Corporate Marketer
Not-for-profit Volunteer

Robin Quattlebaum

Michael Phillips
SVP of Technology &
Innovation
Level Studios

Ariana Raftopoulos
Integrated Marketing Specialist
Xilinx

Felicia Terwilliger
Growth Strategy and Business
Development
Truly Wireless

Andy Wiedlin
Internet Executive & Advisor

OVERVIEW

CH01

Why would anyone want to study marketing? There are lots of reasons. First and foremost (and the reason that you probably bought this book) is that marketing is an important business function. Every business needs a marketing perspective. Marketing may or may not be done by a "marketing professional," but the basic marketing activities need to happen in order for a business to be successful. Because of that, principles of marketing classes are required in almost every business college in the United States.

But marketing can be much more than that. In the developed world, we live in a consumer culture. Understanding marketing fundamentals can help us negotiate the social structure and entertainment opportunities available to us. In addition to being an important business function, marketing fundamentals are skills we can use in our everyday lives. Drawing on lessons learned from economics and social psychology, marketing helps us understand what people want and how they decide to get it.

There are two areas in particular where marketing principles can help you be successful in life: managing your career and personal relationships. Getting a job is a selling situation if ever there was one. You need to understand what a potential employer is looking for and develop a "product" (you) they would want to "buy" (hire you). After you have been hired, marketing fundamentals will help you manage your career. Identifying opportunities and creating solutions are a path to promotion. Using marketing for personal relationships is less obvious but equally effective. Successful relationships come from matching the right product (you) with the selected target market (significant other).

1.1 WHAT IS MARKETING?

Marketing is a word that means different things to different people. For some people, marketing is going to the grocery store every week. For others, marketing means selling something. In business, the term "marketing" could refer to the marketing discipline or it could refer to identifying potential customers for the sales force. In her blog, *Actionable Marketing Guide,* Heidi Cohen identified 72 definitions of marketing used by experienced practitioners in various specialties (http://heidicohen. com/marketing-definition/). Because there can be so many interpretations of the word "marketing," let's take a moment to talk about the definition of marketing we will be using for the rest of this book.

The American Marketing Association defines **marketing** as *the activity, set of institutions, and processes for creating, communicating, delivering, and exchanging offerings that have value for customers, clients, partners, and society at large* (2013). This is a good starting place, and it assumes you understand what all of these terms mean in a business context. We'll spend a lot of time dealing with the processes for creating, communicating, and delivering offerings in the first part of this book. It may be worthwhile to clarify some of the other terms in this definition. Let's take a closer look at value, exchange, stakeholders, and markets.

> "[In college] I always thought of marketing as being one dimensional. When I walked into my new job—marketing lives in everything and it's such a crucial part of your brand if you're in a saturated market. How do you differentiate yourself? How do you get your message to the right person at the right time—the least cost and the highest conversion rate? There's an omni approach to all of these things."
>
> **Felicia Terwilliger**

Value

How do you create value? We start with the concept of utility—utility in the economic sense of being useful. In marketing, **utility** is the usefulness or the **benefit** that a customer receives when he or she uses your product. There are different kinds of utility—things you can use to increase the benefit a customer receives from using your product. Four widely recognized types of utility include form, place, time, and possession. It might be helpful to think of it in terms of a commonly used product, let's say, a cup of coffee. Do you use a cup when you drink coffee? That would be form utility. Do you drink it in the morning? Time utility. Do you brew it at home, or do you stop at a nearby coffee shop on the way to work? Place utility. Do you drink it all by yourself, or do you share it? Possession utility.

Other types of utility can be more subtle. For example, information utility is the benefit you receive from knowing things that other people don't know. In the workplace, knowledge is power. Image utility is the benefit you get from socially consumed products—that is, products you use in the company of others. In our culture, image utility is a very powerful phenomenon. For many products, especially luxury products or status symbols, the real benefit is that others see us using the product rather than in the product itself.

So how do you know if what you do is a benefit for the customer? You may have heard talk about meeting customer needs. From a psychological perspective, a need is a perceived lack of something. More formally, a **need** is the difference between an actual state and a desired state. Some needs are stronger than others. If you drop your cell phone in a puddle, you need a new cell phone. Right now. If you have a toothache, you may want to think about going to the dentist sometime, maybe, if it doesn't get better, let's give it a couple of weeks. In marketing, while we talk about satisfying customer needs, we are really talking about satisfying customer wants. A **want** is a need in the context of cultural and social influences. For example, your basic need may be you are thirsty, but what you want (and what you buy) is a bottle of Fiji® water. You will rarely hear professional marketers talk about satisfying customer wants. We talk about satisfying customer needs. To be successful in creating value for customers, you need to understand both the basic need you are trying to satisfy as well as the cultural and social influences that will determine the customer's final selection.

Features vs. Benefits

You, as the manufacturer, get to decide what goes into the product. From a marketing perspective, it is helpful to think in terms of product **attributes**—features or qualities that are an inherent part of the whole, which we'll simply call **features** for the purposes of this discussion. You have complete control over the features that go in to your product. You have no control over how potential customers will react to the features you build into your product.

Theodore Levitt of the Harvard Business School illustrated the difference between features and benefits with a drill analogy—people don't buy quarter-inch drill bits because they want a drill bit, they buy the ability to make quarter-inch holes.[1] It is the hole, not the drill that provides a benefit to the customer. This is an important distinction. Customers are selfish. They only buy something if there's something in it for them. It is easy to get caught up in internal discussions around how many features a product should have and lose sight of the benefit the customer expects. For proof of this you need look no further than the remote control for a modern television set. There are so many buttons that you can't find the ones that you want to use—on/off, volume, channel. Who knows what those other buttons do.

Which brings us back to value. Now that we understand needs and benefits, we can talk about value. **Value** is a function of the benefits received from a product and the costs associated with obtaining that benefit: value = f(benefits, costs). If the benefits received are greater than the costs to acquire the benefit, the offering has positive value. So far, that relationship is pretty straightforward. However, in marketing, perception is everything. Value is not simply a function of benefits and costs; perceived value is a function of perceived benefits versus perceived costs: perceived value = f(perceived benefits, perceived costs). Take shopping for shoes as an example. For some people, shopping for shoes is a chore. Shopping is part of the cost of the shoes. For other people, shopping for shoes is an enjoyable experience. Shopping is part of the benefit of the shoes. The behavior is the same, but the perception of that behavior can be radically different and have a significantly different impact on the customer's perception of value. Satisfaction is the customer's evaluation of whether or not the product/offering provided the expected benefits.

Exchange

There are three ways customers satisfy a need with a product. They can make it. They can steal it. Or they can buy it. An exchange happens when they buy it. *Merriam-Webster* defines an **exchange** as the giving or taking of one thing in exchange for another.[2] Marketing can only happen when there is an exchange. The basic unit of exchange is a **transaction.** This implies that exchanges should be win-win situations. To be more specific, there are five conditions necessary for a transaction to occur:

1. **You need two or more parties.** You can't exchange with yourself.
2. **Each side needs to have something of value to offer.** This is where perceptions are important. No two people will perceive a specific object to have the same value. Economists call this marginal utility. Because of the differences in perceived value, it is possible to create win-win transactions.
3. **There needs to be a means of communication.** You can't determine the relative value of things and negotiate a transaction unless you can communicate with the other party.
4. **Participation in the transaction has to be voluntary.** When participation isn't voluntary, we call it theft.
5. **It must be appropriate to deal with the other party.** Not everyone who wears a red shirt in a Target® store is an employee authorized to ring up your purchase. There are also legal limitations on who might participate in certain transactions. For example, most contracts made with minors are not legally binding.

Although a transaction is the basic unit of exchange, transactions don't happen in a vacuum. Every transaction is influenced by the individual's history. For example, I once had a bad experience with curry at a Chinese restaurant. Since then, I won't order curry in a Chinese restaurant. Even if it is the first time we've ever purchased a product, a transaction is influenced by our years of experience buying things.

For example, would you consider buying an automobile at Wal-Mart®? No? Why not? You know Wal-Mart will have low prices and that automobiles are expensive, but you don't believe that Wal-Mart is the right place to buy a car.

Relationships

It is unusual for a business to have just one transaction with a customer. It is much more common for a business to have multiple transactions with a customer over time. This is called a customer relationship. Almost all B2B (business to business) marketers and most consumer-oriented businesses think in terms of **relationship marketing**. In this situation, each individual transaction is considered in the context of the larger relationship. Looking at the **lifetime value of a customer**, allows businesses to take a longer-term perspective looking at the anticipated profit from a customer relationship rather than trying to maximize the gain on each individual transaction. With this longer-term perspective, a business might even be willing to lose money on a specific transaction in order to build or maintain a long-term profitable relationship with the customer.

Think about situations where a purchase is a one-time situation. With no expectation of future business and no need to worry about the business's reputation, what is the incentive to treat the customer fairly? When you think about the businesses that have the worst reputations for dealing honestly with customers, they are usually one-time transactions.

From a relationship perspective, the total lifetime value of all customers, or **customer equity**, is an important indicator of the sustainability of a business. Customer equity can be increased by acquiring new customers, by retaining existing customers who might otherwise have left, and by providing additional products to existing customers or increasing "share of wallet." The product/market growth matrix (Chapter 21.3) describes the four basic approaches to increasing sales.

> "Sometimes I feel that the things I learned at business school were not relevant to working in the real world. The most important ingredients, for me, to doing well at work have to do with: being able to collaborate with different groups of people, communicating effectively, and being willing to roll-up your sleeves and get your hands dirty."
>
> Marian Kwon

Stakeholders

Who benefits from marketing? In a successful business, customers benefit, or they wouldn't be your customers. In fact, the first question in marketing is: "Who is the customer?" But customers aren't the only people who benefit from marketing activity. There needs to be a financial return to the investors. Employees need to make a living wage, or there will be nobody available to make the customers happy. Likewise, we need our suppliers, distributors, and other partners to be successful if we are going to be successful.

The **stakeholder** concept recognizes that in order for a business to enjoy long-term success, sometimes called sustainability, there are other entities that need to benefit (or at least not be harmed) from the marketing activity. Human beings are social animals, and we thrive in a healthy community with a good government, low crime rates, and opportunities for socialization and recreation. The stakeholder concept even extends to the natural environment. A business can't be sustainable if there's no air to breathe or water to drink.

It is important for a business to have mutually beneficial relationships with all of its stakeholders: customers, employees, suppliers, distributors, community, government, environment.

Markets

Since this is a marketing text, it's probably a good idea to be clear about what we mean when we use the term "market." Simply put, a **market** is all of the **potential customers** for your product. In economics, they call this effective demand. So what makes a potential customer? First, in order for someone to be a potential customer, that person needs to see a benefit from using your product. This may seem obvious; however, it is hard for some people to admit that there may be people who would never want to buy their product.

Just because someone perceives a benefit in your product, it doesn't make them a potential customer. In order to convert a potential customer into an actual **customer**, there needs to be a transaction. That means a potential customer needs to have the resources necessary to make the exchange happen. For example, even though you might really, really want to own a luxury car, such as a Ferrari, you might not be able to afford it. Even if you could afford it, you may not be willing to spend that much money on a car. And even if you were willing to spend that kind of money, you might not have the authority to do so because you are a wealthy minor and your trust officer needs to approve all major purchases. To put it simply, a potential customer is someone who perceives a benefit in your product and has the money, time, willingness, and authority to make the purchase.

Marketing is a Moving Target

The marketing discipline has evolved over time. At the beginning of the industrial era marketing was less important than achieving economies of scale. This "pro-duction orientation" made products affordable for the masses and assumed that there was a ready demand for these products. At some point, the ready demand was satisfied and people needed to be encouraged to buy. With a "sales orientation," the key to success was to create demand for existing products through personal selling. As markets became saturated and customers had many options for satisfying their needs, the successful companies adopted a "marketing orientation," where the key to success was identifying market segments and creating need satisfying offerings for each segment.

Today, the marketing concept focuses on identifying and satisfying customer needs to ensure a business's long-term profitability. Continued evolution in technology and social structure suggests that in the future, successful businesses might adopt a "relationship orientation"—focusing on the customer experience; or perhaps a "stakeholder orientation"—where the focus is on sustainability and healthy stakeholders; or even a "digital orientation"—using technology to understand and to develop relationships with customers.

1.2 WHAT DO MARKETERS DO?

The major focus of this book is to help you understand the language and theories used in the marketing discipline—in other words, the fundamentals. In addition, we hope you see how these principles can work for you in your business, your career, and even your personal life. The rest of this book is organized around the major activities associated with the marketing discipline: listening to the market, creating need-satisfying offerings, and developing successful marketing programs.

Listen to the Market

In order to be successful, marketers need to understand the capabilities of all areas of the business, not just marketing. In addition, they need to understand the customers, competitors, and the business environment in order to identify and exploit lucrative opportunities. Because of this, marketers tend to be "boundary spanners"; they look beyond the boundaries of their department or business to achieve their goals.

Listening to the market involves scanning the environment to identify opportunities and selecting appropriate target markets. Chapters 1 and 2 look at the characteristics of customers. Chapter 4 looks at gathering and using data to make marketing decisions, and Chapters 5 and 6 deal with identifying and addressing market segments.

Create Need-Satisfying Offerings

Having identified an opportunity, marketers develop products, or offerings, intended to satisfy the needs of the relevant market segments. Chapters 7 through 19 deal with the marketing mix, or tools marketers use to create need satisfying offerings. These are frequently referred to as the four "P's": product, price, place, and promotion.

Develop Marketing Programs

Rarely does a business succeed with just one product. Chapters 20 through 23 present a framework for developing and executing successful marketing programs. This involves managing the mix of products over time, developing and implementing marketing strategies, and measuring results.

Because launching a successful career should be the goal of obtaining a business degree, and because a job search is a natural application of marketing principles, we've included an appendix looking at the use of marketing in your job search.

(ENDNOTES)

1. Levitt, Theodore, 1983, *The Marketing Imagination*, New York/London, The Free Press.
2. http://www.merriam-webster.com/dictionary/exchange. Accessed June 17, 2015.

CONSUMER BEHAVIOR

CH02

Our knowledge of consumer behavior draws heavily on social psychology and on economic theory. While the concepts covered in this chapter are intended to help you do a better job of getting people to buy your products, these same principles apply to many areas of your life beyond buying and selling. This chapter will give you insight into how you and the people you know deal with problems and make decisions; it will also give you an idea of how you may be able to better manage these situations.

2.1 WHAT IS A CUSTOMER?

Simply put, a **customer** is the actual or potential purchaser of your product. A potential customer has a need that could be satisfied by using your product. An actual customer is the end result of a successful marketing program. In order to convert potential customers into actual customers, it is important to understand the process people go through when they make purchasing decisions. There are two principles to keep in mind as we look at the process: buying is problem solving, and people are biased.

Buying Is Problem Solving

People buy things because they have an unmet need. They feel a lack of something in their lives and believe that purchasing a product will fill the void. When you purchase an ice-cold Coke® soft drink on a hot summer day, it is not because you appreciate the beauty of the brown color contrasted with the crystal clear ice; it is because you are really hot and thirsty. As you walk past the refreshment stand with the Coke logo prominently displayed, you remember how refreshing a Coke tasted the last time you were really hot and thirsty.

If we think of it in the abstract, a need is a problem. There is a difference between your actual state (thirsty) and your desired state (not thirsty), and the problem is how to get from point A to point B. This analogy might be useful because the process we use to make buying decisions is the same process we use to solve other problems in our lives.

The way individuals decide to solve their problems by purchasing products is called consumer behavior and is at the heart of the marketing discipline. In this chapter, we focus on the individual customer, or the **consumer**. This is a person who purchases a product for personal enjoyment. Well, maybe not for enjoyment but certainly for personal use. A person may not enjoy having to purchase Benadryl® lotion to treat a poison ivy rash, but the product will help solve the itching problem.

Buying is also decision-making. There are a lot of different ways to quench your thirst. You can have a Diet Coke®, a Cherry Coke®, a bottle of water, a milkshake, a pearl tea, an agua fresca, a sip from a drinking fountain—any of these would solve the problem. So how did you end up purchasing a Coke? Again, the process we use to make a choice from the options available to us applies to more than just marketing.

People Are Biased

In microeconomics, we learned that people carefully consider all the information available to them in order to make the best decision possible. If that were true, all you would have to do is come up with a better product, and people would buy it.

Ralph Waldo Emerson summed this approach up when he said, "If you build a better mousetrap, the world will beat a path to your door."

The truth is that consumers are **biased**. They are neither objective nor impartial when it comes to making decisions such as which product to buy. They don't worry about making the best decision every time. They are simply trying to cope in an increasingly complex world. The good news is that recent work in social psychology and behavioral economics can help us understand how consumers are biased and to take these biases into account in our marketing efforts. A marketer's advice to Ralph Waldo Emerson might be: if you build a better mousetrap, people will beat a path to your door … *if* they know they have mice … *if* they think having mice is a problem … *if* they are aware of your new mousetrap … *if* they believe your mousetrap is better than the one they are already using … *if* they think your prices are fair … *if* it comes with a guarantee … *if* they know how to find your door … *if* you have the mousetrap in stock …

2.2 CONSUMER BUYING PROCESS

Consumer behavior researchers have identified a five-stage **consumer buying process** useful in understanding consumer buying: problem recognition, identify alternatives, evaluate alternatives, decision, and post-purchase behavior (Figure 2.1). People go through this process from top to bottom. You have to recognize you have a problem before you can look for solutions.

Just because you recognize a need, it doesn't mean you will end up making a purchase. You don't go out and buy a new cell phone every time one comes out with a new feature … or do you? You can think of the consumer buying process as a customer funnel with lots of people recognizing they have a need and a much smaller number of people actually making a purchase.

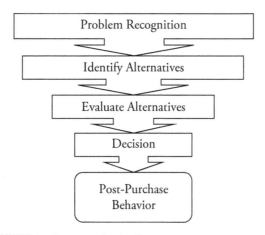

FIGURE 2.1   Consumer buying Process

Limited vs. Extensive Problem Solving

People don't necessarily go through each stage of the consumer buying process every time they make a purchase. If you are hungry for a snack, for example, you may stop by a convenience store and grab the first thing that looks good to you. This is called **limited problem solving**, or automatic purchasing. On the other hand, if you need to purchase a new car, you may spend weeks agonizing over whether or not you really need to replace the car you are driving and then spend a lot of time researching different cars before making your purchase. This is called **extensive problem solving**.

Consumers are much more likely to use limited problem solving than they are to use extensive problem solving when making a purchase. This is because we are **cognitive misers**. A term coined by psychologist Susan Fiske, cognitive miserliness recognizes we spend as little mental effort as possible when solving problems. Limited problem solving helps us make it through the day. If you paid full attention to all of the decisions you have to make in a day—you would never make it out of the front door in the morning.

Since humans are lazy thinkers, there has to be a reason for a person to make the effort needed for extensive problem solving in a purchase decision. Involvement, accountability, and perceived risk[1] are variables shown to have a strong impact on the amount of effort we put into a decision.

Involvement, or ego-involvement, looks at whether the decision is personally relevant to the consumer. When involvement is high, buyers will spend more time and effort to make sure they are making a good decision. They are more likely to use all of the stages of the consumer buying process. When involvement is low, buyers are more likely to use limited problem solving. For example, if a friend were painting his room and asked for your opinion about what color to use, your involvement would be low. If the same friend were painting your room and asked for your opinion about what color to use, your involvement would be high because you would have to live with the color you chose. You would probably put a lot more effort into choosing a color for your room than for a friend's room.

Accountability looks at whether the consumer will be required to explain or justify the decision to someone else. Clearly, people will put more effort into solving a problem if they know others will be looking over their shoulders.

Perceived risk considers how much is at stake if a consumer makes a bad decision—not how much is actually at stake but how much the consumer thinks is at stake. There are both economic and social consequences of a bad purchase. If you spend $25 on a new hat, and it doesn't work out, you're out $25. That's the economic consequence. If you spend $25 on a new hat, and people laugh at you when you wear it in public, what has it cost you? That's the social consequence. Which do you think is worse, the loss of $25 or public humiliation? Many products have a strong **social consumption** element where the benefit we receive from using the product comes from how others react to us when we use the product in public. This is especially true with clothing and luxury goods, or status symbols.

Now you can see why a person might engage in extensive problem solving when purchasing a car rather than when purchasing a candy bar. For the car, involvement is high because safety is at stake; if there needs to be a loan approval, accountability is high; and the social and economic consequences of a bad decision are huge. For the candy bar—who cares?

Stages of the Consumer Buying Process

Now we're ready to look more closely at the consumer buying process. We will describe each stage and what is going on for the consumer at that point. We will also suggest tactics you can use to influence the consumer to purchase your product at each stage of the process. Table 2.1 summarizes these tactics.

Need Recognition

This is also called the problem recognition stage. It is when we first become aware that something is not the way we would like it to be. This awareness can come on suddenly or gradually. If your cell phone breaks, you immediately know you will need a new cell phone. On the other hand, your phone may be working fine, but over time, you are less and less satisfied with it until, at some point, you realize it is time for a replacement. People have been known to "accidentally" break a fully functioning cell phone they are not happy with in order to justify getting a new one.

The stimulus can be internal or external. Hunger is a need that comes on gradually. You finish one meal and are satisfied. Sometime before the next meal, you realize you are hungry again. An internal stimulus for hunger might be your stomach rumbling, letting you know that it's time to eat. An external stimulus for hunger might happen when you walk past a bakery, smell freshly baked bread, and get a craving for something to eat. When a need comes on gradually, an external stimulus (such as the smell of freshly baked bread) can act as a **trigger**, causing a person to suddenly recognize that a problem exists.

Remember, just because we feel a need doesn't mean we'll end up buying something. We can drop out of the process at any time.

One approach to reaching customers at the need recognition stage is to create dissatisfaction with a product the customer is currently using. This might be coming out with a new and improved version of a product, making the customer feel the old product is obsolete. In the fashion industry, this year's fashions replace last year's offerings. Another approach is to provide triggers to stimulate the need in consumers. This can be done with intrusive advertising or by using point-of-purchase displays where consumers are likely to pass (we call these high-traffic areas). Mobile marketing (Chapter 19.5) uses contextual information such as location and search activity from a person's mobile device to infer needs and serve up appropriate ads to initiate the buying process.

Table 2.1 Marketing tactics used in the consumer buying process

STAGE	TACTICS
Problem Recognition	Create dissatisfaction with current products • Planned obsolescence • Fashion Provide *triggers* • Intrusive advertising • Mobile advertising • Point of purchase display
Identify Alternatives	Intrusive advertising Search Engine Marketing Point of Purchase display
Evaluate Alternatives	Personal selling Framing • Emphasize features that favor your product Packaging Website design
Decision	Personal selling Convenience • No money down • Free delivery Limited time offer Guarantee/warranty
Post-Purchase Behavior	Postpurchase advertising After sale service Satisfaction survey Loyalty rewards program

Identify Alternatives

Having recognized a problem, the next step is to figure out our options. We seek a number of alternative solutions that can be thought of as the **awareness set**. The amount of effort people put into identifying alternatives depends on how big the problem is and how difficult it will be to acquire new information. The easiest approach is to go with what we already know. This is called an **internal search,** or a memory-based search. If a person is not happy with the alternatives available after the internal search, then **external search** strategies are used. You may talk to your friends or go on the internet to find information. As a last resort, you may start paying attention to advertisements relating to the problem.

You cannot sell a product to a consumer who doesn't know your product exists. The key in the identify alternatives stage is to make sure your solution is part of the customer's awareness set. This is why intrusive advertising is so important to marketers. You can't expect people to look for information about your product if they don't know it exists. You have to get in their faces. In a retail setting, point-of-purchase displays near the area where similar products are stocked can be an effective way to reach consumers who are looking for a solution for a specific problem. This is where search engine marketing can be very powerful. When you buy the appropriate keyword, consumers doing an internet search related to your product are made aware of your product.

Evaluate Alternatives

We actively consider only some of the alternatives identified in the awareness set. This **consideration set** is a subset of the awareness set. In order to compare alternative products, we need to develop criteria, or features used to make the decision. These are usually based on **attributes**—qualities or characteristics inherent in, or ascribed to, the product. For example, coverage area, ease of use, availability of apps, camera, memory, battery life are all attributes of a smart phone. Different people have different strategies for comparing attributes in a given situation. Some focus in on one specific attribute while others use multiple criteria to make the decision. Many political consumers (voters) use a single-issue strategy to evaluate political candidates. This makes it difficult for politicians to take a stand on a specific issue. They know that every time they take a stand they will lose all of the single-issue voters who disagree with their position on that one issue. It is much safer to acknowledge the issue is important without actually committing to one side or the other.

For people who use multiple criteria, there is a question of how the criteria are weighted. When you look for a new car, which is more important to you, price, styling, resale value, performance, safety? To some people, safety is critical and styling less important. To others, performance is much more important than safety.

The evaluation of an alternative solution is based on the individual consumer's perception of the attribute(s). No two people will have the same reaction to the same attribute. This is where some of the consumer biases start to come into play. First, people may not be aware of (or might not want to admit) their true motivation for buying a product. People buying a BMW might say it is because the car is well engineered and is reliable. They may not be aware that the real reason they are paying $60,000 for a car is because they want others to see them as successful.

Another bias comes from the use of **heuristic** decision-making. Heuristic decision-making uses readily available information based on earlier experiences to make the decision. These can be thought of as rules of thumb, educated guesses, or intuition. Heuristics can be very influential in limited problem solving situations. A typical consumer heuristic is "bigger is better"; when comparing two products, the larger package is perceived as being a better value.

The key to marketing during the evaluate alternatives stage is "framing" or featuring attributes favorable to your product as the basis for comparison. For example, if you were selling coffee that tastes better than everyone else's but is more expensive, you would emphasize taste in your ads. On the other hand, if your coffee were less expensive, you would talk about value in your advertising. The idea is to help the consumer focus on criteria favorable to your product. For many consumer products, the package is a critical tool to help the customer evaluate the product. The quality of the package plays a heuristic role—a well-designed, full-color package suggests a higher-quality product. In an online setting, the look and feel of the website has an impact on how the product is perceived. Labeling provides customers with information they need to make a decision. Finally, it may be helpful to have a salesperson available to help the customer evaluate the alternatives. This is especially true for expensive or complicated products.

Decision

Having decided that one of the alternatives considered is the best solution, the customer needs to be able to complete the transaction. This is where availability and financing come into play. If your product is not available at the time of purchase, customers using limited problem solving may decide not to make the purchase or buy something else. For expensive purchases, consumers may feel unable to afford the product or may procrastinate, postponing the purchase decision until later. Creating a sense of urgency may help the customer to make a decision. Financing can help make the product affordable by spreading the cost over several monthly payments.

In addition to evaluating the attributes of the product, a consumer is likely to evaluate the business selling the product (what is its reputation, is it a local business) when it comes time to make the decision.

The key to marketing to consumers during the decision phase is to make the transaction as convenient as possible (sometimes called, "reducing friction"). Minimize the paperwork associated with the transaction. Make financing available if appropriate, and make sure the customer can get the product home. Free shipping is a nice touch. A salesperson can help identify barriers to completing the transaction and help create a sense of urgency. A guarantee or warranty can help minimize the perceived risk associated with the purchase.

Post-Purchase Behavior

Having bought the product, the consumer will use it. They will either be happy or unhappy with the product, and these experiences will play a role in future purchase decisions. This is one way that brand attitudes are developed (Chapter 9.2).

You may have heard of the term "buyer's remorse." This sometimes happens after a major purchase. You do all of the research, spend a lot of effort making the decision, and immediately after making the purchase, you question yourself and begin to think you did the wrong thing. This is normal human behavior and is based on the psychological principle of **cognitive dissonance**. When there is a difference between who you think you are and who you actually are, there is conflict. To resolve the conflict, you either have to change the perception or change the reality. Because the reality is fixed after you make a decision, buyer's remorse is about changing your perception of yourself.

Imagine you just purchased a car. While you were shopping, you looked at a lot of cars, and the choice came down to either a Lexus™ or a Kia®. After much agonizing, you decided the Kia would be a better choice for you. While not as luxurious as the Lexus, the Kia was a better fit for your budget.

Up until you made the decision, you had been able to picture yourself driving the Lexus. You may have imagined driving it home and seeing the expression on your friends' faces. This had been an attractive possibility for you. Now, having bought the Kia, the possibility of driving a Lexus is gone. Even though you know you did the right thing, for a while, all you can think about are the possibilities that died with the purchase.

This is more likely to happen with high-involvement products and in cases where there were large differences between the alternatives. I mean, if the choice had been between a Lexus and a Mercedes-Benz, it wouldn't have been such a big deal.

Marketers can help minimize buyer's remorse by continuing to communicate product benefits after the sale is complete. This will help the consumer remember why your product was the best choice as he or she adjusts to the reality.

It is also important to build relationships with consumers after they have purchased your product. Satisfaction surveys can help understand consumers' experiences with the product so you can improve your offerings. Post-sale service goes a long way to keep customers satisfied. Loyalty programs offer benefits to repeat customers.

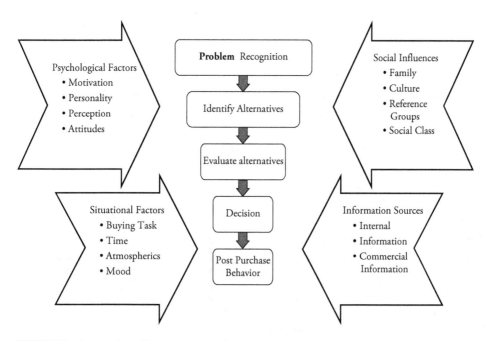

FIGURE 2.2   Factors that affect the consumer buying process

In today's social networked world, many companies are finding it useful to encourage online communities to develop around a product.

2.3 FACTORS THAT INFLUENCE BUYING

Understanding that people go through a similar process when buying products is one piece of the consumer puzzle. Another big piece of the puzzle comes from understanding how each consumer is unique. There are a lot of things going on—psychological factors, social influences, situational factors, and information sources - when we make a purchase decision (Figure 2.2).

Psychological Factors

Each one of us experiences the world in a unique and private way. Our motivations, our personalities, the way we perceive the world, and our attitudes have a powerful impact on our purchasing behavior. Yet these things are invisible to an outside observer. Understanding how these invisible influences shape consumer behavior will make you a more effective marketer.

Motivation

Motivation helps us understand why people do things. Psychologists speak of the difference between where we are and where we want to be as the motivator. Marketers call these differences needs. There are two basic sources of motivation: physiological needs (such as food and shelter) and psychological needs (such as friends and a positive self-image). Some needs are more motivating than others. For example, if you are bleeding, you will take care of the problem right away. On the other hand, if you are unhappy with your current job, you may wait until the right opportunity comes along before doing anything. Abraham Maslow famously described a hierarchy of needs beginning with physiological needs and moving through several stages until reaching the highest-level need—the need for self-actualization (Figure 2.3). He proposed that people have to satisfy their lower-level needs before they can be motivated by higher-level needs. In a consumer culture, the majority of people have enough to eat and a safe place to live. This is why social factors (belongingness and ego needs) can have such a powerful impact on consumer buying.

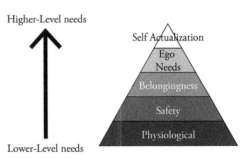

FIGURE 2.3   Maslow's Pyramid

Personality

Personality deals with an individual's self-concept, or the way we see ourselves. Most of us have at least two self-concepts: an actual self-concept, or the way we really see ourselves, and an ideal self-concept, or how we would like to see ourselves. This is important to marketers because in a consumer society, we use products to reinforce our self-concepts. Can you see how influential a Nike® commercial showing fit, healthy people might be to an individual struggling to lose a few pounds? Buying those shoes makes you feel as if you, too, can be a performance athlete.

There has been a lot of work done in the area of personality, and researchers have identified many traits where people may differ. These include traits such as innovativeness, self-confidence, sociability; the list is much too extensive to cover in an introductory marketing text.

Many businesses use the Myers Briggs Personality Inventory (www.myersbriggs. org) as a tool for helping people to understand themselves and to work with each other. This personality test develops a profile based on four dimensions: extrovert/ introvert, sensing/intuition, thinking/feeling, judging/perceiving. Once you have established your profile, there is information about your personality and information about how you interact with other personality types.

Perception

Perception deals with the way we interpret the world around us. Remember people are cognitive misers and do as little thinking as possible to solve a problem. The result is that consumers don't look for the best solution to a problem. They settle for the first solution that works. This leads to subtle but powerful biases in the way we perceive the world. Selective attention, selective interpretation, and selective retention are all examples of this selective perception.

Selective attention means that we ignore things that are present. Take for example the following sentence:

> *Love of money is*
> *is the root of all evil.*

Most people who read this sentence won't notice the word "is" appears twice: at the end of the first line and again at the beginning of the second line. If the problem is to understand the meaning of the sentence, "Love of money is the root of all evil" does the job. No need to put in any more mental effort. You don't need to see the second "is" to understand the meaning of the sentence, so you don't see it. More importantly, you don't know that you missed anything.

Consider the implications of this for your marketing communications. Consumers simply do not see much of what is in front of them, especially if there is no reason for them to pay attention. How many advertisements did you see during your morning commute? On the way home tonight, try to count the number of advertising messages you see. You will be amazed at how many ads are out there. (If you are driving a car, be careful to pay attention to the road while you are counting.)

Selective interpretation means we make assumptions about things based on what we already know and look for things that support our assumptions. This is sometimes called confirmation bias. A common optical illusion illustrates this beautifully. What do you see when you look at the following figure?

Most people describe this as a white triangle on top of three black circles. If you look closely, you can almost see the lines connecting the circles. But they aren't there. There is no triangle. So why do most people see a triangle that isn't there? In elementary school, we learned that a triangle has three angles and three sides. When we see the three angles, we make an assumption that it is a triangle. This requires much less mental effort than trying to describe three black circles with a pie-shaped wedge taken out of each one. Having decided it is a triangle, the brain wants to see three sides to confirm the assumption.

Have you ever remembered someone telling you something and later denied ever having said it? It might be selective interpretation at work. Maybe you heard what you wanted to hear rather than what was actually said. This has powerful implications for marketers. Think about it in the context of green marketing. If people believe that commercial cleaning products are bad for the environment, they will make an assumption that every commercial cleaning product is bad for the environment. It can be difficult for a company like Clorox®, which makes a line of green cleaning products, to overcome these assumptions.

Selective retention recognizes that even our memories are biased. It is easier for us to remember things that are consistent with what we already believe, and we tend to forget things that don't "fit." One theory of memory suggests that we remember things in categories.[2] Say for example, you try a new candy bar, and you hate it. The candy experience gets filed into memory in two categories: "things I have tried" and "things I hate." Over time, the link between the two categories weakens. Maybe a couple of months later you are looking for a candy bar and you notice the one you tried earlier. You search your memory and remember the candy bar in the "things I have tried" category. Having found the candy bar in memory, there is no reason to continue thinking about it, so you don't remember that you didn't like the candy bar. Here another phenomenon called the **familiarity effect** kicks in. As a rule, we like things we are familiar with and dislike things we are unfamiliar with. So, because it's familiar, we try it again!

This is why name recognition is so important to many aspects of marketing. People who don't have a strong opinion about a product will go with the familiar. This is especially true in politics. People who don't know a lot about a candidate will vote for the one whose name is familiar to them.

Perceived risk deals with how people interpret the possible consequences of a decision. While some people deal with risk on a day-to-day basis and are very good at assessing it (just watch the World Series of Poker on television), most of us are not very good at judging risk. Behavioral economists Khaneman and Tversky describe the **risk aversion principle,** which shows people weigh the negative consequences of a decision much more heavily than the positive consequences. "Fear appeals" in advertising succeed by highlighting the negative consequences of a purchase decision (Chapter 17.2).

Attitudes

An **attitude** is a learned predisposition to respond to an object or to a class of objects in a consistently favorable or unfavorable way. Remember, we tend to make assumptions about things based on what we already believe. Attitudes are how we hold many of these beliefs. You can't just have "attitude." An attitude needs to be about something. And attitudes have to be either positive or negative. You can have a strong attitude or a weak attitude, but you can't have a neutral attitude. There are two components to an attitude: a cognitive component, composed of facts and beliefs; and an affective, or emotional component.

You aren't born with attitudes; they have to be learned. You develop attitudes about products through experiences with the product, or post-purchase evaluation; and by observing others' reactions to the product. Attitudes tend to be stable, but they can change over time.

The reason this is important to marketers is because the concept of branding (which we will talk about in Chapter 9.1) is based on developing attitudes about your product. Think about your favorite brand. How did you come to like it? How long have you liked it? Do you have an emotional connection to the product? How long would you stay loyal to the product if you started having bad experiences?

Social Influences

The people around us can have a profound influence on our purchase decisions. We learn from observing others. Some of the major social influences on buying behavior are family, culture, reference groups, and social class.

Family

We learn how to be consumers from our families. Studies have shown that children begin to have brand preferences as early as age two, and by the time we are 16 years old, many of the consumption patterns we take with us for the rest of our lives have been formed. These early years are an especially vulnerable time because attitudes are being formed, but our judgment isn't fully developed until our mid-20s (this explains a lot about the decisions teenagers make).

In addition to incubating our consumer desires, families also act together to make some consumption decisions. There are several roles each family member might play in deciding what the family should buy: information gatherer, influencer, decision-maker, purchaser, and user. If you've ever been in a crowded supermarket on a Saturday afternoon, you've probably seen a parent pushing a cart full of influencers and information gatherers (especially when going through the cereal aisle).

Culture

Culture is a set of values, ideas, and attitudes shared among members of a group. As with the family, many patterns of consumption, especially food and fashion, are determined by the culture in which we grew up. Certain rituals (birthdays, bar and bat mitzvahs, quinceañeras, weddings, funerals) can be significant consumption occasions.

A **subculture** is a group of individuals within a larger cultural setting that shares unique values, ideas, and attitudes. It is a way for people to maintain a sense of identity within a larger population. Because people have more freedom to choose the subcultures with which they identify, this can be a powerful opportunity for marketers, who can create products to support this chosen identity. It has been said that everybody is Irish on St. Patrick's Day, and people buy into this subculture by wearing (or consuming) green colored products on March 17.

"Data is half of it. The other half is knowing what to use the data for."

Beverly Connelly

Reference Groups

A **reference group** is an actual or imaginary individual or group that has a significant effect on a person's evaluations, aspirations, or behavior. In other words, we look to other people for cues on how we should live. There are two major kinds of reference groups—opinion leaders and identity groups. **Opinion leaders** are those to whom we look for cues or advice. One kind of opinion leader, called a market maven, is a person you know who is expert about something. These people's opinions are helpful when we buy expensive, complicated products such as computers or cars. Celebrities are another kind of opinion leader. A lot of people admire celebrities and want to be just like them. Having a celebrity endorse your product will appeal to fans of that celebrity. Marketing Evaluations, Inc. publishes a "Q" score, or popularity quotient, that measures the popular appeal of celebrities.[3]

The other type of reference group is an **identity group**. These are people you use to define your personal sense of identity in several ways. Membership groups are people you fit in with. Aspirational groups are people you want to be like. Dissociative groups are people you wouldn't be caught dead with. In a consumer culture, we signal our membership in these groups with socially consumed products such as clothing or accessories. People who claim to be nonconformist frequently demonstrate this nonconformity by using dissociative groups. A person who is against the mass-market consumer culture and corporate America will demonstrate this nonconsumer attitude by purchasing handmade or socially responsible goods. Ironically, anti-consumerism is a consumption decision.

Social Class

Social class refers to the relatively permanent, homogeneous divisions in a society into which people sharing similar values, interests, and behavior can be grouped. The determinants of social class vary from culture to culture. We generally think of social class in terms of an upper class, a lower class, and a middle class. In the United States, social class is largely determined by source of income (inherited wealth vs. earned wealth vs. living paycheck to paycheck), occupation (white collar vs. blue collar), and education (high school degree vs. college degree).

Socially consumed products such as cars, clothing, and even where we choose to live are highly influenced by class considerations.

Situational Factors

While much of what we think about how consumers make purchase decisions is internal and psychological, at some point, a person has to go shopping. The physical experience of shopping has an immediate and powerful impact on purchasing behavior. It doesn't matter how hard you've worked to create a desire for your product if customers can't find it at the store, or if the e-commerce site is down. A rude salesperson can be a real turn off. The buying task, time, atmospherics, and mood are all things that can change dramatically from situation to situation.

Buying Task

The amount of effort a person puts into the buying process depends on the purpose of the purchase. Most of the time, buying is a chore we need to get done. Grocery shopping, running errands, and other chores are routine tasks that beg for limited problem solving. Other occasions call for more extended problem solving. When buying a gift for another person there is a social risk to the gift. That calls for more attention to the purchase. Sometimes, people treat shopping as a form of recreation. Spending Saturday afternoon in a shopping mall is a way to unwind after a hectic week. Retailers need to understand why customers are buying the products offered in order to create the best shopping experience for the customer.

Time

Time has an impact on purchase decisions from both a chronological perspective and from an available time perspective. From a chronological perspective, it makes a huge difference what season of the year or even what time of day it is. There is not a lot of demand for Valentine's Day cards in October, and it is hard to sell breakfast sandwiches in the afternoon. From an available time perspective, the issue is how much time we have available to us. As a rule, people are short of time—the clock is always ticking. We simply don't have enough time to do everything we need to get done. This means consumers are looking for convenience in their transactions and will reward marketers who make finding and buying products simple. Just look at the explosion in the use of online banking as a convenient alternative to ATM machines, which are a convenient alternative to bank tellers in retail banking.

Atmospherics

Atmospherics deals with the environment in which the purchase decision is made. This includes the physical environment (store layout, merchandise signage) and social surroundings (is it crowded? busy? relaxing?). Is the website graphically appealing, fast loading, and simple to navigate? These elements are important in inviting customers into your retail setting. If you have ever walked down a street with lots of retail stores or even strolled through a shopping mall, you can tell just by looking whether or not a particular store has a good "vibe." In December, many stores play holiday music and introduce cinnamon and peppermint scents into the air to get people in a holiday mood. We'll talk about using atmospherics to build a store identity in Chapter 15.6.

Mood

The last situational factor we'll discuss is mood, or how you feel emotionally in the moment. This is probably the most volatile situational factor as your mood can change in a second. Think about it. When you are in a bad mood, nothing tastes good, nothing looks good, and you just want to go home. How do you feel when you are in a good mood … better yet, have you ever fallen in love? Every experience took on a special meaning - our song, our restaurant. Everything was wonderful, and price was no object. This is the difference mood can make.

Employees in service businesses play a critical role in managing customer moods. The Aveda® chain of toiletries plays quiet music and offers you a cup of "relaxing tea" when you step into its stores.

Information

The last major influence on the consumer buying process is the information available to consumers when they make their decision. As discussed earlier, the easiest information to access is information already in memory. In most cases, this is all the information people need to make a decision. However, when consumers do actively seek additional information, they have two sources—social information (from friends) and commercial information (from marketers). Clearly, social information, or word of mouth, is the more persuasive source. This has two implications for marketers. The first is to understand that commercial sources of information (advertising, press releases, websites) are the easiest to use but have a relatively weak influence on consumer buying. As we'll discuss in Chapter 17.2, it takes lots of time and money to build brand awareness using advertising. The second is to recognize the potential of some of the internet-based communication technologies such as social networking, Twitter®, and blogs to bridge the gap between social and commercial sources of information.

(ENDNOTES)

1. Kardes, F. R., 1999, *Consumer Behavior and Managerial Decision Making*, Reading, MA: Addison-Wesley, 144.
2. Wyer R. S., and Srull, T. K, 1989, *Memory and Cognition in its Social Context*, Hillsdale, NJ: Lawrence Earlbaum and Associates.
3. http://www.qscores.com.3.1

BUSINESS MARKETS

CH03

n his book, Marketing Insights from A–Z: Concepts Every Manager Needs to Know,[1] Philip Kotler, currently the S. C. Johnson Distinguished Professor of International Marketing at the Kellogg School of Management at Northwestern University, observes that while the vast majority of marketing activity is from one business to another (B2B), the major focus of "Principles of Marketing" textbooks is on business to consumer marketing (B2C). Marketing educators defend this disconnect by observing that most marketing principles apply regardless of whether the customer is an individual or another business. However, there are significant differences between individuals and businesses, both in the problems they solve with their purchases and with their approach to solving these problems. Given the size of the B2B market, chances are good you will be dealing with other businesses rather than individual consumers at some point in your career.

3.1 WHAT IS A BUSINESS CUSTOMER?

Broadly speaking, the difference between a business customer and an individual consumer is that the business customer doesn't get to personally enjoy the purchase. Business customers would include **industrial customers**—businesses that buy things in order to produce finished goods and components for other businesses to use; **resellers**—businesses that buy things in order to resell them at a profit; and **institutions** such as government, educational, not-for-profit organizations (sometimes called NGOs or non-governmental organizations)—that purchase goods and services to run the organization.

In many cases, the difference between a business purchase and a consumer purchase is why the product was purchased. For example, if you buy a bag of potato chips for a snack, that would be a consumer purchase. If you bought that same bag of potato chips, but rather than eating it as a snack, served it at a sales meeting, it would be a business purchase.

North American Industry Classification System

One way of classifying businesses is to use the North American Industry Classification System (NAICS). The system was developed by the Office of Management and Budget (the largest office within the Executive Office of the President of the United States) as a way to organize statistical information collected by various federal agencies.

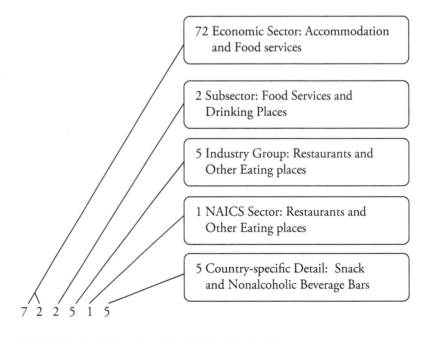

72 Economic Sector: Accommodation and Food services

2 Subsector: Food Services and Drinking Places

5 Industry Group: Restaurants and Other Eating places

1 NAICS Sector: Restaurants and Other Eating places

5 Country-specific Detail: Snack and Nonalcoholic Beverage Bars

7 2 2 5 1 5

FIGURE 3.1   North American Industrial Classification System

The **NAICS** is a six-digit code where the first two digits designate the largest business sector, the third digit designates the subsector, the fourth digit designates the industry group, the fifth digit designates the NAICS industries, and the sixth digit designates the North American Country. Figure 3.1 illustrates the NAICS code for snack and nonalcoholic beverage bars.

The reason this is important is that every five years the US Census Bureau conducts an economic census (www.census.gov/econ/) which provides a wealth of business information organized by the NAICS code. For most industries, you can find information on the number of businesses, number of employees, payroll, and annual revenue. The good news is that this information is available for free, and some of it is available at the zip code level. The bad news is that the information is relatively old—the most recent economic census was published in 2012. Data for the 2017 economic census is collected in 2018 and released starting September 2019. Even though the information is dated, this is still a great place to start developing a plan for a new business.

As an example, suppose you were thinking of opening a coffee shop near the San Francisco State University campus. The economic census could give you a sense of the business landscape to help you make an informed decision. Looking up NAICS code 72 (Accommodation and Food Services) we find in zip code 94132 (the zip code for SF State) that there are 456 establishments employing 6,325 people with an annual payroll of $177 million. A little interpolation gives us an average of 14 employees per establishment and an average annual wage of $27,900. Zeroing in on NAICS code 722515 (Snack and Nonalcoholic Beverage Bars) we find there are seven establishments in the zip code, three of them with one to four employees, two of them with five to nine employees, one of them with ten to 19 employees and one with 20 to 49 employees. Obviously, you would want to do quite a bit more research before investing any money in a coffee shop near campus, but you can see how just a few minutes of research can give you a sense of the business landscape.

3.2 CHARACTERISTICS OF BUSINESS MARKETS

Now that we understand what a business customer is, we can look at some of the ways they are different from an individual consumer. Taking the perspective of a manufacturer hoping to serve this market, let's look at these differences in market structure, the nature of demand, and buying objectives.

Market Structure

There are several ways that the **B2B** market differs from the **B2C** market, some of them obvious, some of them not so obvious. One of the obvious differences is that business transactions tend to be much, much larger than individual purchases. Take groceries, for example. On a weekly trip to the grocery store I might pick up one or two boxes of cereal (unless cereal is on super-sale, in which case I might buy ten or 12 boxes). I buy my cereal from a local reseller—the grocery store. Because I am not the only person who frequents that store, in order to make it possible for me to buy one, two, or even 12 boxes of cereal, the grocer needs to buy hundreds if not thousands of boxes of cereal each week for the store.

It also follows that there are fewer customers in the B2B market than there are in the consumer market. In all likelihood, the store where I bought my cereal is part of a national chain with hundreds or thousands of stores. It would be very inefficient to have each individual store manager handling all of the buying for all of the products for each store. It makes more sense to have a professional buyer managing the cereal purchases for the entire chain. So while there may be millions of individual consumers deciding whether or not to buy a particular brand of cereal, in the business market, there may be only hundreds or thousands of resellers deciding whether or not to buy a particular brand of cereal. In February 2015, the Chain Store Guide (chainstoreguide.com), a market research firm covering the food service industry, listed 3,100 grocery chains and 4,100 individual retail grocers for a total of 7,200 grocery resellers in the United States.

Finally, many industries have a high level of geographic concentration, where a small area accounts for a large share of an industry's activity. For example, Silicon Valley in Northern California has a high concentration of technology companies while the Detroit Michigan area has a high concentration of automotive businesses.

Buying Center

It might be worthwhile to take a moment to talk about just who does the buying in business markets. Unlike individual consumers, business customers buy things for a living. As you can imagine, when your whole career revolves around purchasing, you get pretty good at it. The business buyer is likely to have had specialized training in negotiation, and because a typical buyer looks at a relatively small number of products, the business buyer has a very good understanding of the products available and the reputation of the companies behind these products. Sometimes the B2B buyer knows more about the seller's product than the salesperson does.

It is also common for more than one person to be involved in a business purchase decision, especially with a high-involvement purchase. A **Buying Center** includes all of the people involved in making a business purchase. Membership in the buying center may be relatively stable, or it may change from purchase to purchase as different people have different skills to bring to the table. When approaching a business customer it is important to understand the different roles people in the buying center might be playing. An *initiator* is the person who recognizes the need for a purchase. *Users* are the people who will be using the product, while *influencers* are people who won't be using the product, but will have a say about the kinds of products that are considered. The *decider* is the person who is responsible for making the decision to buy. For a reseller, the decider is probably a professional buyer.

Marketing Yourself

When you are looking for a job, you are marketing yourself to a business customer. It might help your job search if you were able to identify the buying center roles in the company you hope to work for. The initiator is the one who decides there's an opening to be filled. The user is the person who will end up being your manager. Many companies require multiple interviews as part of the hiring process. These interviews allow others in the company (influencers) to get a feel as to whether or not you would make a good colleague. In a job search, the decider is probably the same person as the user. Gatekeepers are any people who keep you from meeting with the people with the authority to hire you. In many large companies, the human resources department plays the role of gatekeeper. Its job is to sort through the thousands of applications received for each opening in order to pass a handful of promising prospects through to the interview process.

Finally, *gatekeepers* are people whose role it is to protect the people inside the company from unwanted attention from people outside the company.

Demand

Because businesses are not buying products for personal satisfaction but are buying products in order to provide a benefit to the end user, the demand for some business products (especially for component parts) is **derived**. The demand for your product does not come from your business customer, but from the ultimate consumer your business customer serves. Take spark plugs, for example. If you have purchased an automobile, a lawn mower, a snow blower (for those who live in the North), or anything with an internal combustion engine, a spark plug was included. As a spark plug manufacturer, my sales forecast depends on the sales forecast for automobiles, lawn mowers, snow blowers, etc. Because spark plugs are only useful as a component in an internal combustion engine, there is nothing I can do to increase demand for spark plugs per se.

It also follows that since demand is derived, demand (especially for component products) is inelastic. If you remember from your microeconomics course, inelastic demand means that large changes in price have a small impact on the quantity demanded. Let's go back to the spark plug example. The average new car costs around $30,000. A car manufacturer may pay less than a dollar for a spark plug, so the manufacturer's cost for spark plugs in a six-cylinder car would be around six dollars. If the price of the spark plug doubles—a 100% increase in price—what impact would that have on the demand for cars? Well, the spark plugs went from being .0002% of the cost of the car to being .0004% of the cost of the car. The only way a car customer would even notice that the cost of the spark plugs increased would be if the manufacturer chose to pass that price increase through to the customer.

Even then, the increased cost would be negligible—not enough to deter a customer from buying the car. Similarly, a decrease in the cost of spark plugs—even if we gave them away for free—would not influence people to buy more cars.

I don't want to minimize the importance of price in B2B products. The point is that when demand is derived and when demand is inelastic, negotiating the price of spark plugs is much more important in the transaction between the spark plug manufacturer and the automobile manufacturer than it is in the transaction between the automobile dealer and the end user.

Buying Objectives

Another more subtle difference between individual consumers and business customers involves what they hope to accomplish with the purchase. As we discussed in Chapter 2, individual consumers may not be clear about their motives and may not be aware of some of the hidden costs associated with making a transaction. A professional buyer recognizes that purchasing is a business cost and needs to be minimized.

Minimizing cost is much more than negotiating the lowest price. Business customers are much more likely to recognize non-price factors such as ordering cost, handling charges, inventory costs, transportation costs, return policies, and quality. For example, the cost of replacing a faulty spark plug that has been installed in a new automobile is an order of magnitude larger than the cost of buying a spark plug that will not need to be replaced.

Many college students, especially students who don't have a lot of experience working in corporate America, tend to think of corporations as large buildings, product brands, and busy executives. It is important to understand that when you deal with a business, you don't deal with a corporation. You deal with a person—an individual—a human being with all of the foibles of a human being—who works for the corporation. While the primary objective is to minimize the cost of purchasing, there may be personal objectives, such as a desire to look good in order to earn a promotion, a desire to be liked, or other personal idiosyncrasies, playing a role in the decision.

3.3 BUSINESS BUYING PROCESS

As we discussed in Chapter 2.2, the consumer buying process is a template for how human beings solve problems. This problem-solving process is just as valid for solving business problems as it is for solving individual problems. Pretty much everything associated with individual purchases applies to business purchases. However, there are issues at each stage of the buying process that apply specifically to business customers.

Problem Recognition

For business buyers, it makes a big difference whether this is a first-time purchase or whether you have purchased the product before. For first-time purchases, sometimes called a new buy, or **new task buying,** business buyers are more likely to use extensive problem solving. This is especially true when the purchase is expensive or complex, such as choosing an internet security firm to protect the company's databases. From a marketing perspective, the earlier you can become involved in a first-time purchase, the more likely you are to have a positive influence on the results of the decision. This is why networking is so important in the business world. It is through your personal contacts that you are likely to get early awareness of a selling opportunity. Ideally, if you have a personal relationship with the person facing a new task buy, you may be able to frame the decision in a way favorable to your product. For example, if you work for a cybersecurity firm and discover a friend is looking to implement an internet security solution, you might be able to give your friend some pointers about what to look for and what to avoid when hiring an internet security firm.

When a business has purchased a product before, sometimes called a rebuy, the company already has experience buying the product and is less likely to use extensive problem solving. For routine purchases, or a **straight rebuy,** there is no reason to pay a highly trained person to negotiate a deal that has already been made. Businesses today are likely to automate routine purchases. With automated purchases, the buyer and seller will meet periodically to negotiate the terms of the deal, but the actual ordering and reordering is automatic.

A **modified rebuy** occurs when a business has experience purchasing a specific item but for some reason, needs to pay attention to the transaction. This may be because there is a reason to be dissatisfied with the seller's current product, because the requirements of the business have changed, or maybe because a new competitor has entered the market. This is the reason salespeople continue to call on business customers even when the customer is not buying from them. There is always a chance that dissatisfaction with the competitor's product has created the opportunity for a modified rebuy. In his book, *Swim with the Sharks without Being Eaten Alive,*[2] Harvey Mackay describes a "strong second-place" strategy, where if you stand in second place in enough lines long enough, sooner or later you are bound to move up to first place in some of them.

> "The world's just gotten a lot smaller because of the internet. I think on a global level now versus when I was buying media for nationwide programs. It's a very different mindset to think global. I have to be cognizant of all the things that pertain to certain regions of the world … I get up at 6 in the morning, 5:30 actually, I wake up and check my mail because in the six hours I've been sleeping a whole day has gone by."
>
> **Lauren Nguyen Cohen**

Identify Alternatives

Business customers are much more likely to be proactive in seeking solutions to their problems. Rather than simply shopping for a product, a business might publish a set of product specifications and invite other businesses to develop products that meet those specifications. This RFP (request for proposals) often includes the quantity requested and delivery schedules. Going one step further, some companies may ask for competitive bids in their RFP. In a competitive bidding situation, a company might invite several businesses to bid for a contract, with the winning contract going to the lowest bidder. The downside is that the winning bidder is held to the terms of the contract even if some costs had not been considered at the time the bid was submitted and may end up losing money on the contract.

Evaluate Alternatives

Business buyers are also more likely to consider nonfinancial costs when evaluating alternative solutions. There may be a reciprocal arrangement where a company's vendors for some products may be customers for other products. Keeping that relationship healthy may be an important consideration in the buying process. A business buyer needs to be concerned about whether a potential vendor has the production capacity and technical capability to deliver an acceptable product. It is a good business practice to have more than one potential supplier for a product. That way you are not at the mercy of your supplier if there is an emergency or a sudden price increase. Some large companies handle this by having an approved **vendors list** (or approved bidders list for competitive bidding situations). Local managers would have the authority to purchase from the approved vendors list without having to go through a formal approval process.

 While price will always be an important factor for business buyers, price is not the only criterion for making the purchase decision. Actually, business buyers are looking for the lowest cost, not necessarily the lowest price. They recognize there are costs in addition to price such as financing, inventory, and the cost of repairing the damage caused by defective components. In addition to price, service is an important consideration in business purchases. The timing of deliveries and who will be responsible for honoring customer warranties play a role in the decision.

Decision

The actual purchase decision is far more complicated in a business setting than it is for an individual consumer. Unlike consumers, businesses have the option of either building their own solutions or buying a product from someone else. If a proposed solution is likely to generate a competitive advantage, it would make sense for a business to try to create the solution "in-house." On the other hand, in today's highly competitive business landscape, there may be activities or products currently developed in-house that could be supplied more efficiently by an outside supplier. By **outsourcing** noncritical activities, a business can focus its resources on the activities and products that are most valuable to the company.

Having made the decision to outsource and purchase a solution from an outside vendor, there are some other things to consider. Do you buy the product or lease it? You'll need to negotiate specific terms of the purchase, including financing, payment schedule, delivery dates, etc. Many times, businesses will create a formal contract that lays out in detail the terms of the deal and is signed by all parties. Although some verbal contracts are legally binding, in business it is always good to "get it in writing." Sometimes, rather than negotiating a formal contract, businesses will generate a MOU (memorandum of understanding), which details the key points in the agreement. Even when there isn't a document signed by both parties, you can create a written record by simply sending a communication (such as an email, or memo) that summarizes what you believe was agreed to by yourself and the other party. This gives the other party a chance to correct any misunderstandings.

Post-Purchase Evaluation

While relationships are important in consumer marketing, they are fundamental in B2B. Business purchases tend to be long-term cooperative relationships focused on creating value for the end customer. This recognizes that while not all businesses in the value chain may be selling directly to the end user, all businesses in the value chain play a role in creating need-satisfying offerings for the end user. When there are problems with a B2B product, the problem not only affects the two companies who negotiated the purchase but may also affect the end user. It is important that problems are resolved in a way that, ultimately, doesn't harm the relationship with the consumer.

(ENDNOTES)

1. Kotler, Philip, 2003, *Marketing Insights from A–Z: Concepts Every Manager Needs to Know,* Hoboken, New Jersey: John Wiley & Sons.
2. Mackay, Harvey B., 2005, *Swim with the Sharks without being Eaten Alive,* New York: HarperCollins.

MAKING MARKETING DECISIONS

CH04

No one in their right mind, when faced with a choice that could affect the future of their business, would say, "Which of these alternatives will cost me the most money and do the most harm to my company?" Yet bad business decisions are made every day. The reality is that there is no way of knowing whether a decision is a good business decision or a bad business decision at the time you make it. You only find out whether it was good or bad after you have made the decision and deal with the consequences. The best you can do when faced with two or more alternative courses of action is to make a *defensible* decision. A decision is defensible if you have systematically considered the factors that may affect your decision (which we will discuss in more detail in Chapter 20) and have carefully evaluated the information available to you at the time. In this chapter, we will look at how to use information to make defensible marketing decisions.

4.1 WHAT IS A DECISION?

A business decision is a situation in which you are faced with two or more alternative courses of action and make a conscious choice to select one alternative. If there is only one possible course of action, then there is no decision to be made. Marketers are called upon to make many decisions every day. Most of them are minor decisions with relatively minor consequences (i.e., "Which restaurant would be an appropriate place to take a client to lunch?"). Some of them are significant decisions with consequences critical to the business (i.e., "How much money should be allocated to each communications medium in your promotions budget?"). This chapter will focus on big decisions—decisions where the consequences are major and require significant effort to make the correct, I mean defensible, choice.

The Value of Information

One of the key principles in marketing is never to spend money on something unless you have a clear idea of what benefit that expenditure will have for your business. In today's business climate, you will rarely have all the information you would like to inform your decision, and there will never be enough time to give each decision all the attention you would like to. Gathering marketing information is an expense. So how much money should you invest in researching a question? The standard marketing answer applies—it depends. It depends on how much is at stake in the decision and on how difficult it will be to gather the information you need.

One way to establish a benchmark for your research expenditure is to look at the value of perfect information. Let's take a very simple example. Suppose you wanted to launch a new product. There are two new product concepts in the pipeline, and you only have the resources to launch one of them. If the product you choose is successful, it will generate $1 million in revenue. If the product launch is unsuccessful, you will only generate $500K in revenue. You don't know which of the two products will be successful, so if you have no information, you have a 50% chance of guessing correctly. What would be the maximum amount you would pay for perfect information—so you would know exactly which of the two products will be the successful one?

Using the expected value of a decision, if you have a 50% chance of earning $1M and a 50% chance of earning $500K, the expected value of the decision with no information would be $750K. That means if you made the same decision over and over again by guessing, you would get it right half of the time and get it wrong half of the time. With that in mind, what is the most you would be willing to pay to know which product to launch? Well, if you get it right, you will expect to earn $1M, and if you just guess, you will expect to earn $750K, so you wouldn't be willing to pay more than $250,000 for perfect information.

In the real world, you never have perfect information, so you wouldn't spend anything close to $250,000 for market research to support this decision; however, the exercise will give you a sense of the scope of the decision—how much is at stake and how much value better information will add to the decision.

Sometimes a business will pay for research when there is only one alternative course of action. This **pseudoresearch** is not done to inform a decision but rather to provide support for a decision that has already been made. Pseudoresearch may be unintentional—such as when a brand manager orders market research for a project because it is part of the company protocol; there could be negative consequences if the research wasn't done, even though it wasn't used to support the project. Other times, pseudoresearch might be intentional—for example, when an herbal supplements company pays for research to demonstrate the effectiveness of its products.

"Half of all statistics are made up."

Neil Cohen

Data vs. Information

A datum is a fact or, at least, something you believe to be true. In today's connected world, getting data is easy. You can Google anything and get lots of data (I Googled "anything" and instantly got more than 400 million results). So the issue is not getting data; the issue is sorting through the mountains of data at your fingertips to find the facts you need.

Data becomes information when it is used to make a decision. When you have filtered out the key data you will use in making a decision, synthesized it, and given it some context, it becomes information. As you become more adept at making decisions using information over time, the ability to appraise past, present, and future options can help make the business more intelligent, more capable of using information to generate profits.[1]

So what keeps businesses from becoming more intelligent? The answer is human and technological barriers. As human beings, we make mistakes working with data. For example, we may not enter all of the data we are requested to, or our big ego keeps us from doing boring tasks. Do you always enter the warranty information after buying something? From a technological perspective, many information databases were developed before the internet and aren't able to communicate with other information systems. These **data silos** are gradually being updated as companies gain better access to their history.

4.2 MARKETING INFORMATION SYSTEM

One way to manage all of the information coming at you is to think of it in terms of a **marketing information system**. Many companies have developed marketing

Marketing Information System
Conceptual Framework

Internal Sources of Data
Customers
Vendors
Previous results
Market research

External Sources of Data
Marketing intelligence
Databases
Syndicated research
Industry-level data

Technology to Manage Data
Hardware
Software
Connectivity
Security

Uses for Information
Progress reports
Data mining
Decision support system
Marketing dashboard

FIGURE 4.1   Marketing Information System

information systems that include some or all of the elements we will discuss here and have been very successful in the marketplace. From a conceptual perspective, a marketing information system looks at what information is available to decision makers, the technology used to manage information, and the people who will be using the information to make decisions. Figure 4.1 illustrates the elements of a marketing information system framework.

Sources of Information

There is a wealth of potential information available internally as well as a number of external sources that can be used to make decisions. Most businesses collect data for multiple reasons in order to make the business function effectively. Customer information such as sales history, contacts, customer service logs, pricing information, and vendor information are of obvious interest to marketers. But there is much more information available that may not have been collected specifically for marketing purposes but could potentially be valuable. Information such as production schedules, internal communications, social media posts, financial data, and company history can also be included in a marketing information system. In addition to information routinely collected, there may be occasions when specific information is needed to support a decision. In that case, the company may conduct market research to supply that information. We'll talk more about market research later in this chapter.

In addition to internal sources of information, a good marketing information system includes data created outside of the company and available to anyone. Many industry trade groups collect data on an industry-wide level as a service to their members. The Census Bureau collects national-level data, such as the economic census organized by NAICS code, and it is available for free. **Syndicated research** firms such as JD Powers (covering the automotive industry) or Nielsen (covering the media industry) conduct research for an industry and sell it to the individual companies working in that industry. The Nielsen ratings of television audiences can determine whether or not your favorite show is picked up for another season.

Many companies conduct marketing intelligence as a way to monitor developments outside of the company. This can involve monitoring the general business climate as well as the competition. There are a number of ways to gain intelligence on your competitors. Monitoring social media for posts by and about your competition can provide useful insights. Many vendors sell to more than one company in an industry. These vendors may be able to provide information about some of their other customers who may be your competitors. And there are any number of creative approaches to understanding what's happening with the competition. Information gathering could be as simple as driving by a competitor's place of business to note how many cars are parked in the parking lot. For a manufacturer, a crowded parking lot is an indication of strong business activity. For a retailer, a crowded parking lot suggests strong customer support.

Technology to Manage Data

We live in a computer-mediated world. The technology used to build a marketing information system is critical to its effectiveness. There are a number of issues to be addressed when looking at the technology. The first is what hardware is included. Is the data stored on a company server or in the cloud? Does the system support mobile devices such as cell phones or tablets, and if so, which devices are supported? Will the company allow people to use their own devices for business (sometimes called BYOD for "bring your own device") or require employees to use company-approved equipment? Equally important is the software used in the system. Do you want to go with an external supplier such as Salesforce or Marketo, which specialize in marketing information, or do you want to adapt internal systems? Which employees will have access to the data, and how deep into the database are they able to go? Are customers or only (selected) employees given permission to access the data? Who has the ability to make changes to the information? And finally, what steps have you taken to ensure the security of your database? What will you do if you get hacked?

Uses for Information

The most important element of a marketing information system is the people who use it. There are three basic ways in which marketers use information to inform their decisions: routine reports, data mining, and support for ad hoc decisions. Most marketing information systems generate routine reports showing progress towards meeting quarterly or annual goals. Some systems generate these reports in real time; others generate them periodically. One kind of report that helps focus management attention where it is most needed is called an exceptions report. While monitoring progress towards goals, an exceptions report may flag specific areas that are performing better or worse than expected. With this information, managers can easily identify where their attention is most needed. More and more, marketing managers are using a marketing dashboard (Chapter 22.2) to keep their fingers on the pulse of the organization. Just as the dashboard on a car allows the driver to monitor key performance metrics (such as the rate of speed and how much fuel is available), a marketing dashboard specifies a small number of key marketing performance metrics (KPIs) and monitors them in real time.

Data mining recognizes that although the information may have been collected for a specific purpose, now that it exists it may generate insights to improve other areas of the business. In addition to the information collected internally, data mining may include external databases as well. By integrating and analyzing these databases, companies are able to better manage customers. Customer acquisition develops a profile of existing customers and then uses that profile to identify people who are not yet customers but have the same characteristics as people who are customers. Customer retention and customer abandonment make use of the Pareto principle (80% of your business comes from 20% of your customers; 80% of your problems come from 20% of your customers) to identify highly profitable and unprofitable customers. Customer retention programs monitor the activity of highly profitable customers and may generate activity to stimulate business if a valuable customer seems to be losing interest in the company.

Customer abandonment programs identify customers whose lifetime value may be negative and gently discourage them from continuing to do business. For example, in a retail setting, when a customer returns a product to the store, the customer service representative may check the customer's record and handle the customer differently depending on his or her purchase history. A high-value customer (one who makes frequent purchases) might have no problem returning a product. An unprofitable customer may have a hard time returning a product, especially if the customer has had an unusual number of merchandise returns in the past.

Another data mining activity, **market basket analysis**, looks at massive amounts of purchase data and identifies relationships between products. Whenever you buy something from Amazon.com, you see market basket analysis at work. Before you complete the purchase of your product, the computer suggests other products you might like to buy based on people who bought the product you are considering.

The third way managers use the marketing information is as a decision support system. Rather than generating routine reports anticipating a manager's information needs, a decision support system serves as a source of information when a manager needs to make an ad hoc or one-of-a-kind decision. For example, suppose a traditional mail order company is considering opening a physical location in order to have a better brand experience for customers. One question would be where do you locate the first store? When Land's End was faced with that situation, it analyzed its shipping data and looked for the zip codes where its customers lived. The best place to put the first store is where the customers already are.

In order for a decision support system to be effective, the information needs to be current and as broad as reasonably possible. At the speed of business today, when you need to make a decision, you don't have time to go back and enter the data into your system. The information needs to be available at the time you need it. Not only does it have to be available, but it also needs to be available in a format that managers can use to make a decision. Ideally, information can be downloaded to an analytical package or spreadsheet where the manager can analyze the information. And finally, the people using the system need to have an understanding of how to use data to support decisions. At a bare minimum, anyone in business should be able to run a simple analysis on a spreadsheet. If you need to run very sophisticated analyses, you can hire a consultant.

4.3 BIG DATA AND MARKETING ANALYTICS

Big data is the hot topic in business today. There is so much data generated by devices connected through the internet that the massive amount of data available is beyond the reach of traditional analytical techniques. IBM estimates we create 2.5 exabytes (2.5×10^{18} bits) of data each day.[2] To put this in perspective, it is estimated that all human knowledge up until 1999 was about 12 exabytes of data.[3] From a technical perspective, big data simply refers to data sets that are too big for traditional database analytical packages, such as SQL, to handle.

Big data can be characterized in terms of the four "Vs": volume (we're talking petabytes[i] here), velocity (real-time high frequency and streaming data), variety

---

i One exabyte = 1,000 petabytes

(numeric, text, network, images, video), and veracity (reliable and valid).[4] Google, for example, receives more than four million searches per minute and processes more than 20 petabytes (20×10^{15}) of data each day, or seven exabytes per year.[4] Now that's big.

In marketing, big data is frequently discussed in the context of **marketing analytics**—the methods for measuring, analyzing, predicting, and managing market performance in order to maximize effectiveness and return on investment (ROI).[5] Marketing analytics supports marketing decisions in four major areas: customer relationship management, or CRM (Chapter 19.6); personalization; optimizing the marketing mix (product, price, promotion, distribution); and privacy and security. One major concern in data security is the "mosaic effect," where personal information that should be private is revealed when integrating different data sets.

4.4 MARKET RESEARCH PROCESS

There may be situations where the only way to generate the information needed to support a decision is to create it from scratch. **Market research** is the systematic gathering, recording, and analyzing of data with respect to a specific customer group in a specific geographic area. Because creating new information requires spending money—either by hiring an outside firm to conduct the research or by paying internal staff to conduct the research—a systematic research process can increase the likelihood of a successful outcome. Most researchers use a process involving at least five steps: define the problem, develop the research plan, collect data, interpret the data, and act on the result of the research (Figure 4.2).

FIGURE 4.2   Marketing Research Process

Define the Problem

The first, and most important, step of the research process is to be clear about why you are conducting the research. Most research projects have two dimensions. The first dimension is to clearly define the business problem you are trying to address. If there is a decision to be made, what are the alternative courses of action, and what factors might help you determine if one alternative is better than the others? Who is the customer/market being studied, and are there others in the company who will be affected by the results of the research? The business problem might involve multiple sources of information, including original research as well as secondary sources of information.

The second dimension is to define the research question. What information are you trying to develop in order to support the business decision? **Exploratory research** is conducted when the alternatives are not clear. The goal is not to answer specific questions but to figure out which questions need to be answered. **Descriptive research** is conducted to find answers to specific questions. The goal of descriptive research is to find correlations or relationships between variables. For example, if I increase my advertising spend, will sales increase? For most business research, establishing a correlation between variables is sufficient to answer the research question. However, descriptive research can't establish whether one thing causes another—only that there is a correlation.

The most famous example of the difference between correlation and causation is the well-known relationship between ice cream cone sales and murder rates in big cities. Whenever ice cream sales increase, there is a spike in murder rates. Does this mean ice cream turns people into murderers? Obviously not. What is happening is that both ice cream sales and murder rates go up when days are longer and the weather is hot. If it were important to prove that ice cream causes violent crime, **causal research** would need to be conducted to establish cause and effect.

Develop the Research Plan

Having decided that market research is necessary to support an important decision, you need to develop a plan to answer the research question. This involves identifying any constraints or limitations that may affect the research, identifying the data needed, and putting together a plan to collect the data you need.

Constraints

The two biggest constraints on market research are time and resources. Many market opportunities are short-lived, and if the research is to be of value, it needs to be completed in time to implement the results before the opportunity evaporates. If it is unlikely the research will be completed in time to be of use, it would be a waste of money to conduct it.

In corporate America, the term "resources" is a code word for money or for things that cost money. Financial resources are the dollars needed to conduct the research. If you are working with an outside market research firm, the financial resources will be the amount needed to pay the research firm for its work. If you are conducting the research in-house, you will need to budget for salaries, equipment, and data collection. In addition to the direct financial costs of the research, you will need to take into account the amount of time and effort it will take to oversee the process. Managerial attention is a critical resource needed to conduct successful research.

Identify the Data Needed

Assuming you have the resources needed to conduct the research, the next step is to determine the data needed to support the decision. The type of data needed depends heavily on the research objectives. Exploratory research frequently uses qualitative (nonnumerical) data such as interviews or direct observation of behavior. Descriptive research requires quantitative data (numbers) that can be subjected to statistical analysis. Most business research is cross-sectional, meaning data is collected at a specific point in time. Longitudinal, or time-series, research is less common because it requires multiple data collection efforts, each costing money. Longitudinal research is done when identifying a trend is an important consideration. For example, political candidates conduct repeated polls over the course of the campaign to determine whether the candidate is gaining or losing ground to the opponent.

Causal research requires a formal **experiment**. A formal experiment has to meet five conditions: a theoretical framework (specification of the variables involved and a prediction or hypothesis about how the variables will interact), a dependent variable (measures the result of the experiment), one or more independent variables (the things you are testing), a control group, and a probability sample (a random sample is an example of a probability sample). Sometimes it is difficult or even impossible to meet the conditions for a true experiment. A **quasi-experiment** is a study that doesn't meet one or more of these conditions. The most common reasons for conducting a quasi-experiment are the inability to generate a probability sample and an inability to have a control group.

> "It's no longer about being really clever and coming up with the big hash tag line and making the art and copy marriage work really well. It's about being able to prove everything out and to show this performance. ... I think the advent of CRMs, Web technology, and analytics has put a lot more pressure on being a marketer."
>
> **Marketing Professional**

There are several factors to consider in developing a data collection plan. First, because many of the issues we deal with in marketing revolve around customer perceptions (i.e., satisfaction, loyalty, purchase intention), it may not be possible to measure the variable directly. We can't look into a customer's head to see whether he or she is satisfied with a product, but we can use indirect measures to infer what is going on. If a customer makes a repeat purchase of our product, that would imply satisfaction. With indirect (sometimes called latent) variables, it is helpful to use more than one measure to increase the likelihood of a correct inference. In addition to looking at repeat purchases, you could monitor social media to look for positive or negative comments about the product or ask customers to fill out a satisfaction survey. By the way, the single most effective indicator of customer satisfaction on a satisfaction survey is to ask, "Would you recommend this product to a friend?"

Another issue is whether to use secondary or primary data. **Secondary data** is information that already exists. This might be data collected internally, such as sales or billing data, or it may be research conducted by another company. The obvious advantage of secondary data is timeliness. Since it already exists, you have access to it immediately. Because secondary research was created for some other purpose, it has been paid for. You may have access to the data for free or for a fraction of what it would cost you develop the data yourself. The problems with secondary data are that it may be out of date, it may not directly address your research question, and you have no control over the methodology.

Primary data is just the opposite. Since you are creating it from scratch, it can be costly in terms of money and time. However, because you are developing the data specifically for your research question, you have complete control over the methodology and can be sure the information addresses your question directly. It makes sense to look for secondary data first and only conduct primary research when there isn't relevant secondary research available and when you can justify the expense of conducting original research.

A third issue is whether or not you are going to interact directly with the participants while collecting the data. Interactive techniques such as focus groups, telephone interviews, and video chats can be especially helpful in exploratory research because you have the ability to clarify responses or ask follow-up questions. Sometimes, especially when developing new products, it is helpful to provide a concept or prototype of a product. Customers are not always good at visualizing new ideas, so giving them a starting point for the conversation makes it easier for them. The disadvantage of interactive methods is that they are expensive. You have to pay a person to interact with the participants. When you are conducting multiple interviews, lack of consistency among interviewers can be a problem.

The most common methods for collecting data without interacting with the participant are questionnaires and direct observation. Online questionnaires are popular because they are relatively inexpensive to administer, and the results from online surveys are similar to traditional paper and pencil surveys. Companies like SurveyMonkey or Qualtrics allow you to create the questionnaire (or survey instrument) online, there are no printing or postage costs, and the results are automatically tabulated. Questionnaires are best suited for descriptive research, as there is little room for respondents to tell you about the things you don't ask. Have you ever filled out a questionnaire and had difficulty answering a question because it was missing the point?

Actions speak louder than words. Observation is a way of collecting data based on what people do rather than on what they say. In addition to watching video of customers in action, there are many opportunities to collect behavioral data. When you scan your loyalty card at the supermarket, the store is collecting a lot of information about your shopping, including what time of day you shop, whether or not you look for sales, what products you purchase, how you pay, etc. The challenge with observational data is that it can be difficult to interpret. Your computer, your phone, your car, or even your thermostat are generating mountains of behavioral data every minute.

Collect Relevant Information

There are three qualities that separate "good" data from "bad" data: validity, reliability, and generalizability. Validity addresses the question, "Are you measuring what you think you are measuring?" In marketing, many of the things we study are difficult to measure. So we focus on what is easy to measure rather than on what we want to study. For example, when measuring the effectiveness of a banner ad, it is easy to measure the "click-through rate," the number of people who were served the ad and clicked on it to see the offer. But the click-through rate doesn't take into account all of the other ads a person might have seen related to the product. It may be that a persuasive television ad seen earlier caused the person to click on the banner ad.

Reliability speaks to the quality of the measurement. If you repeat the same measure over and over, will you get the same result? The closer the measurements are to each other, the more reliable the measurement is. Many of the variables we study in marketing are probabilistic, meaning that multiple measurements will vary but follow a distribution around a mean value, which we treat as the true value. The shape of a distribution curve will vary from variable to variable, and we use statistical methods to estimate the true value of a variable.

Generalizability looks at whether the results from a sample represent the larger population. It is impractical to survey everybody in the population to find out what is going on. Usually, we base our inferences on a sample of the population. The way the sample is collected determines whether or not the findings are representative of the entire population. A **probability sample**, or a sample where every person in the population has a known chance of being included, is required for generalizability. The most common probability sample is a random sample where everybody in the population has an equal chance of being included in the sample. Sometimes, when we want to zero in on a specific segment of the population, we use a stratified random sample. Rather than giving everyone in the population an equal chance of being included in the sample, a stratified sample might draw twice as many samples from the segment (or strata) we are interested in. Even though not everybody has an equal chance of being included in the sample (the lucky segment is twice as likely), we can account for the difference statistically.

Sometimes it is just not feasible to use a probability sample. If you don't know in advance the size of the population you are studying, you can't use a random sample because you can't say that each person had an equal chance of being chosen. Many market research projects use a **convenience sample**. A convenience sample is just what it sounds like: you survey the people who are convenient to you. When you see someone standing outside a shopping mall asking passersby questions about a product, this is an example of a convenience sample. Similarly, a Facebook poll would be a convenience sample, as the people who respond are likely to be friends of the person publishing the poll. While a convenience sample won't allow you to generalize your findings to a larger population, it may be adequate to provide the information you need. Remember, market research is a means to an end, not an end in itself.

Another nonprobability sample is called a **snowball sample**. A snowball sample is used when you don't know in advance who is in the population you want to study. The idea is to start with someone you know is in the population and then tap into that person's network to find others. After surveying the first person, or seed, you ask that person if he or she knows of others who might be appropriate for you to survey. As you talk to more and more people, the snowball grows, giving you access to more people in the population of interest. When you start hearing the same names over and over again when you ask for referrals, the snowball is probably complete.

Avoiding Bias in Research

When dealing with market research, the term "bias" doesn't mean you are being unfair; it simply means that what you are measuring may not be what you thought you were measuring. Some numerical biases can be handled through statistical techniques. Other forms of bias can come from poorly developed data collection techniques.

Face validity asks the question, "Does this make sense on the face of it?" Given the population you are studying, does it appear that the questions you are asking will give you the answers you seek? There are several things to consider when developing a questionnaire. Is the language appropriate? Are the questions clear and unambiguous? Is the sampling protocol appropriate to the situation?

In market research, we communicate in the language of the customer. If the target audience is likely to include non-native English speakers, are the questions translated to the language of the customer? Ideally, you would have someone fluent in the language translate the question from English. Then, have someone else translate the question from the other language back to English. Does the retranslation mean the same thing as the original question? Even within the English language, some words have more than one meaning and could be misunderstood. For example, if a doctor asks you about your diet, they are talking about the nutritional quality of the food you eat. If anyone else asks you about your diet, you will tell him or her about your weight-loss program.

There are many ways questions can be unclear. A double-barreled question is when you unintentionally ask about two things in the same question. If you ask, "Are you satisfied with your recent purchase and customer service?" you won't know whether the respondent is referring to the product or to the customer experience. A loaded question is one that uses emotionally charged language or tries to steer you to a particular response. Framing is when you set the context of the question in order to encourage a specific interpretation of the facts. Framing can either be neutral—giving the respondent enough context to answer the question effectively— or framing can be persuasive—encouraging the respondent to interpret the facts in specific way. Neutral framing is critical to unbiased research results. Persuasive framing is an important tool for advertising and personal selling, but it should be avoided in market research.

54   Develop Findings

Having collected the information you need to support your decision, the next step is to analyze and interpret the data and present the findings to the people responsible for making the decision. At a minimum, you should be comfortable carrying out some of the basic statistical analyses you can perform in an Excel spreadsheet, such as descriptive statistics (mean, mode, median), cross tabulations, correlation, and simple regression analysis. Unless you are a market research specialist, you probably won't need to know some of the more advanced statistical techniques, such as multidimensional scaling, multivariate regression, and structural equation modeling. If these techniques are necessary to understand the data, you will need to work with someone with advanced training who can help you understand why these techniques are necessary and how they can inform the decision you are facing.

It is rare to have perfect information, so it is important to recognize how some of the choices you made in collecting the data might impact the decision. Any assumptions you made in the process, such as assuming a secondary research report would apply to the decision at hand, need to be taken into account. There is a temptation to read more into the findings than are really there. If you found customers were highly satisfied with a particular product, it might be tempting to say, "Customers are satisfied with our products." This is called overgeneralization.

The final step in the analysis is to make your recommendation. Based on the results of your research, which of the alternatives would you recommend, and on what are you basing the recommendation? It is not enough just to report the statistical results. You have a responsibility to explain how the results help make the decision.

A major research project might require a formal report of the results. A typical research report starts with an executive summary, describes the methods used to gather and interpret the data, discusses the analytical findings, discloses any limitations, and makes a recommendation.

An executive summary is just that—a very short summary of the project, including a statement of the research question and the findings. Some people think of it as an introduction to the research and don't want to "give it all away" on the first page. It may help to understand how decisions are made in large organizations. Senior-level decision makers don't have time to delve into the details of a research report. They just want the "top-line" results. If the senior decision maker agrees with the recommendation, the report will be handed off to a junior-level person responsible for implementing the decision. This person will need to see the details of the report in order to execute the decision.

Take Marketing Actions

Unless this was pseudoresearch, you will act on the results of the research. Using the criteria established in advance, you will choose one or more of the alternative courses of action and implement the decision. Only after the decision has been implemented can you determine whether or not it was a good decision. There are two dimensions to evaluating the results of a research project. The first is to evaluate the decision that was based on the research. The second is to evaluate the process itself.

4.5 USING MARKET RESEARCH

The goal of a "Marketing Fundamentals" textbook is to give you enough information to be an effective consumer of market research rather than to train you to be an expert market researcher. So how do you become an effective consumer of market research? The first step is to put the research in context. Does the research relate to the decision(s) you make at work? If so, are the top-line results informative—do the results of the research help you choose among the alternatives you face? If the research appears to be helpful, take a deeper look to assess the quality of the research. If it is a primary research report, does the methodology support validity, reliability, and representativeness? If it is a secondary research report, it is especially critical to look at the sampling to decide whether the results are representative of your customers. Many times, you will see research reports cited in various media outlets. Try to find a copy of the original research project to make sure the findings reported in the news are consistent with the original research. Sometimes, a reporter will only emphasize the parts of the research that support a good story. If possible, take a look at the questions that were used to see if they were clear, unbiased, and on topic.

(ENDNOTES)

1. Liautaud, B. (2001). *e-Business intelligence: Turning information into knowledge and profit.* New York: McGraw Hill.
2. Retrieved from http://www-01.ibm.com/software/data/bigdata/what-is-big-data.html
3. Enriquez, J. (2003, Fall/Winter Special Issue). The data that defines us. *CIO Magazine.*
4. Wedel, M., & Kannan, P. K. (2016). Marketing analytics for data-rich environments. *Journal of Marketing, 80*(6), 97–121.
5. Wedel, M., & Kannan, P. K. Kannan. (2016). Marketing analytics for data-rich environments. *Journal of Marketing, 80*(6), 97–121.

SEGMENTATION AND TARGET MARKETING

CH 05

The first question we always ask in marketing is: "Who's the customer?" When you have created a new product and are excited about its potential, there is a temptation to think, "Who wouldn't be a customer for this?" We are so in love with our great idea, we can't imagine anyone not being as excited as we are. The reality is that if you can't say who your customers **aren't,** you don't know who your customers **are**. Segmentation, targeting, and positioning (covered in the next chapter), sometimes called STP, is the process used in marketing management and in strategy development to focus your marketing efforts on the people who would most benefit from your product.

5.1 WHAT IS A MARKET SEGMENT?

If you remember from Chapter 2.1, a customer is someone who perceives a benefit in your product and has the money, time, willingness, and authority to make the purchase. In his seminal work on competitive advantage,[1] Michael Porter (a Harvard Business guru) identified three generic business strategies: being the low-cost producer, differentiation, and focusing on a specific group. As there is only room for one low-cost producer in any industry, the majority of businesses need to provide value beyond what is available from the low-cost producer. By definition, this added value will increase the cost of providing a product. In order to recover the added cost and, hopefully, to earn a tidy profit, we need to be sure what we add is something the customer values enough to be willing to pay for the extra cost. Segmentation attempts to identify the customers who have the money and willingness to buy your particular version of the product.

There's a little bit of a paradox when it comes to marketing. We know that each individual is unique, yet we speak of mass markets where we treat everybody the same. The solution to this paradox comes from The Law of Truly Large Numbers. If you have a large enough group of people, anything can happen. If there are one million people and there is a one in 1,000 chance of something happening, it will happen 1,000 times. The point is, if you have a large enough group of people, there should be a subset of that group that sees the value in what you're offering and is willing to pay for it. When we are looking for a market segment, we don't have to look at the whole person, we only need look at that part of the individual with respect to our product. When it comes to pets, some people like dogs, and some people like cats. Regardless of how different dog lovers might be in other areas of their lives, we know that they all have a love of dogs in common.

Both the differentiation strategy and the focus strategy succeed by finding subsets of the population who value what you're offering above the low-cost alternative. A differentiation strategy appeals to multiple segments while a focus strategy, sometimes called niche marketing, zeros in on a specific group.

Definition of a Segment

In order to be called a **market segment**, the subset you are looking at must meet four requirements. First, the people in the segment must be similar to each other in that they see the value of what you offer and are willing to pay for it. Second, they must be different from those outside of the segment with respect to your product. This is where the idea that if you can't say who your customers aren't, you don't know who your customers are comes from. You don't want to waste time and money marketing to people who don't see the value in what you're offering.

The third requirement is that you have a means of communicating with the people in the segment. If you can't reach someone to tell about your product, that person can't possibly see the benefit in what you're offering, much less place an order with you.

And finally, the segment in question needs to be economically viable. There has to be enough potential demand in that segment to make it worth your while. How big does a segment need to be in order to be economically viable? It depends. A large corporation might need to see the potential to make millions of dollars before investing in a segment. A local coffee shop might be viable with a few hundred regular customers.

Table 5.1 Properties of a Market Segment

PROPERTY	RATIONALE
Similar to each other • people who see a benefit in your product	You are looking for people who are similar to each other because they see the value in your product or service. They may differ in other areas of their lives.
Different from everyone else • people who don't see a benefit in your product	If you are not clear about who is not in the market segment, you waste money marketing to people who aren't potential customers.
Reachable	In order to create transactions, there needs to be a way to communicate with people in the segment.
Economically viable	There must be enough potential profit in the segment to justify the expense of marketing to it.

5.2 BASES FOR SEGMENTATION

There are any number of variables you can use to try to identify profitable market segments. We will discuss several of the most common segmentation variables in this section. There are a couple of things to keep in mind as you consider which variables would work best for you. First, although we discuss each variable separately, it is common to use several variables in combination to identify a segment. Second, by no means is this list exhaustive. If you find a way to identify promising segments no one else is using, you are likely to have the field to yourself. This is how fortunes are made. One of the goals of data mining and marketing analytics is to discover new variables that help explain customer behavior in order to identify new segments.

Business Segmentation

Business customers are an obvious candidate for segmentation. While businesses use many of the same products as do individual consumers, their reason for buying is different. In this way, businesses are similar to each other and different from individual consumers. Because the business segment is so large (the 2012 Economic Census listed 5.7 million businesses in the United States), it can be helpful to further segment the business market. Common segmentation variables include geographic region, size of business, industry, and product usage.

The business segment is reachable because businesses don't try to hide. Most businesses make a significant effort to make themselves known to the public. Some of them even put a sign up in front of the building and try to call attention to their website. There are many organizations who maintain directories of businesses. Most industry trade associations keep a membership roster with information on member companies. Local chambers of commerce keep lists of local companies that are members. And there are commercial providers of information about potential business customers. Hoovers (www.hoovers.com), a commercial source, has information on more than 80 million potential business customers.

The same sources you use to identify business customers can help determine the economic viability of the segment.

Geographic Segmentation

Geographic segmentation recognizes that buying patterns will be different depending on where you live. People living in Boston are more likely to buy snow blowers than people living in Tampa, Florida. People living in Los Angeles are more likely to buy surfboards than people living in Oklahoma City. In addition to the climate and physical location, different regions may have different cultures as well. Fishing is a big deal if you live in northern Minnesota, and what happens in Vegas stays in Vegas.

Geographic segmentation is very reachable. Every city has local media outlets, such as television stations, newspaper, outdoor advertising, and many national publications have regional editions that allow you to focus your message on a specific area. Event marketing is a good way to communicate with people in a specific location. Sporting events, community festivals, Little League baseball teams are all looking for corporate sponsors.

Physical location is an important criterion for products that have high transportation costs or are highly perishable. Having the product close to the customer saves money, reduces spoilage, and improves customer service.

Demographic Segmentation

The most common way to segment markets it to use demographic variables such as age, gender, income, education, ethnicity, occupation, stage in life, nationality. This is because these variables are relatively easy to measure and yield useful differences. Here are some of the implications of these demographic variables.

Age

There are a number of ways age can be used to understand potential market segments. One of them is that we go through biological changes as we grow older. Babies need diapers, and grandparents need glasses. The aging process is well understood, and people at different ages will value different products.

Cohort marketing recognizes that groups of people of the same generation will have many experiences in common. The music we listen to, the political picture, and even hairstyles will vary from generation to generation. While there is disagreement about the exact boundaries for the various generations, there is consensus around the importance of these generational differences to marketers. Jean Twenge, a generations researcher, defines the various generations as follows[2]:

Table 5.2 Generational Cohorts

COHORT	BORN	POPULATION (MILLIONS)
Baby Boomers	1946–1964	76
Generation X	1965–1979	62
Generation Y (Millennials)	1980–1994	57
iGen	1995–2012	74

If you are looking to launch a career after graduation, you may find encouragement in these numbers. Seventy-six million Baby Boomers are nearing retirement age, and as they retire, it will create a need for people from succeeding generations to take their places. Just sayin'.

Families buy a lot of products, and many of the products purchased are related to where they are in the **family life cycle**. We start out young and single. Next, we may or may not get married. SINKS (single income, no kids) and DINKS (double income, no kids) are two segments particularly attractive to marketers. Some families include children (full nest), and their purchase patterns change as the children leave home to begin their own family life cycle (empty nest).

Ethnicity

Both race and culture play a role in consumption patterns. For example, a Nielsen (www.nielsen.com) report suggests that African Americans shop more frequently but spend less per trip than other ethnicities and consume more television; Hispanics shop less frequently but spend more per trip and are heavy smartphone users; Asians/Pacific Islanders shop less frequently, spend more per trip, and are more likely to buy when products are on sale. They watch less TV and stream more content on the internet than other groups.[3]

It is important to make a distinction between ethnic segmentation and stereotyping. **Stereotyping** is assigning a characteristic to a group based on race, nationality, etc., that has been perpetuated in a society. Segmentation based on stereotypes leads to discrimination, alienation, ignores diversity within an ethnic group, and is a waste of marketing dollars. Ethnic segmentation is about identifying genuine needs associated with a particular group in order to provide superior value. One way to minimize stereotyping is to have an ethnically diverse marketing team. The marketing team should reflect the ethnic makeup of the market it is trying to serve.

Psychographic Segmentation

Psychographic segmentation looks for differences between people based on their personality, lifestyle, attitudes, or values. You may question whether this meets the reachability requirement for a segment. How do you know whether or not someone is looking to improve his or her diet? You can't look into peoples' brains (yet!) to see how they feel. While it is true that you can't measure someone's food preferences, you can reach them indirectly. You can assume people who subscribe to *Food & Nutrition* magazine are careful about what they eat, and you can reach them through the magazine and its website.

There are a couple of commercial psychographic segmentation approaches widely used in marketing. The VALS™ profile from Strategic Business Insights classifies people into eight psychographic segments based on primary motivation and access to resources. Nielsen's PRIZM classifies people into 66 categories based on demographics and behavior. To get an idea of how psychographic segmentation works, go to Nielsen's zip code lookup page (https://segmentationsolutions.nielsen.com/mybestsegments) and see if the descriptions of your neighborhood apply to you.

Buying Behavior Segmentation

Actions speak louder than words. Looking at how customers behave while buying your product can be a good basis for segmentation. People look at products differently depending on the outlet where they buy, the benefit they receive from the product, how much experience they have with the product, or even the occasion for the purchase. When it comes to buying a cola drink in a grocery store, you would likely buy a six pack or a case; you wouldn't care if it was cold or not because you aren't going to drink it in the store, and price would be an important factor. In a restaurant, you would want your cola to be cold with lots of ice and come in a glass, so you could drink it right away.

By understanding the specific benefit customers look for in a product, marketers can add value to their offerings. Some people buy aspirin to get relief from a headache and are concerned with how fast it will take effect. Others buy it for relief from arthritis and need it to be strong enough to provide relief. Still others buy it to help prevent heart attacks and need a smaller dose than other users. Providing extra strength pain reliever for arthritis sufferers and baby-dose pain reliever for those with heart issues makes it easier for each segment to acquire the benefit they desire.

Segmenting based on usage can provide useful differences. When it comes to fast food, 33% of Americans don't eat at fast food restaurants, 25% eat fast food less than once a week, 22% eat fast food weekly, and 19% eat fast food more than once a week. The heavy users (pun intended) who eat fast food more than once a week would be a more attractive segment than those who eat fast food less than once a week.

First-time buyers have a higher level of involvement with a purchase than repeat customers. Knowing what to expect and having experience with the product reduces risk. Recognizing this, some marketers design different experiences for first-time customers and for repeat customers. For example, service staff at a restaurant with an unusual format may ask if you have dined at the establishment before. That way, they can help the new customer know what to expect. Repeat customers understand the format already.

Finally, the occasion for the purchase makes a difference in a customer's approach to the purchase. You probably spend a lot more time selecting a gift for a special person in your life than you do when you make your weekly trip to the grocery store.

5.3 TARGET MARKETING

A **target market** is simply the segment or segments out of all the segments you have identified that you choose to go after. Looking back to the three generic strategies, you can choose an undifferentiated or mass-market strategy, a focus or niche market strategy, or, more commonly, a multisegment strategy.

The first step in selecting a target market is to evaluate all of the segments you have identified to find the ones with the most potential. Things to consider include: How big is the market potential for each segment? Is a segment is growing or shrinking? How many competitors are also targeting the segment? How difficult will it be to reach the people in the segment? How well does the segment fit in with other business activities—can you create synergies? In addition, there may be other reasons for targeting a particular segment. For example, many fashion-oriented businesses target well-known celebrities, sometimes going so far as to give the product away for free in the hope a star will be seen using the product. Even though this strategy isn't profitable, it may help the product appear to be trendy.

Here is an example of a simple matrix to help evaluate market segments. Suppose we've identified five potential market segments and want to evaluate their relative attractiveness based on market size, market growth, competitive intensity, the cost to communicate with people in the segment, and the fit with our existing business. On one axis we've listed the five segments under consideration. On the other axis, we've listed the criteria for evaluating the segments. In this simple example, we've weighted each criterion equally and rated them on a scale from one to ten, with one being the least attractive and ten being the most attractive.

Table 5.3 Example of an Evaluation Matrix

	SEGMENT				
	A	B	C	D	E
Market size	6	4	7	4	6
Market growth	8	3	5	3	2
Competition	2	6	3	4	1
Cost to reach segment	8	5	2	7	9
Fit with business	4	3	6	2	1
Overall	28	21	23	20	20

After evaluating the various segments, you would rank them from most promising to least promising based on their overall score. Then starting with the most promising, you would select as many segments as you have the resources to handle. In this example, we would first target segment A with an overall rating of 28. The growth rate is attractive, it is relatively inexpensive to reach customers in this segment, and we will face stiff competition, but overall it seems to be the most attractive segment. If we have the resources to target another segment, our second choice would be segment C with an overall rating of 23. This segment is not as attractive from a market standpoint, but we would have a strong competitive position. We would continue to select segments as long as we have the resources needed to market to them effectively. This approach helps maximize your profits by addressing the most promising segments first.

Market segmentation is a way to answer the question, "Who is the customer?" It is a basic input into the development of marketing plans (Chapter 21.3). A marketing mix needs to be developed for each segment you choose to target.

(ENDNOTES)

1. Porter, Michael E., 1985, *Competitive Advantage: Creating and Sustaining Superior Performance,* New York: Free Press.
2. Twenge, Jean M., *iGen: Why Today's Super-Connected Kids are Growing Up Less Rebellious, More Tolerant, Less Happy—and Completely Unprepared for Adulthood,* Ney York: Atria Books, 2017.
3. http://www.nielsen.com/us/en/insights/news/2011/dissecting-diversity-understanding-the-ethnic-consumer.html. Accessed March 11, 2015.

POSITIONING

CH06

The concept of positioning—managing customer perceptions of your brand relative to perceptions of competitive brands—was originally developed by Al Ries and Jack Trout[1] in the 1980s as a way to cut through advertising clutter (the fact that we are bombarded with more advertising messages than we could possibly pay attention to). Today, understanding how customers perceive your brand relative to the competition is critical to reaching the right people with the right message. In fact, many marketers feel positioning is so important to effective marketing that they consider it to be the fifth element of the marketing mix—product, price, place, promotion, and positioning—the five "P's"

6.1 WHAT IS POSITIONING?

If I ask you to name the first brand that comes to mind when I say the word "soda," you are likely to mention Coke® or Coca-Cola®. Why? For more than 100 years, the company has been promoting the product in ways that have since become part of our culture. For many of us, Santa Clause is a jolly white-bearded man wearing a bright red coat (the same color as the Coke label) and enjoying a refreshing glass of Coca-Cola. Coke taught the world to sing, and when we open happiness, we have a Coke and a smile.

The Wyer and Srull "bin" theory of memory[2] suggests that people tend to remember things in categories (schema). We store our memories in chronological order—the most recent memory is at the top of the category. Over time, through repetition, one trait may become the exemplar—a sort of label for the category. When the category has been well established in the mind, the first thing we think of when we access the category is the exemplar. It requires additional mental effort to search further in the category. Coke is the exemplar for the category "soda."

In the consumer buying process (Chapter 2.2), we learned that when people are evaluating alternative products, they choose the first acceptable solution rather than conducting an exhaustive search to find the best solution. The first place people look for solutions is in memory, and we tend to search memory by category. Because of this, you can see how being the exemplar for a category in a customer's mind gives a powerful advantage to the brand that occupies that position. If a person is thirsty and looking for a soda, the first thing that comes to mind is a Coke, and if a Coke is good enough, the search ends there.

If my product is 7UP®, I will need to give customers a reason to look beyond the category leader in order be selected.

Positioning is understanding how customers perceive your brand and managing their perceptions relative to competing brands. Ideally, you want to create a market position where your offering is clearly superior to the competition.

"When in doubt, just reach into your well of empathy and just think about whatever the target user or customer is going through. Think about their entire life. Think about the layers of context that they are bringing to the [brand] experience you are building and see what comes up. The headline is 'have empathy.'"

Justin Garrett

6.2 HOW TO ESTABLISH A MARKET POSITION

The easiest way to become the category leader is to create the category. In addition to offering something novel, you are creating the category customers will use when they search for the product and automatically become the exemplar for the new category. This **pioneering effect** is one of the advantages of being first to market with a truly innovative product. When the Haloid Photographic Company (now Xerox® Corporation) came out with the Xerox 914 plain paper copier in 1959, it created the category for plain paper copiers. Today the Xerox brand name has become so powerfully associated with the copier category that the company is in danger of having the brand name become the generic name for the category.

Another way is to create a subcategory where your brand can be the exemplar. In our culture, nobody cares about who comes in second. In sports, second place is sometimes referred to as first loser. It is better to be the exemplar in a small category than it is to be second place in a larger category. One of the most famous examples of creating a market position by owning a subcategory is 7UP. In the soft drink category, 7UP barely registers against Coke and Pepsi®. However in 1967, the 7UP company positioned its soda as an alternative to colas with the "Uncola" campaign and became the exemplar for the category of sodas other than Coke or Pepsi.

The last way to create a market position in the minds of consumers is to use promotional mix (Chapter 16.3). Because customers pay very little attention to things they aren't interested in, it is very expensive to buy the exposure needed for your product to be perceived as a category leader by customers.

Process for Creating a Market Position

There are three basic steps to creating a market position. First, you need to understand how your product is currently perceived in the marketplace. Second, you need to determine what position you want your product to have. And finally, you need to develop a plan to take you from where you are to where you want to be.

Figure Out Where You Are

Many businesses don't have a good understanding of how their customers perceive them. There are many reasons for this. First, the principle of selective perception (Chapter 2.3) suggests that we are more likely to hear positive things than negative things about our product. Second, the information you get from the people around you is likely to be filtered. Your sales force, your suppliers, and consultants are good sources of information about your product as well as competitors' products, but they are likely to emphasize the positive in their reports.

So where do you go to get the unvarnished truth? One good source is people who complain to you and company critics. For every customer who complains, there are nine who don't complain to you (but then give you a bad review on social media), so it is critical to listen to the few who are willing to share their displeasure. Social media and the blogosphere are where people are willing to share their opinions and are a good source for understanding customer perceptions of your product. Just as people who work for you tend to put things in a favorable light, people who don't like you will emphasize the bad things.

Your goal is to weigh both the positive and the negative information to come up with an honest and balanced view of how customers perceive your product as compared to the competition. Systematic approaches such as an internal marketing audit, a SWOT analysis (Chapter 21.3), or market research can help weigh positive and negative perceptions of your company and its products.

Figure out Where You Want to Be

There are several approaches to identifying an attractive market position. In this book, we'll talk about a couple of them: perceptual mapping and using a positioning framework. Both of these approaches are very robust, meaning they work well under a variety of circumstances. The concepts are useful if you are a small business working things out on the back of a cocktail napkin or a large corporation investing thousands of dollars for more sophisticated analyses.

Perceptual Mapping. A perceptual map is a tool that takes two key product attributes and shows the relative position of each competitor graphically on a 2 × 2 matrix.

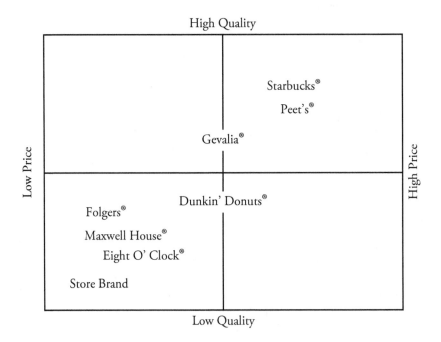

FIGURE 6.1   Perceptual Map for Ground Coffee

It is important to identify attributes that are important to the customer for the map to be relevant. For simple analyses, you may start with your judgment of which attributes are most important to customers. More sophisticated analyses will use advanced statistical tools to help identify key attributes and the relative position of products on the map.

Figure 6.1 is a made-up example of a perceptual map for the ground-coffee market based on the attributes of perceived quality and perceived price. We can see that Starbucks® and Peet's® coffee are perceived as high-price/high-quality brands while Folgers® and Maxwell House® are perceived as lower-price/lower-quality brands. Store brand coffee is seen as low price/low quality while Gevalia® coffee is seen as moderate price/higher quality.

If you were planning on introducing a new brand of ground coffee, where on this map would you want to position it? Would you go against Starbucks and Peet's in the premium-price/premium-quality category, or would you compete in the crowded low-price/low-quality category? There is very little competition in the high-price/low-quality category, but it wouldn't make sense to come out with a high-price/low-quality product. In the upper left quadrant, it looks as if a high-quality/lower-price product would have little competition.

There are other things to take into consideration before choosing a target position. How big is the market potential for the chosen position? Is the category growing or shrinking? Are there other key attributes that should be taken into consideration in determining a target position?

Three Circles Positioning Framework. The limitation of the perceptual mapping approach is that you are limited to exploring two attributes at a time. The three circles strategic framework, adapted from Joel Urbany and James Davis strategic insight framework,[3] allows you to consider multiple product attributes or even multiple products in developing a market position. This approach uses a Venn diagram with three circles: one representing your product (or products), one representing your competitor's (or competitors') product, and the third representing your customers' needs.

The intersection of all three circles is "The Bar." This represents the things valued by the customer that everybody in the industry is doing. You won't be able to develop a unique market position by emphasizing these attributes, but you need to offer them to be taken seriously in the industry. For example, in the hospitality industry, having a clean hotel room with television and a working bathroom is the "bar". You won't be able to differentiate based on having a clean room, but if your rooms aren't clean you will lose customers.

The area labeled "Your Unique Position" refers to attributes of your product that are valued by the customer and not available from your competition. These are attributes you can use to create a distinctive market position. "Competitor Unique Position" refers to attributes your customers value and that they can only get from your competition. These are areas where you are vulnerable to your competitor's positioning strategy. The "Opportunity to Strengthen Position" area represents things the customer values and nobody is currently providing. This represents opportunities to develop new products or to add features that can strengthen your position relative to the competition.

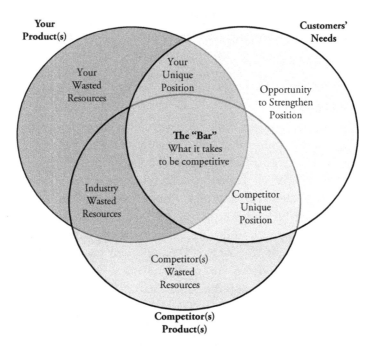

FIGURE 6.2   Three Circles Positioning Framework (Adapted from: Joel E. Urbany and James H. Davis, "Strategic Insight in Three Circles," Harvard Business Review, 2007.)

Another valuable contribution of this approach is that it recognizes there may be features or products you are offering that aren't valued by the customer. This is simply a waste of resources. Identifying and eliminating them can free up resources to invest in more productive areas. Eliminating attributes that everyone in the industry offers and are not valuable to your customers will allow you to lower the cost of your product or to boost your profit margins without affecting customer satisfaction. Many hotels still offer amenities such as newspaper delivery and telephone extensions in the bathroom area. In a world of digital media and cell phones, these amenities are wasted as they are no longer valued by customers.

Figure out How to Get from Point A to Point B

Having established where we are and where we want to be, we need to develop a plan to get us to the desired market position. What changes will we have to make to the product and other elements of the marketing mix to occupy the desired position? Does the company have the resources to support the change? What will the competitors' response be to your new position, and will you be able to defend the new position against competitors if the positioning is successful?

6.3 REPOSITIONING

Unless you are coming out with a new product, establishing a new position in the market involves repositioning from the current position to the desired position. There are two basic approaches for repositioning a product: positioning against the competition and positioning against yourself.

Positioning against the Competition

One of the ways to communicate a new market position is to use an existing category leader as a point of reference. The goal of head-to-head positioning is not to show how you are different than the competition but to show how you are better than the competition. You can position based on the same attributes—Coke and Pepsi have been playing this game for decades—or you can show that you are superior to the category leader on a specific attribute. For example, Jolt® cola famously positioned itself against the category leader with the slogan "All of the sugar and twice the caffeine," at a time when people were questioning the health benefits of caffeine-laden, sugary drinks. The downside of head-to-head comparisons is that in order to make reference to the category leader, you have to mention the category leader, which reinforces the category leader's position.

Another way to position against the competition is to show how you are different than the category leader in order to create a new sub category in which you can be the exemplar as 7UP did with its "Uncola" campaign.

Repositioning against Yourself

What happens if your initial positioning strategy fails? Perhaps it is because you didn't understand customers' perception of the positioning attributes. When the Miller Brewing Company first came out with Lite® beer, it was positioned as a diet beer. The way that they lowered the calorie count was to reduce the alcohol content. The product flopped. Men tend to be the heavy users for beer, and men were not interested in a diet product. In an attempt to reposition, Miller recognized that reducing the alcohol content made it easier to drink more of it. The new market position—"tastes great, less filling"—struck a chord with beer drinkers, and the rest is history. Today, lite beers are the largest category of mass-market brews.

(ENDNOTES)

1. Ries, Al, and Jack Trout, 1981. *Positioning: The Battle for Your Mind, New York: McGraw Hill.*

2. Srull, T. K., and Wyer, R. S., 1980, Category accessibility and social perception: Some implications for the study of person memory and interpersonal judgments, *Journal of Personality and Social Psychology, 38(6), 841–856. doi:10.1037/0022-3514.38.6.841.*

3. Urbany, Joel E., and James H. Davis, "Strategic Insight in Three Circles," *Harvard Business Review*, November 2007.

PRODUCT DEVELOPMENT

CH07

We have no control over how customers perceive our products. When creating new products, we can only control the features we build into them. It is up to our customers to decide if there is value in what we have done. This leads to a phenomenon I call "Stupid Customer Syndrome": you know that yours is the best product out there because of all the great features you've built into it, but customers are too stupid to appreciate what you have done. In business markets, the term is "disloyal" customers: even though yours is the best product on the market, your customers betray you by purchasing from a competitor a product you would be happy to provide. The reality is that customers are not stupid. They don't care how hard you worked on a product or how difficult it was to make. All they care about is what's in it for them. Don't blame the customer if the market isn't buying what you are selling.

7.1 WHAT IS A PRODUCT?

In Chapter 1.1, we talked about the concept of exchange, where, in order to complete a transaction, each side had to bring something of value to the other party. At its most basic, a product is the "something of value" marketers bring to the table. While we normally think of a product as something physical (a gallon of milk or an automobile), a product can be intangible (a college education, a musical performance) or a combination of both tangible and intangible benefits (a new car with a warranty). From a marketing perspective, a **product** is a bundle of tangible and intangible attributes that provide value to customers in exchange for money (or something else of value). This broader definition of a product encourages creativity in developing need-satisfying offerings for potential customers.

It is important to make the distinction between attributes, or features of products, and benefits. A **feature** is something that the manufacturer has control over. We add features in the hope that they will provide a benefit to the customer. A **benefit** is the perceived value of the feature as determined by the customer. Each customer will perceive the benefit associated with a specific feature differently.

Levels of the Product

While this textbook definition of a product frees us up to be creative in thinking about our products, I've found the "**levels of a product**" concept developed by Philip

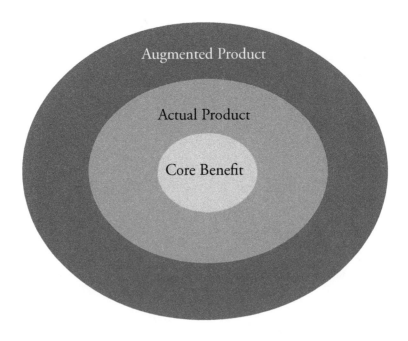

FIGURE 7.1 Levels of the Product (Adapted from: Philip Kotler, "Figure 12.5," Principles of Marketing, pp. 369, Prentice Hall.)

Kotler, building on the work of Theodore Levitt, to be very useful in developing products to meet the needs of customers.

According to Kotler, product development begins with the basic need being satisfied and then builds the bundle of tangible and intangible attributes on that base. This approach looks at the product as having three layers: the core benefit, an actual product, and an extended or augmented product.

Core Benefit

At the heart of any product is the **core benefit**, or basic need you are satisfying for the customer. Remember that people perceive things differently, so the same product may be providing a different core benefit for different people. For example, many people choose to enjoy a cup of coffee in the morning. For some people, a cup of coffee is a much-needed jolt of caffeine to get their day started. For others, a cup of coffee is a warm beverage to help ease the transition from night into day. And for still others, a cup of coffee is a rich, flavorful complement to a delightful breakfast.

From a marketing perspective, it is important to remember that for each of these customers, there is only one benefit to a cup of coffee. In essence, a cup of coffee could provide three different core benefits. This understanding is an important basis of positioning, as discussed in Chapter 6.1.

Actual Product

The **actual product,** or "what's in the box," is the form the product takes when the customer buys it. While this is what we usually think of when we think of a product, in reality, it is simply a benefit delivery system—a way to get the benefit to the customer. There are many different ways to deliver the same benefit to a customer. For example, if the core benefit is a much-needed jolt of caffeine to get the day started, the actual product could take the form of a cup of coffee, a can of cola, an energy drink, a cup of tea, or a caffeine pill; the list is endless.

This is where creativity in marketing comes in. One way to attract customers is to develop a more effective way of delivering a core benefit they are already enjoying.

Augmented Product

The **augmented product**, or extended product, places the actual product in the context of the marketing mix: product, price, promotion, and distribution. This is where marketers can enhance the benefits received and satisfy additional needs. For example, when I make a cup of coffee at home, I'm getting my caffeine fix, but when I stop by my neighborhood Starbucks, I can purchase a blueberry scone to enjoy with my coffee, sit back and check my emails with their Wi-Fi hot spot, and maybe try a seasonal brew they may be featuring.

The augmented product can be used to develop relationships with customers as well as to increase the value of the customer relationship by including other benefits in the product/service bundle.

BMW Ultimate Service is a beautiful example of using the augmented product to build customer relationships. When you purchase a new BMW automobile, in addition to the car, you receive free routine maintenance for 4 years or 50,000 miles. This requires you to visit the dealer regularly, where you can see the latest models while your car is serviced and washed at no charge to you. This way, BMW helps to make sure you have a positive experience with your car, and when it is time for a new car, you know right where to go for your next one.

7.2 NEED FOR INNOVATION

Today's customers are moving targets. With rapid technological change, customers are regularly presented with new ways of satisfying their needs. Economic theory tells us that if you have a highly profitable product, it will attract competition until the profits have disappeared. In today's global marketplace, the competitive pressure is accelerating. In order to be consistently successful in this environment, businesses need to continuously reinvent themselves by developing a stream of new products.

One study (Tretheway, 1998) looked at businesses that were leaders or laggards in terms of profitability and found that profit leaders had 39% of sales from new products while profit laggards had 23% of their sales from new products. To get 39% of sales from new products every year, in effect profit leaders have to reinvent themselves every two and a half years. Profit laggards reinvent themselves every 4 years. Any way you look at it, you need to be able to innovate to stay successful in business today.

A business can take either a reactive or proactive approach toward new product development strategy. The reactive approach seeks to develop new products to defend its market share against competitive offerings or to make up for declining sales in maturing markets. The proactive approach embraces new products as a way to achieve a sustainable competitive advantage and seeks to develop processes that support innovation. More and more companies are recognizing the importance of a proactive approach to new product development.

What Is New?

Innovation is not easy. There are good ideas that never make it to market and bad ideas that do make it to market. As many as 80% of new products fail. This is not an easy number to estimate because definitions of what is new can vary considerably.

The Federal Trade Commission defines a new product as something that is significantly changed and less than 6 months old.

From a customer perspective, it may be helpful to think of new product introductions as being on a continuum from very small, incremental changes at one extreme to radically new innovations at the other extreme. Within this continuum, we see many types of new product introductions.

A **continuous innovation** is small, incremental change to an existing product. These "new and improved" products are created to position the product relative to the competition or to reinvigorate interest in a mature product. While these incremental changes are relatively easy to do, they are also easy to imitate and seldom lead to a sustainable competitive advantage. Much of what is happening in the soft drink industry is based on continuous innovations. In the cola industry, caffeine free, diet caffeine free, and cherry diet caffeine free were all incremental innovations introduced and quickly imitated by the competition.

Toward the middle of the innovation spectrum you see **dynamically continuous innovations**, or new ways of delivering the same benefits to customers. These "new to the customer" products require some consumer education for people to understand how the new product replaces an existing solution the customer is using. This space also contains new products that are the result of convergence or synergies created by the combination of two or more technologies. eBay became successful by combining the variety of a flea market with innovative bidding software to create an electronic marketplace.

At the farthest extreme of the new product spectrum is the disruptive, or **discontinuous, innovation**. These are radically new products that have the potential of changing the way we live. The risk of failure is high because it requires changing people's habits and may require extensive education. However, the rewards can be just as great. A company that develops a successful disruptive innovation can create a significant and sustainable competitive advantage for years to come.

7.3 NEW PRODUCT DEVELOPMENT

There has been a lot of research around how companies develop and introduce successful new products. The following seven-step **new product development process** is consistent with most of these findings.

New Product Strategy

What role does new product development play in your company's overall strategy? Are new products seen as an opportunity to create a competitive advantage in the marketplace, or are new products seen as a way to replace revenue lost through declining markets or to aggressive competitors? What systems do you have in place to support the new product development process? Strategies used by companies that have been successful in developing new products include creating a new product development

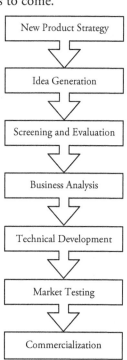

FIGURE 7.2 New Product Development Process

department or testing laboratory and using cross-functional teams of marketing, production, design, engineering, and finance people to speed up the development process and minimize wasted efforts. Some companies select a "product champion," or a promising individual, to be accountable for the new product as it goes through the process. If the product is successful, the champion will become the product manager.

Idea Generation

Where do great ideas come from? The answer is, you never know. That's why it is important to cast as wide a net as possible when trying to come up with new product ideas. Customers, employees, and suppliers may have ideas for new ways to serve your customers. Critics or customer complaints are a frequently overlooked source of new product ideas—remember, when a customer takes time to complain about your product, he or she is telling you there is an opportunity for a better product. Professional design firms can work with you to facilitate the creative process and to identify products to fit with your existing product mix.

Screening and Evaluation

While more is better during the idea generation stage, there is no way to seriously consider each proposal that comes up. Rather than stifle creativity, develop the list of possible ideas first—without critiquing the ideas—and then later, when the muse is exhausted, weed out the impractical or impossible ideas.

During this phase, it may be helpful to develop product concepts (prototypes, designs) for some of the more promising ideas. This allows you to better flesh out the idea. Many companies are using the internet to ask their customers to help in the prototyping process.

Business Analysis

This is the point where reality sets in. Having identified a product concept that seems to be attractive to your customers, you need to pause and make sure the idea makes sense from a business standpoint. Based on the feedback from the proto-typing, you need to develop a preliminary business plan for the product. What is the target market for the product? How much will it cost to develop the product? What will it cost to launch the product once developed? What is the forecasted demand for the product? This is a situation where a pro forma income statement is a useful planning tool. A pro forma income statement is based on estimated sales and estimated expenses and gives an early indication of whether or not the product might be profitable.

Technical Development

Now that you've given a green light to the project, you need to develop a prototype, or example of the product as you intend to sell it. This allows you to identify any manufacturing issues and is another area where customer input can be valuable in determining the features of the final product. Rather than building a physical model of the new product, many companies are using computer simulations as a way to save time and money in developing a prototype.

Design—Blending Form and Function

One of the ways marketers turn features into benefits is through the user experience, or "UX," as it is sometimes called. They study users to gain insights about stated and unstated user needs. They then work with designers and product development professionals to create meaningful UX. The UX gives form to the intended benefit in a way that helps the customer perceive the value in your new product. A good design is both useful and pleasing to the eye. When evaluating a product's design, customers use "SAFE" criteria: social (status), altruistic (expression of the greater self), function, and esthetics (beauty).[1]

There are two schools of thought on how to develop the UX. With the *design-driven* approach, customer input is discouraged in the early stages of development. The belief is that when it comes to truly innovative products, customers don't know what they want and designers and product developers are better able to judge user needs because they themselves are users[2]. On the other hand, the *user-centric design* approach is more collaborative, seeking frequent feedback from customers as the design progresses.

IDEO (see https://www.ideo.com/about/), a major product design firm, uses a three-stage user-driven "Design Thinking" process involving inspiration, ideation, and implementation to help develop new products[3].

Room to Fail

In order to grow, you need to take risks. In order to take risks, it needs to be OK for you to fail. Failure is an opportunity to learn. We learn more from our failures than we do from our successes. However, we don't want to keep learning the same lesson over and over.

Market Testing

Because introducing a new product can be very expensive, and because the failure rate for new products is high, many companies choose to introduce the product on a limited scale to see how customers respond to the actual product. This is especially true for radically new products. The test can include the entire marketing mix—including advertising, pricing, and distribution—or it can be a limited test focusing on one or two areas of concern.

The disadvantage of a test market is that it can be expensive to do, and it takes time. When Proctor and Gamble (P&G) introduced the Swiffer cleaning product, it chose to do extensive test marketing because the product was so new. In the meantime, the S. C. Johnson company was able to develop a competing product, the Pledge Grab-it, and bring it to market before P&G in some areas.

Some companies are now using crowdfunding sites such as Kickstarter or Indiegogo as a market-testing tool. While the company may already have the resources needed to fund the new product, it may still launch a crowdfunding campaign to validate the concept by gauging interest of potential customers.[4]

Commercialization

Having determined that this is a viable new product, the final stage is to introduce the product to the marketplace and incorporate it into your product mix. The big question here is whether it would be better to roll out the product nationally or globally or whether it would be better to introduce the product on a limited scale and increase distribution as demand for the product grows. The advantage to a global launch is that you gain economies of scale and market penetration. The disadvantage is that a national or global launch is very expensive should the new product fail to find an audience.

The advantage of limited introduction is that the start-up costs are minimized. If the product is a success at the local or regional level, you can use revenue from the product to fund the next level of expansion. The disadvantage of a limited product introduction is that it gives competitors an opportunity to imitate the product.

7.4 NEW PRODUCT ADOPTION

Developing innovative products is only half of the equation. Customers have to buy them. They have to believe the new product is a better solution than the one they are already using. The **new product adoption process** describes how individuals decide to purchase new products, and diffusion theory describes how populations adopt new products.

New Product Adoption Process

Researchers have identified six stages consumers go through in the process of incorporating a new product into their purchase patterns. This is what marketers call a

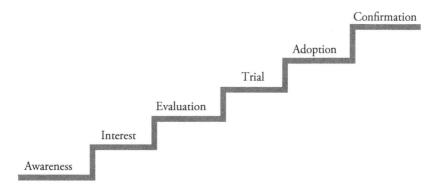

FIGURE 7.3   Product adoption process

product adoption. Each stage of the process—awareness, interest, evaluation, trial, adoption, and confirmation—has implications for a successful product launch.

Looking at the adoption process in stages allows for a better understanding of why a particular product succeeded or failed. Two key metrics are first-time purchase (Did awareness, interest, and evaluation lead to a trial?) and repeat purchase (How many customers ended up adopting the product after giving it a try?). First-time purchase relates to the effectiveness of your marketing program; repeat purchase relates to the value customers perceive in the product offering.

Awareness

New products are, by definition, unsought products because customers can't search for something they've never heard of. Most people do not actively seek out information about new products (remember cognitive miserliness from Chapter 2.2), so it is up to the marketer to reach out to customers with interruptive communication in order to get their attention.

Interest

Consumers are very good at ignoring marketing communication, so it is important to engage the customer quickly. You need to clearly demonstrate the advantage the customer will gain by adopting your product. For some products, this is relatively easy. You may have seen someone demonstrating a novel toy in a shopping mall kiosk, street fair, or even in an airport. All you have to do is see the toy in action, and you can understand how much fun it could be.

Evaluation

Having broken through the customers' defenses, you now have an opportunity to persuade them to buy your product. It is important to have the information people need to evaluate the product available in an easy-to-understand form. For simple products, an attractive package can provide the necessary information. For more complicated products, it may be necessary to have someone nearby to answer questions.

Trial

Sometimes called a trial purchase, this is the customer's first transaction involving the product. This is very similar to the decision stage of the consumer buying process discussed in Chapter 2.2.

Adoption

Having tried the product, the customers can decide whether the product is a fit for their lifestyle. If it is a fit, you can begin building a relationship with the customer around the product.

Confirmation

Repeat purchases are the acid test for new product adoptions. It can be very expensive to get customers to try a product for the first time. Many people try a new product once; a much smaller number become regular customers. A new product becomes profitable when people purchase it for a second time, a third time, and, eventually, become regular customers. This is why it is important to look at both first-time purchases and repeat purchases when evaluating the success of an introduction.

Factors That Affect New Product Adoption

Certain characteristics of new products can make it easier or harder for customers to make the adoption. Here are five factors that can affect whether or not consumers adopt a product.

Relative Advantage

Is the product a significant improvement over the solution the customer is already using? The bigger the relative advantage, the easier it is for customers to adopt the product.

Compatibility

Does the product fit with the customers' lifestyles, or will they need to change their behavior in order to use the new product? It is very difficult to get consumers to change their behavior. Think of any weight-loss program you have ever seen. The ones that work are the ones that require you to change your eating habits and exercise regularly. But many people are willing to spend good money for a pill that promises you can lose weight without exercise.

Complexity

How difficult is it for the customer to see the advantage of adopting the new product? The harder the customers have to work to understand the value of what you are offering, the less likely they are to make the effort.

Trialability

If it is possible for the customer to experience the benefit from the product before making the purchase, there is a better chance for an adoption. This is why many food companies introduce new products by giving away free samples in the grocery store.

Observability

Is there a visible difference between the new product and the product it is replacing? This makes it easier for customers to adopt the new product. One reason for the success of the Toyota Prius hybrid car is that it looked different than any other car on the road when it was introduced.

> "You can spend lots of time reading white papers and the latest articles about innovation and the future of technology, but to really understand something, people need to see it demonstrated or experience it firsthand. I've personally found it very effective to invest in having Creative Technologists on my teams—people that can quickly build, hack, and create a prototype and put it in front of someone and say, 'See, this is why this technology matters—look at this—this is what you can do with it. Imagine the possibilities!'"
>
> **Michael Phillips**

7.5 DIFFUSION OF INNOVATIONS

Diffusion of innovations theory looks at how large populations adopt new products over time. There are five waves, or stages, as different types of people within the population make the decision to adopt. These stages are product specific. One person may be an innovator when it comes to electronic products but a laggard when it comes to new food products.

Innovators

Innovators are the people who live on the bleeding edge and need to have the latest and greatest version of a particular product. They actively seek out information about new products in development and may blog on the topic. Innovators represent about 2.5% of the people who will adopt the product.

Early Adopters

Early adopters are people who want to be innovative and recognized as knowledge-able by their friends. Marketers need to make an effort to reach out and commu-nicate with these early adopters, as their opinions can be very influential to others considering the product. Early adopters represent about 13.5% of the people who will eventually adopt the product.

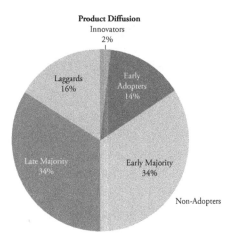

Product Diffusion

FIGURE 7.4   Product Diffusion

Early Majority

The early majority are people who like to be up to date but not cutting-edge. They can be reached by advertising. The early majority represents about 34% of the people who will eventually adopt the product.

Late Majority

The late majority are people who are more cautious about new products. They want to see that the product is effective and reliable before purchasing. They are more influenced by word of mouth than by advertising. The late majority represents another 34% of the people who will adopt the product.

Laggards

Laggards are people who will only adopt the new product when the solution they are currently using becomes ineffective or they need to replace a product that is no longer available. Laggards represent the last 16% of people who will adopt the product.

Nonadopters

It is important to remember that not everybody will see a benefit in a particular product. This means there will always be a number of people who will never adopt the product. There are still people in the United States who do not own a television set.

(ENDNOTES)

1. Kumar, M., & Noble, C. H. (2016). Beyond form and function: why do consumers value product design? *Journal of Business Research, 69*(2), 613–620.
2. Verganti, R. (2008). Design, meanings, and radical innovation: A meta-model and a research agenda. *Journal of Product Innovation Management, 25*, 436–456.
3. Brown, T. (2008). Design thinking. *Harvard Business Review, 86*(6), 84–92, 141.
4. Kaul, G. (2015, June 28). Big firms tap crowds for funds. *San Francisco Chronicle.*

PRODUCT MANAGEMENT

CH08

Few, if any, successful businesses have just one product and one target market. For long-term success, you need to manage an ever-evolving assortment of products to meet the needs of your current customers, to attract new customers, and to create opportunities to strengthen the relationship (and to increase revenue) by offering related products of interest to your customers.

8.1 PRODUCT LIFE CYCLE

One of the most basic principles of marketing is the idea of the **product life cycle**. This theory assumes that product categories (more so than individual products or brands) have a limited life and go through four distinct stages, each stage having a different profit profile and requiring different strategies for success. The life cycle is defined by two curves—sales and profit—whose shape will vary from product category to product category (Figure 8.1).

As you can see from this simple illustration, the sales curve starts at zero when the product is introduced. Sales increase slowly for a while and then begin to take off. Eventually the sales curve flattens out and then begins to fall off. The profit curve starts below zero because you will always have development costs before the product is ready for market. Profits rise steadily until the sales curve takes off at which point the profit curve backs off and continues to decline over time. We will explain why this is as we talk about each of the stages.

Introductory Stage

The first stage of the product life cycle is the introductory stage. This is when the product is first being introduced to the market. Because the product is new, awareness is low, and sales start out slowly. In the introductory stage, you are likely selling to innovators and early adopters. These are the people who want to have the latest and greatest and will actively seek out new products. The goal in the introductory stage is to generate **primary demand**, or first-time buyers, for the product. As nobody really knows about the product, there is no point in trying to show how your offering is better than another. The key issues during the introductory stage are market entry and pricing approach.

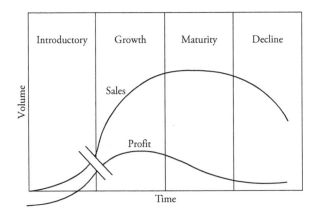

FIGURE 8.1   Product Life cycle

The most aggressive approach to market entry is to be first to market, or **first mover**. The advantage of being first to market is that you will have the market to yourself, will have a strong position in the newly created category, and will be at a competitive advantage should the product prove to be successful. The disadvantage of being first mover is that most new products fail, and the first mover bears the cost of that failure.

Rather than risking a product failure, the **second mover** holds back until the new product concept has proved to be successful and then enters the market either by acquiring the first mover or by launching a similar, competitive product.

Typically, smaller, more nimble companies are first movers as they have little to lose and everything to gain should the product be successful. Larger, well-capitalized companies tend to be second movers. The downside risk associated with a product failure would be a negative impact on earnings and a depressed stock price. We see this dynamic playing itself out every day in the tech industry. There are hundreds of small startup operations developing the next big thing. When an application begins to show promise, the startup is bought out by Google, Facebook, or another of the tech giants.

Pricing

The issue in pricing in the introductory stage is how quickly you can recover the development costs and begin showing a profit. A **skimming** approach sets prices very high initially to recover costs quickly. Innovators and early adopters are willing to pay a premium in order to have the most current product. As demand increases and economies of scale begin to kick in, you can begin lowering the price to attract more buyers while maintaining higher profit margins. Because profit margins are high, competitors begin to enter the market, putting additional pressure on prices. This pattern has been repeated over and over in the consumer electronics industry. A new product category (wide-screen televisions, Blu-ray players, 3-D television, 4K ultra high def) is introduced at very high prices, and as demand picks up, prices fall.

Penetration pricing sets the initial price relatively low to increase market share as quickly as possible and to discourage competitors from entering the market. Profit margins are smaller with the lower prices, so it takes longer for the product to become profitable. This approach is widely used with **consumer packaged goods** (i.e., soap, breakfast cereal, cough medicine) where the product is expected to reach a mass audience very quickly. The advantage is that the lower price stimulates demand, developing the market much more quickly. The lower profit margins discourage competitors from entering the market, allowing you to build a strong market position.

Growth Stage

Once demand for the new product expands beyond the early adopters and moves into the mass market, sales (and profits) begin to increase rapidly. The law of economics says that when there are profits to be made, competitors will enter the market. As competition intensifies, profit margins begin to be squeezed although the industry is still attractive because high growth more than compensates for shrinking margins. Because there are now more competitors, the goal in the growth stage is to differentiate the product to appeal to different market segments. This is where STP (Chapter 5) and branding (Chapter 9) become important. Customers now understand the product category, and your job is to explain why your offering is superior to others on the market.

The Development Gap

Many new products never make it past the introductory stage of the product life cycle. This **development gap** (sometimes called the "valley of death") occurs because early stage buyers (innovators, early adopters) are much more forgiving than the mass market (early and late majorities). Early stage buyers are more willing to make an effort to receive the benefit from the new product. For the product to make the transition to the mass market, the early majority needs to see a clear benefit to adopting the product. As a case in point, look at 3D TV. Following the success of 3D movies like Avatar (a James Cameron spectacle), 3D TV was seen as a way to bring the excitement of 3D into the home. It was hoped this would be the "next big thing," injecting new life into the home entertainment industry. Unfortunately, a lack of "must-have" 3D movies, and the need to mess around with battery operated goggles proved to be too much for the technology to make it to the mass market[1].

Maturity Stage

At some point, sales for the new product level off as there are fewer first-time buyers to fuel growth, but a steady replacement market keeps sales strong. Declining profits force out all but a few strong players in the market, and these competitors compete fiercely to maintain their market share. Many of the products we buy every day are in the maturity stage of the product life cycle. Coke® and Pepsi® have been slugging it out in the soft drink market for years, with each point of market share worth millions of dollars. As fierce competition and level sales make raising prices a challenge, mature stage companies seek to increase profits by reducing operating costs. The goal during the maturity stage is to maintain market share and to extend the life of the product.

Maturity Stage Strategies

Two basic maturity stage strategies are incremental innovations and repositioning. Incremental innovations attempt to extend the maturity stage by making small changes (innovations!) to the product. In recent years, the detergent industry has come out with liquid detergents, scented detergents, unscented detergents, detergents with fabric softener, detergents with bleach, concentrated liquid detergents, detergent pods (please don't eat the pods), high-efficiency detergents, … you get the idea. Each "new and improved" variation is an attempt to renew interest in the category. Because incremental innovations are easily imitated, there is a constant flow of "new and improveds" to stay one step ahead of the competition.

Repositioning is an attempt to extend the life of the product by finding new market segments or new uses for an existing product. The Church and Dwight Company, makers of Arm and Hammer™ baking soda are masters at repositioning. Their flagship product—baking soda—has been around for more than 150 years. While the market for baking soda products is mature, the company has introduced several products based on other properties of bicarbonate of soda. Arm and Hammer toothpaste relies on the hygienic properties of baking soda, Arm and Hammer carpet deodorizer takes advantage of the odor absorbing property. And parents of school-age children can download the recipe for Play Clay, which uses baking soda as a key ingredient.

Decline Stage

Eventually, demand for a product begins to fall off. The product may be out-of-date or have been replaced by a better alternative. Whatever the reason, there is still some residual demand for the product. While most of the benefits the product offered may be obsolete because of the introduction of superior products, or because the product is no longer in fashion, some customers may still have a reason to buy it. One hundred years ago, oil lamps were a popular choice for indoor lighting. Today, electricity has replaced oil lamps for indoor lighting. However, you can still find oil lamps if you look hard for them. Some people use them for emergency lighting or camping. Others use them for decorative purposes. In parts of the world where electricity is not available, oil lamps are still widely used. The point is that while oil lamps are clearly yesterday's news, there is still a residual demand for the product.

In the decline stage, there may be one or two competitors left in the market. Because there is little you can do to stimulate demand for an obsolete product, the goal is to maximize the profit rather than to try to grow the business.

Decline Stage Strategies

There are two alternatives for managing a decline stage product: **milking the product** or exiting the market. Because the upside potential for the product is limited, a milking strategy involves cutting costs wherever possible and continuing to carry the product as long as it is profitable to do so. It is pointless to invest in new features or product improvements in the decline stage as there won't be enough interest in the product for you to recover your costs.

At the point where the product is no longer profitable or where the profitability is too low to justify allocating resources to continue selling it, it is time to exit the market. In many cases, you can divest the product by selling it to another company that finds the product line more attractive than you do. By selling off marginal product lines, you can free up resources to invest in more attractive markets. If there are no companies willing to buy the discontinued product, then you may have to simply shut down production and move on to better things.

8.2 FASHIONS AND FADS

Fashion is an area of the economy that lives and dies by the product lifecycle. To be clear, we need to define a couple of terms. A **style** is a distinctive mode of presentation or performance. A **fashion** is an accepted and popular style. A style may be enduring and come in and out of fashion over time. Fashion marketing involves altering superficial characteristics of a product to make a product feel out-of-date even if the product is perfectly functional. Most of us have articles of clothing in the back of our closets that fit perfectly, look like new, and we wouldn't be caught dead wearing them. Why? Because they are out of fashion.

I believe fashion marketing works because of two competing social principles. We want to be part of a group, and, at the same time, we want to be unique. One of the ways we construct our social identity is through the products we adopt. Because styles are constantly changing, it creates opportunities to express our individuality through fashion. For example, wearing blue jeans is a signal a person has adopted a casual lifestyle. Yet no two people will wear the exact same type of jeans. There are trendy designer jeans, vintage jeans, Levi's® original jeans, and private label jeans.

Fashion products may have a life cycle from a few months to several years. Although we usually think of clothing when we think of fashion, there are fashions in furniture, cars, and even in houses.

A **fad** is a product with a very short life cycle. It comes out of nowhere, is all the rage for a while, and then disappears. Do you remember the Giga Pets™ craze in the late 1990s? Maybe you still have one of these virtual pets sitting in the back of a drawer somewhere, batteries dead and starved for attention.

> "I think the reason [company] hired me is because they had over-hired the previous years for engineers and very quantitative people. What they liked in me is that I could read and write and present information in a consumable way, and I've let that be my edge throughout my career. I've really leaned on that—that I am never the best analytics person in the room. I am never the most imaginative person in the room. But I am frequently the one who can crystalize things into phrases or even into presentations."

Justin Garrett

Fashion Adoption

The fashion cycle, similar to the product life cycle, suggests that fashions spread across social classes in three stages. The distinctiveness stage is when the style is new and eagerly sought by trendsetters. In the emulation stage, the fashion becomes more popular. In the economic stage, the fashion is mass-produced and is available at lower prices to the masses.

This is why following trends is so important in the fashion industry. While marketers have been criticized for promoting fashions that may have a negative impact on society, designers would counter that they can't make a trend fashionable, they can only identify where styles are headed in order to stay ahead of popular tastes. Sometimes styles are adopted by one group after another in successive waves. Trickle-down fashions originate with upper classes and migrate downward toward the middle while trickle-up fashions originate with lower classes and migrate upward. Futurists like Faith Popcorn (www.faithpopcorn.com) can help marketers identify emerging trends.

Fashion and Inventory

Because fashions have a limited life, and because fashions lose value over time, inventory management is critical to success, especially in industries with short fashion cycles such as clothing or toys. These products have a very short selling season, and relatively long lead times, so forecasting is an important activity. For example, the toys you buy at Christmas were probably ordered in July.

If you order too much inventory, you might have to reduce the price in order to get rid of it before the next season rolls around. This has a tendency to cheapen the brand because it appears to be less exclusive. Some high-end fashion houses will destroy unsold inventory rather than put it on sale, but this can be an expensive proposition if you have a lot of unsold inventory.

If you order too little inventory, you are leaving money on the table. It is expensive to create demand for a product. Because fashion merchandise loses value over time, customers are not willing to wait for your inventory to be replenished. There is an upside to not having enough inventory as scarcity makes a fashion more distinctive for those who manage to buy it and can enhance the image of the brand.

The ideal is to have just enough inventory to satisfy demand without having to discount extra merchandise. Zara®, a trend-setting fashion clothing company, solves this problem by creating a very fast manufacturing and delivery system. Rather than ordering the bulk of its inventory before the season begins, it has the ability to quickly restock the items that are selling the best. The money it saves by not having to discount merchandise covers the extra costs of the supply chain.

8.3 CLASSIFYING PRODUCTS

It may be helpful at this point to talk about how marketers classify products. There are a couple of advantages to looking at classification systems. Because they are a systematic way of looking at a category, classification systems (or taxonomies) can help make decisions defensible. Also, because they look at differences in how products are used, taxonomies can help create useful market segments.

Business Goods

Business goods are used by business customers to create products for the eventual end user. Generally speaking, there are three types of business goods: goods intended for resale, goods used to create other goods, and goods used to support the organization. Goods intended for resale are finished products that use an intermediary (usually a retailer) (Chapter 15) to reach the end user.

Goods used to create other goods are things such as raw materials, processed materials, and component parts. Goods used to support the organization are things such as equipment, maintenance, and repair; they are business services that are consumed in the manufacturing process.

Consumer Goods

Consumer goods are products that will be used by the purchaser in its present form (although some assembly may be required). Durable goods, or hard goods, are products that last a long time and aren't consumed in one use. Nondurable goods, or soft goods, are consumed in one use or last a short time (usually less than three years).

Consumer goods can also be classified by how they are purchased. Understanding how products are purchased can help you better align your marketing efforts with customers' expectations.

Convenience Products

Convenience products are frequently purchased staples, impulse products, and emergency goods. One way to understand convenience products is to think of anything you would find in a convenience store, such as 7-Eleven®. Customers don't want to spend a lot of time and effort shopping for convenience products. Outlets that carry convenience products should be located near the customer and have long operating hours. Many convenience stores are open 24 hours a day.

Shopping Products

Shopping products are things people are willing to expend a significant amount of time and effort before purchasing. They may shop at multiple outlets and use extensive problem solving to make the final decision. Clothing and appliances are generally considered to be shopping products. Outlets that carry shopping products should be located near other outlets to make it easier for the customer to compare. This is why shopping malls have so many shoe stores.

Specialty Products

A **specialty product** is something for which a customer will not accept substitutes. It has a unique characteristic that makes it singularly important to the customer. What makes a product unique is in the eye of the beholder. Many people have food preferences for which they will accept no substitute. Because the product is seen as unique, the customer will actively search for the product. Having a presence on the internet can make these specialty products easier for customers to find.

Unsought Products

Unsought products are products that a customer doesn't know about (and therefore can't look for) or products a customer does know about but doesn't want to think about. Many people don't like to talk about life insurance because it reminds them they are going to die. Regardless of whether the customer is aware of an unsought product, you need to use intrusive communication to reach these people during the identify alternatives stage of the buying process.

> "Technology and trends change so quickly. I think you need to be flexible, adaptable and always open to learning at every stage in your career."
>
> Marian Kwon

8.4 PRODUCT MIX

The **product mix** describes all of the products an organization offers for sale. The starting point is to consider each individual item you carry. Retail organizations speak of SKU's, or stock keeping units, as the most discrete product item. A **product line** is a group of product items that have some characteristics, customers, or uses in common. What constitutes a product line will vary dramatically from company to company. Some larger organizations may even have product lines within product lines. For example, Macy's® has a men's department. Within the men's department, there are lines for men's clothing, activewear, big and tall, men's shoes, etc. Within the men's clothing line, there are lines for dress shirts, formal wear, underwear, suits, etc. Let it suffice to say that each organization will develop product lines that make sense given the customer base and the competitive landscape. From a management perspective, it is helpful to think of the product mix as having two dimensions: length (sometimes called depth) and width (sometimes called breadth).

Product Line Length and Breadth

The **length of a product line** speaks to the number of individual product items in the line. A short product line has only a few items in it. A long product line has many items in it. The length of a product line is a way to target more than one market segment. Each item in the product line might appeal to a different customer. Take, for example, a coffee shop. You would expect the coffee shop to have a line of coffee drinks (or ready to serve drinks or hot beverages—you can see how the definition of a line could vary depending on the focus of the shop). Each item in the line—regular coffee, decaf coffee, expresso, cold coffee, lattes, cappuccinos, etc., will appeal to a different type of customer. Thinking back to the levels of the product concept in Chapter 7.1, each item in a product line delivers a core benefit to a different segment within the need class.

The **width of your product mix** speaks to the number of different product lines you carry. A wide product mix will have several different product lines. A narrow product mix will have one or just a few different product lines. Product line width allows you to address other needs of your target market(s), strengthening the relationship and increasing your share of wallet—the total amount of money an individual customer will spend with you. In the coffee shop example, once you have a customer in the store for his or her chosen type of coffee, you might offer a line of food items (snacks, baked goods, sandwiches, salads) for the customer to enjoy along with his or her coffee. You might also have a line of coffee paraphernalia (coffee beans, coffee mugs, coffee brewers, filters, t-shirts, recorded music) so the customer can enjoy the coffee shop experience at home.

So what about tea? Would you have a separate line of tea items, or would you consider tea items to be part of the coffee/hot beverage line? The answer would depend on your understanding of how your customers view coffee versus tea and the marketing strategy for the shop.

Product Mix and Retail Positioning

The product mix can be used to help position a retail operation. A product mix that is wide and deep would appeal to a wide variety of customers and give them lots of choices. This is the approach used by full service retailers such as Macy's or JC Penney®. A product mix that is narrow and deep is an approach used by specialty retailers or niche marketers. A comic book store wouldn't carry much beyond comic books, but a comic book fan would be able to find the latest issue of his or her favorite comic at the store. A product mix that is wide and shallow would offer variety but not much choice within a category. When you go to a Costco® wholesale store, you will find an array of different products but usually only one choice per category. A product mix that is narrow and shallow might be placed in high-traffic areas to allow for convenience. A person traveling in an airport will be able to buy a book in newsstand, but the selection will be very limited.

From a manufacturing perspective, it is important to consider the product mix of potential retail partners as you develop your marketing strategy. You would want to focus on retailers that carry a line in your category. If you are selling the most popular product in your category, you might find distributors with both shallow and deep product lines. If you are selling a more specialized product, you would want to consider retail outlets with a long product line.

Product Management Strategies

You can see that with a variety of products, a variety of target segments, and the dynamic nature of the markets as products move through the product life cycle; managing the product mix can be a challenge. A product manager, or **brand manager**, is a person responsible for marketing a product or group of products. Each product in the line is evaluated in terms of how well it fits with the current market situation. If the product is not performing optimally, the product manager might choose to modify the product to better meet customer needs, change the target segment for a better fit, or even reposition the product to emphasize a different attribute.

From a product line perspective, a manager may decide to add product items to a line to appeal to different customers or remove items from a line if the items aren't selling. Two factors to consider when adding to a product line are cannibalization and synergies. **Cannibalization** recognizes that when you add a product to appeal to new customers, some of your existing customers may prefer the new offering to the one they were currently using. Ideally, the incremental sales increase from the new product will more than offset the cost of adding the item and the lost sales from existing product lines. Sometimes, a company will add a product to the product line even if it only appeals to existing customers. If we don't offer the product, a competitor might, and then we would lose the customer altogether.

A synergy is when the combination of two or more products has a combined impact greater than simply adding the impact of each individual product. In layman's terms, 1 + 1 = 3. Because you already have experience dealing with the items in a product line—advertising, sales techniques, distribution, etc., you may have a relatively low marginal cost of adding a new product to an existing line. Thus, you have the benefit of offering a new core benefit at a lower cost than trying to introduce an unrelated product.

Product Portfolio

One widely used approach to managing the product mix is to use a portfolio approach such as the one originally developed by the Boston Consulting Group (BCG). The BCG portfolio uses a 2 × 2 matrix as a screen to evaluate the various products in the mix. One axis rates market attractiveness, the other axis rates your relative market position. Products in the upper left quadrant, high market attractiveness, high relative position, are called stars. These are products that have growth

103

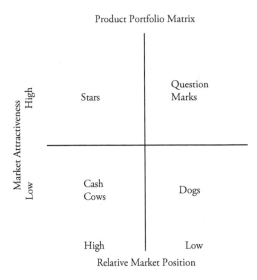

Product Portfolio Matrix

Market Attractiveness

High — Stars | Question Marks

Low — Cash Cows | Dogs

High | Low

Relative Market Position

FIGURE 8.2 BCG Matrix

potential and will likely be profitable in the future.

These are the products where you want to put your strongest marketing effort. As these products move through the product life cycle to the maturity and decline stages, growth potential is less. These cash cows generate positive earnings and cash flow that can fuel the growth of the stars. Ideally, you would want a product portfolio with a balance of stars and cash cows for sustainability. But what if you have no stars or cash cows? Then you would need to invest in developing a product that is in an attractive market, but your market position is weak. Hopefully, you can improve your market position and turn them into stars. Dogs are products where you have a weak market position and the market has low growth potential. These should be eliminated so you can focus your resources on more promising areas.

8.5 PRODUCT QUALITY

Quality is in the eye of the beholder. A customer's perception of value is a function of perceived benefits less the perceived cost of obtaining the benefit (Chapter 1.1). So whether the customer perceives value in your product is the first indicator of product quality. It is important to understand customer expectations so as not to overengineer a product. When you build features into a product that aren't valued by the customer, it has no impact on the perceived quality and simply increases your costs.

The second component of product quality is consistency. Does your product deliver the same customer experience time after time? For physical products, consistency is delivered through quality management programs such as the ISO 9000 standards for production efficiency (www.iso.org). With services, consistency is delivered through effective training programs and well-defined business systems. The McDonald's® Corporation sells more hamburgers than anyone else in the world. Why are McDonald's hamburgers so popular? I don't think anyone would claim that McDonalds makes the best tasting hamburger. What makes the chain so popular is the consistency of experience. Wherever you are in the world, you know what to expect from a McDonalds.

(ENDNOTE)

1. Katzmaier, David, "With a bullet to the head from Samsung, 3D TV is now deader than ever," *Cnet.com,* March 1, 2016.

105

BRANDING

CH09

Branding is one of the most visible aspects of marketing. As consumers, most of our interactions with companies, and even with the world in general, are through branded products. We love our favorite brands. Literally. We are emotionally attached to our favorite brands. In our consumer culture, brands are so important that we sometimes define who we are in terms of the brands we use. Are you a Prius kind of person or are you more of a Mercedes person? Some Apple "fanboys" have an almost religious attachment to the brand. Nike followers will go as far as to tattoo the company logo on their bodies.

The branding concept is so powerful that it extends into areas beyond the marketing of products. The idea of a personal brand was introduced by business guru Tom Peters in the late 1990s. Since then, the idea of personal branding has spawned a whole industry of self-help, consulting, and career advice, all designed to help you make the most of "Brand You."

9.1 WHAT IS A BRAND?

When someone describes you to a potential employer, they use a bundle of descriptive words. They may describe you as "punctual, capable, professional," etc. The adjectives represent how that person sees you. You know you are so much more than that, but you would hope people use those kinds of adjectives when describing you to a potential employer. In order to be perceived as "professional," you dress in a certain way and act in ways that support the impression. You try not to act in ways that would create a negative impression. You are managing your "brand." This is what brand managers do. They engage in activities that create and reinforce positive impressions of the product and reduce the negative.

At its most basic, a **brand** refers to a name, term, design, symbol, or any other feature that identifies one seller's goods or services as distinct from those of other sellers. More importantly, a brand is a promise you make to your customers. As long as what you promise is perceived as valuable by your customers, and as long as you keep your promise, your brand will have value.

From a customer perspective, a successful brand is an assurance of quality and increases customer loyalty. The successful brand is the exemplar of the product category and will be the first thing that comes to mind when a customer thinks about the category. Through branding, a company creates a relationship with the customer. If we think of a brand as an attitude, this relationship has both a cognitive and an emotional component. When a brand becomes truly successful, customers develop a sense of ownership of the brand. This is why companies who change the brand without the participation of customers risk the kind of emotional backlash that the GAP® felt in 2010 when it changed its logo. The negative reaction from customers on social media quickly caused the company to change back to the original logo. Increased customer loyalty and the ability to support higher prices are some of the benefits of a strong brand.

From a competitive standpoint, a successful brand is a significant barrier to entry. Increased customer loyalty and the ability to support higher prices are some of the benefits of a strong brand. Brand equity refers to the value to a company of a well-known brand name. Each year, Interbrand (interbrand.com) publishes a list of the world's most valuable brands from publicly traded companies. To give you an idea of the degree of advantage a strong brand can bring, the world's most valuable brand in 2015 was Apple, worth an estimated $170 billion dollars.[1] A newcomer hoping to compete against Coca Cola® will have to overcome more than 100 years of positive brand associations, the cumulative impact of billions of dollars in advertising expenditures over the years, and over $78 billion in brand equity.

Types of Brands

There are two basic dimensions to categorizing brands: geography and ownership. A brand can be local, regional, national, or even global. Local and regional brands are usually owned by intermediaries, while national or global brands are owned by the manufacturer. There are exceptions. The Old Dutch brand of potato chips is a regional manufacturer's brand, and President's Choice is an intermediary's brand that has gone international.

Whoever owns the brand owns the relationship with the customer and receives the benefits of branding. A manufacturer's brand (producer's brand) is owned by the manufacturer. Most of the brands we are familiar with are manufacturer's brands. Ford, Apple, Coke, IBM, and Microsoft are manufacturer brands.

A distributor brand (private-label brand, store brand, house brand) is owned by an intermediary, usually a large retail operation. Walmart's Great Value, Costco's Kirkland Signature, and JC Penney's Arizona jeans are all examples of distributor brands. In addition to owning the brand relationship with the customer, distributor brands frequently carry a higher margin for the retailer. In order to introduce a successful private-label brand, the retailer's position needs to be distinct enough for a brand promise to have meaning, and its reputation needs to be strong enough to signal the quality of the brand.

A generic brand (or no-name brand) represents an attempt to market products without the benefit of a brand name. The idea is that by eliminating the high cost of advertising to support a brand name, you can provide the product at a significant savings to the consumer. This strategy has not been successful with consumer products. Without advertising, demand for generic products is lower, so generic products don't benefit from the economies of scale associated with branded products. This takes away from the savings associated with generics. Also, retailers prefer to support private-label brands over generic products because store brands can represent a savings to the customer while improving margins for the retailer. One area where generic brands have become popular is in prescription pharmaceuticals. Once a prescription drug has come off patent, chemically identical generic drugs can offer consumers significant savings over the branded drug.

9.2 HOW TO CREATE A BRAND

Not all products lend themselves to branding. Ideally, the product has something unique about it that allows you to differentiate it from similar products. The benefit customers receive should be consistent in order to be able to keep the brand promise. It should be a product that customers repurchase frequently in order to benefit from brand loyalty, and the potential market should be large enough to benefit from economies of scale in production and advertising expense. Finally, it should be easy for customers to be able to identify the product by its brand. The most common products to be branded are called **consumer packaged goods**. These are the items you see on the shelves of stores every day.

Building a brand is a process. If you remember from Chapter 2.3, a brand can be thought of as an attitude existing in a customer's memory. Current thinking in brain research suggests we form memories by creating connections among brain cells. When one neuron is repeatedly involved with the firing of another neuron, metabolic changes take place, making it more likely these same cells will fire together in the future, or "Neurons that fire together, wire together." Over time, this process creates cell assemblies representing a concept or a symbol in memory. One neuron can participate in many concepts, and neurons from different concepts can overlap.[2]

An associative network model (Mitchell, 1982) looks at these concepts as nodes in a memory network. Linkages between nodes (concepts) define their relationship with each other, and the strength of the relationship will vary. Each time a concept is recalled, approximately six related concepts are recalled with it. The context of the memory search will affect which related concepts are retrieved with a specific memory. This suggests marketers can influence the nature of the concepts associated with a specific brand by managing the context in which the customer accesses the brand memory. These (hopefully positive) associations become stronger each time the brand is recalled.

Customer-Based Brand Equity Model

Kevin Keller, an international leader in the study of brands, uses associative memories to develop a **Customer-Based Brand Equity Model** (CBBE).[5] The CBBE model suggests marketers must go through four successive stages in order to develop an effective brand: (1) establish the brand identity, (2) create the appropriate brand meaning, (3) elicit positive brand responses, and (4) form a brand relationship with the customer.

Brand identity relates to a customer's ability to recall from memory and to recognize a brand. The key criteria for brand identity are depth and breadth. Depth relates to how easily a customer can recognize a brand, and breadth relates to the number of different circumstances where a customer will be able to recognize the brand.

Now that a customer has the brand concept in memory, the next question is "What does the brand mean to the customer?" The CBBE model looks at brand meaning in terms of performance and image. Performance relates to the functional benefits a customer gets from using the product, and image speaks to the psychosocial aspects of the brand. The goal is to develop strong positive associations that are unique to the brand.

Once a brand attitude has meaning to a customer, the next step is to develop positive brand responses. This includes both brand performance and brand imagery. Brand performance looks at judgments around product characteristics, while brand imagery looks at some of the feelings associated with the brand, such as "What type of person uses the product" or "What is the brand's personality?" Ideally, the brand response will include positive associations that involve both head (cognitive) and heart (emotional) elements. Segmentation, targeting, and positioning (Chapters 5 and 6) will help identify customers with whom the brand will resonate.

The ultimate goal of the CBBE model is to develop strong positive relationships around the brand. The real benefits to the marketer come when a customer is loyal to the brand, has a personal connection to the brand, feels a sense of community around the brand, and actively engages with it. The more intense a customer's feelings and the more willing a customer is to engage with the brand, the stronger the brand equity.

Brand Expression

Brand expression refers to all of the ways a company communicates the brand experience with its customers. It starts with developing the name, positioning, logo and identity design, message strategy, advertising copy, website design, marketing materials, and company culture to support the brand promise. This can cost anywhere from a few thousand dollars for a startup to hundreds of thousands of dollars for a large corporation. This is part of the context you manage as a brand manager. Some activities create new and unique associations, while other activities reinforce favorable associations. You want there to be strong positive associations when a customer recalls your brand.

The most visible element of brand expression is the brand name. A good brand name should be short and easy to pronounce, memorable, likable (Twitter), meaningful (Mr. Clean), adaptable, transferable, and protectable. The U.S. Patent and Trademark Office (uspto.gov) maintains the Trademark Electronic Search System (TESS), an easy-to-use search engine for trademarks. A few minutes with TESS will let you see if the brand name you are considering is available or if another company is already using it.

"Branded content is the new 30-second commercial."

Neil Cohen

9.3 HOW TO PROTECT A BRAND

Once you have succeeded in creating a strong brand, you will need to protect it. This involves claiming and defending the legal right to use the brand as well as keeping your brand promise even in the face of adversity.

Legal Protection

Being the first to use a brand name in business gives you rights to that name. However, in order to get legal protection for your brand, you must register it. A

trademark (or service mark) is the equivalent of a brand name for registration purposes. A trademark is defined as any word, slogan, symbol, design, or combination of these things that identifies the source of your goods and services and distinguishes them from the goods and services of another party. In the United States, the U.S. Patent and Trademark Office (USPTO) handles trademark registration for national marks, and each state has a trademark office to register trademarks at the state level. Registering a trademark with the USPTO costs $200–$400 in filing fees. The USPTO registers trademarks but does not take legal action against potential infringers, so you can figure another couple of thousand dollars in legal fees for an uncontested registration. Registering a trademark at the state level is less expensive but does not provide national coverage.

After registering the trademark, you are required to document that you are actively using the name, or you will lose rights to the name. The USPTO requires filings every 10 years (plus 5 years after the initial registration) to keep a trademark "alive."

Finally, you will need to protect your trademark against unauthorized uses, such as imitation, counterfeiting, or appropriation. **Infringement** is the legal term for unauthorized use of a trademark or service mark on or in connection with goods and/or services in a manner that is likely to cause confusion, deception, or mistake about the source of the goods and/or services. When you notice someone is infringing on your trademark, you need to respond or risk losing protection.

Common Usage

Ironically, you can have a brand name that is so successful it becomes the generic name for the product category. In that case, you can lose the trademark protection for that name. Aspirin and Escalator are two brand names that have come into common usage. Xerox®, Kleenex®, and Band Aid® have become so well known that they are in danger of falling into common usage. One way to prevent a strong brand from falling into common usage is to use it as an adjective rather than as a noun or a verb. We hear of Xerox brand copiers rather than Xeroxing or making a Xerox. This emphasizes the distinction between the brand name and the product category. Because we speak of Googling something when we search for information on the web, the Google® name may be in danger of falling into the common usage.

Keep Your Promise

Legal protections preserve your right to a distinctive brand, but unless you keep your brand promise, the legally protected brand will have no value to your customers. Keeping the promise involves not only delivering a consistent brand experience but managing customer's perceptions of the brand. The real test of a brand promise comes when there is a choice between short-term profitability and the reputation of the brand. It could be as simple as abandoning a new logo (as the GAP did in response to customer outcry) or as serious as recalling millions of dollars' worth of product during a safety scare (as the Johnson & Johnson company did during the Tylenol® poisonings in 1986). In both of these situations, maintaining a positive perception of the brand was more important than short-term profitability.

9.4 BRAND STRATEGIES

Developing a successful national brand can be very expensive. In addition to the hundreds of thousands of dollars invested in creating the brand identity, there may be millions of dollars in advertising and other marketing communications needed to give customers the repeated exposure to the brand in order to develop a positive attitude. There are both short-term and long-term benefits to this marketing effort. In the short term, advertising creates attention and awareness for the brand. Over the long term, carryover effects can support the brand well after a particular ad campaign is run. For many companies, especially consumer-oriented companies, brands are some of their most valuable assets. When deploying the brand in the marketplace, there is a trade-off between maintaining the uniqueness of each brand while trying to make the most of the financial investment required to establish the brand.

Individual Brands

The purest form of branding is to create an individual brand for each product/market you are targeting. The advantage is that you can match the brand expression with the target to have a clear and unique brand identity. The disadvantage is that it is very expensive to create a brand, so the target market needs to be big enough to support an individual brand. A multibrand strategy is when you create multiple individual brands in the same product category. Each brand is targeted toward a different market segment, and customers might not be aware that the competing brands are owned by the same company. Proctor & Gamble, a leading consumer package goods company, uses a multibrand strategy in several categories. When you are looking for a laundry detergent; if you choose Cheer®, Daz®, Era®, Gain®, Ariel®, Dreft®, Fairy®, Bold®, Lenor®, or, of course, Tide®, you are choosing a P&G brand.

A fighting brand strategy is when you create a new individual brand (usually at a lower price point) to compete with successful competitors without diluting the image of the original brand. Whole Foods® Market introduced 365® by Whole Foods Market to appeal to customers turned off by perceived high prices associated with the flagship brand.

Family Brands

Family branding, or umbrella branding, uses one brand for several products. The brand promise covers a range of products rather than one specific product. When you go through the canned soup aisle in a supermarket, you will be greeted be a wall of red-and-white cans—the trademark for Campbell's soups. It would not be cost-effective to develop a separate brand identity for each flavor of condensed soup. Instead, the Campbell's brand covers all flavors of soup. It doesn't matter which flavor you select; you can be assured that the flavor and quality will be consistent with the Campbell's brand.

Another approach to family branding is to create a number of distinct subbrands under a single family brand name. This approach is common in automobile marketing. The Toyota brand is a master brand for several distinct passenger car brands in order to support a **price lining** strategy. Each offering is intended to appeal to a different economic segment using a good, better, best approach. The Yaris is the entry-level offering, very affordable but not very fancy. The Corolla and Camry are more upscale, offering more features at a higher price point. The Avalon is the most luxurious passenger car in the Toyota lineup, appealing to those looking for the features of a luxury car but not ready to trade up to a Lexus (another Toyota-owned master brand).

"When you think about how much has changed in the last twenty years, I could never have predicted that. Now in the next five, ten, fifteen, twenty years, will there be that kind of change? You've got to be willing to accept and embrace change because it's not going to stop or slow down for anyone. Because change is so quick, you're never going to know everything. You have to stay humble and keep learning because that's how the world is happening around us."

Marketing Professional

The advantage to the family branding strategy is that it spreads the cost of building the brand over several products. From a customer perspective, the assurance of quality extends to every product in the brand family. Family branding also lowers the cost of introducing a new product under the brand umbrella. A **line extension** (or flanker brand) is when you offer a new product to an existing product line. Usually this is a new flavor or a new size—the incremental innovations characteristic of the maturity stage of the product life cycle. Customers who are happy with the Campbell's soup brand will be more willing to give a new flavor in the lineup a try. The risk with line extensions is **cannibalization**. Some of the gains you make from the new product come from customers who were already using a different version of the product.

A **brand extension** is when you introduce a product in a new category under the family brand. The advantage is that brand-loyal customers will be more likely to give the new product a try, greatly reducing the cost of introducing the new product. The risk with a brand extension is **brand dilution**, the weakening of a brand through overuse. As the range of products under the family brand becomes more diverse, what does the brand promise mean? Starbucks® has been experimenting with grocery store products such as Starbucks coffee ice cream (now discontinued) or cold-bottled Frappuccinos. Does the Starbucks brand promise mean hot, cold, or frozen coffee? And should one of these products fail, what impact would it have on the Starbucks brand?

The disadvantage of family branding is that it dilutes the brand. Do customers have the same expectations of a luxury car that they do from an economy car? So what does it mean when a car is a Toyota?

Leveraging Brand Equity

As a brand becomes more successful, there are opportunities to benefit from the brand without the need to introduce new products. Licensing arrangements are where you sell the right to use your trademark on unrelated products to another company. For example, there seems to be an inexhaustible demand for Coca-Cola collectibles—everything from baseball caps to home decor to toys and games; if it has the Coke logo on it, it will sell. Licensing generated more than one billion dollars for the Coca-Cola Company in 2014.[5] Cobranding arrangements and ingredient branding are where the popularity of your brand is used to help market another product. In the case of cobranding, the perceived quality of your brand gives a boost to the cobranded product, while the marketing of the cobranded product increases awareness of your brand. Thus, when General Mills announces that Cocoa Puffs cereal is now made with real Hershey's chocolate, it reminds consumers that Hershey's is a quality product. Intel broke new ground with its Intel Inside campaign for microprocessors: a product usually considered a component part was given a consumer-oriented branding campaign.

9.5 PACKAGING

A **package** is the container used to protect, promote, transport, and/or identify a product. For consumer products, especially for consumer packaged goods, the package is an important tool for expressing the brand identity. A package provides functionality, perceptual benefits, and communication to customers.

Functional Benefits

The package provides protection for the product and also helps meet the needs of wholesale and retail partners. When it leaves the manufacturer, a product may have multiple layers of packaging. The primary package is the container for the actual product. A secondary (master package, overpack) may hold one or several primary packages for shipping. The secondary package is more functional and keeps the primary package from being damaged while being shipped to the retailer.

Whether the ultimate destination is a retailer, an individual consumer, or another business, the package needs to be designed to make life easier for the end user. For industrial products, the package may be designed to plug into a manufacturer's assembly line. For consumer products, the package needs to be designed in a way that facilitates sales. For example, if a retailer is going to display the product by hanging it on a hook, the package needs to have a hole near the top so it can be hung from that hook. If a different retailer will display the same product on a shelf, the product needs to be square to allow for stacking. Some retail master packages are designed so that they can be turned into freestanding display units if necessary.

Some consumer packages are designed to provide utility to the consumer even after the product has been consumed. Altoids® mints come in handy little metal boxes. After the mints are gone, the box is just too useful to throw away. I use it to keep small things inside, and each time I see it, I'm reminded of Altoids mints.

Perceptual Benefits

You may not be able to judge a book by its cover, but you can definitely judge a product by its package. The quality of the package is a heuristic that signals the quality of the product. If you have ever purchased an Apple product, the brand experience starts with the package. The box is elegant, and everything fits inside perfectly. Obviously, the product is well designed. For some products, the package is everything. Would you purchase perfume that came in a plastic bottle? The look and feel of the package is an important element of the brand image. That is why it is rarely a good idea to scrimp on the primary packaging to cut cost. A high-quality full-color package is a signal that what is inside is high quality.

Communication

Packages have been called the "silent salespeople." When customers are looking at the package, they are well along in the buying process—probably at the evaluate alternatives or decision stage. Have you ever been in a grocery store and noticed a person holding up two different products and reading the package? The package is the last chance you have to make a case that your product is the solution to the customer's problem. All of the questions a customer might ask at the point of purchase should be answered on the package. You have complete control over what the customer will see at this point.

Labels

A **label** is the term for the information attached to or on a product for the purpose of naming it and describing its use, its dangers, its ingredients, its manufacturer, and the like. There are several kinds of information included in the labeling for your product. Obviously, there should be brand information, as the whole point of branding is to help customers make the connection between the brand experience and the product.

Some of the information on the label is required by law. For example, food products must provide nutrition information, and tobacco products must contain a warning about the hazards associated with smoking in a format specified by the U.S. Food and Drug Administration. In California, companies are required to disclose if a product contains any chemicals known to cause cancer or birth defects.

Other warnings or certifications should be included on the label even if they are not required by law. Some products are inherently dangerous or could be dangerous if misused. There should be a warning about any dangers associated with the product. These warning labels help keep customers safe and can protect the company from liability should a product cause an injury through misuse. This is why hair dryers carry a label warning you not to use them in the shower. Many products, especially food products, rely on third-party organizations to certify the quality of the product. Knowing that the eggs are USDA Grade A and that the peanut butter is kosher is important to many customers.

After taking these requirements into account, the rest of the label is yours to describe the product. You may want to offer suggestions on how to use the product, describe the benefits of using your product, or point out features that may set you apart from the competition—anything you think might help a customer choose your product over someone else's.

9.6 WARRANTIES

A **warranty** is a statement that the product is fit for the purpose being claimed and describes what the seller will do if the product performs below expectations or is defective in some way. It is a description of how far you will go in order to keep the brand promise associated with the product. Warranties can be either express or implied.

Express Warranties

An **express warranty** is clearly stated, usually in writing. It describes the minimum standard of performance for the product and what the manufacturer will do if the product fails to meet the standard. A **full warranty** offers satisfaction guaranteed, no questions asked. Full warranties are rare as the cost of honoring the warranty can be huge. You are likely to see full warranties with lower-cost items because the lifetime value of a customer is greater than the potential loss on a single transaction.

Limited Warranties

A **limited warranty** is where a manufacturer specifically excludes things that will be covered by the warranty. As the saying goes: "The large print giveth and the fine print taketh away." This is to limit the potential cost of the warranty and to protect the manufacturer from legal liability should there be a problem with the product. Typical limitations include putting a time limit on warranty claims, excluding damage caused by the customer or abuse of the product, liability for other damage caused by a defective product, etc. In cases where there is a potential for injury if the product is misused, the limited warranty may list specific instances of improper use. Again, don't use that hair dryer in the shower.

When a person is injured by a product, a manufacturer may be held liable for damages even if the product was not defective and if the manufacturer did nothing wrong. For a product that is inherently dangerous (like a hair dryer), anyone involved with the manufacture and distribution of the product may be held liable for damages through **strict liability**.

Implied Warranties

Implied warranties are based on the assumption that a product will perform as represented. If you sell a watch that doesn't tell time, **warranty of merchantability** would imply that the sale is void because a customer would reasonably expect a watch to tell time. If a person specifically asks you for a watch to be used while surfing, the **warranty of fitness of purpose** would imply that the watch is waterproof. The **warranty of title** implies that you have the authority to sell the watch. Unless specifically limited in the express warranty, these implied warranties are binding on any product you sell.

(ENDNOTES)

1. Retrieved from https://www.rankingthebrands.com/The-Brand-Rankings.aspx?rankingID=37
2. Domingos, P. (2015). *The master algorithm: How the quest for the ultimate learning machine will remake our world.* New York: Basic Books.

3. Mitchell, A. A. (1982). Models of memory for measuring knowledge structures. In A. Mitchell (Ed.). NA-Advances in Consumer Research, Vol. 9 (pp. 45–51). Ann Arbor: Association for Consumer Research.
4. Keller, K. L. (2001). Building customer-based brand equity: A blueprint for creating strong brands. Working paper at the Marketing Science Institute.
5. Retrieved from http://www.retail-merchandiser.com/index.php/reports/retail-reports/1754-the-coca-cola-company

SERVICES

CH10

What is a service? It has been argued that all products are services at the point of consumption. A car provides personal transportation services when you drive it, and a can of peas is a nutrition delivery system. Most products have both tangible and intangible attributes. Something as tangible as a can of peas purchased at the grocery store might include intangible attributes such as serving suggestions or a way to contact the manufacturer with questions. Everything we talk about related to product marketing applies to all products whether they are physical or intangible. However, when a product is mostly intangible, there are some unique issues to consider. Understanding and properly addressing these issues around intangibility can help focus your resources where they will be most effective.

10.1 WHAT IS A SERVICE?

An intangible is something you can't touch—it has no physical presence. If a product is a bundle of tangible and intangible attributes, it may be helpful to think of products on a continuum from mostly tangible attributes (a can of peas, a hammer) at one extreme, mostly intangible attributes (legal advice, digital downloads) at the other extreme, and a varying blend of tangible and intangible attributes (a resort hotel, a tanning booth) are in between the two extremes. A **service** would be a product that consists primarily of intangible attributes. This could involve intangible attributes of the core product as well as services accompanying the sale as part of the extended product. A good, on the other hand, would be a product that consists primarily of tangible attributes.

There are many intangibles we might not normally think of as services that benefit from this approach. For example, many public figures (politicians, entertainers, athletes) present a public image or personality that may not reflect the complexity of the individual. As cognitive misers, we don't want our heroes to be multifaceted. Professional sports leagues would like fans to focus on the heroics performed during the game rather than on less than exemplary behavior that can happen off the field. Tourist boards and chambers of commerce promoting physical locations, especially vacation destinations, try to create a brand image around the experience associated with the place. You can visit Disneyland®, the Happiest Place on Earth, while the Las Vegas Convention and Visitors Authority wants to assure you that "what happens in Vegas stays in Vegas." In addition to people and places, ideas can be marketed as intangible products. Political campaigns are built around the effective marketing of ideas as well as a candidate's personality.

10.2 CHARACTERISTICS OF SERVICES

Defining a service as a product that consists mostly of intangible attributes is subjective; at what point does a good become a service as you move along the continuum? Once you understand the characteristics of a service and how to address them in your marketing, you will be in a better position to decide whether or not these techniques would apply to your offerings. There are four unique characteristics of services: intangibility, variability (sometimes called heterogeneity), perishability (or the inventory problem), and inseparability.

Intangibility

By definition, a service is primarily intangible. So how do you market a product that the customer can't touch or see? The basic approach to the **intangibility** issue is to find some way to make the product "real" in the mind of the customer. There are four strategies you can use to help the customer get in touch with the service: visualization, association, physical representation, and documentation.

Visualization is a strategy where you help the customer form a mental picture of the service. While you can't show the service, you can show the customer through pictures and words what it would be like to benefit from the service. When the Disney Corporation shows pictures of families having fun meeting costumed characters, going on thrill rides, and looking gratefully at the parents who made the experience possible, who wouldn't want to bring his or her family to the Happiest Place on Earth. When the H&R Block® company wants to interest you in its tax preparation services, it shows pictures of the billions of dollars in unnecessary taxes paid by people (who we assume didn't use H&R Block).

Association is a strategy pairing an intangible product with a something tangible that the customer likes. Drawing on the principles of classical conditioning, the idea is that over time the positive feelings associated with the known object will transfer to the service. Thus, the Prudential Life Insurance Company has a representation of the Rock of Gibraltar in its logo and invites you to "own a piece of the rock" because it is important that life insurance products stand the test of time. This is an area where celebrity endorsements and sponsorships can be particularly effective. We know that Priceline® will always find us the best deal on travel arrangements because Kaley Cuoco says so. Of the 29 million people who play golf in the United States, 79% have a net worth over $100,000.[1] Is it any wonder that financial services companies are lining up to sponsor events on the PGA Tour®?

Physical Representation attempts to make the intangible tangible by creating something physical associated with the service. If you have ever been to a Broadway musical, you received a copy of *Playbill®* magazine that includes the program and biographies of the actors in the show. Many people keep these as physical reminders of the experience they had attending the show. But if you really want to remember the experience, be sure to stop by the lobby where you can purchase full-color souvenir programs, t-shirts, recordings, and other physical representations of the show. A diploma is a physical representation of your education. Upon successful completion of the program, you are given a piece of paper that you can hang on the wall as proof that you are very smart.

A **documentation** strategy uses the concept of social proof to make the service real. One approach is to document past performance. The McDonalds® Corporation reminds us that it has sold billions and billions of hamburgers over the years. All of those billions and billions of customers can't be wrong. Many local businesses emphasize the year they were established as a way of documenting their ability to perform. If the service wasn't any good, customers wouldn't come back, and they would quickly go out of business.

Another approach is to document capability to perform a service through certifications or diplomas. In medical offices, doctors proudly display the ornate diploma that tells you they are, in fact, trained medical professionals. If you've ever been to an automobile repair shop, you are likely to see dozens of certificates documenting that the staff have been trained to perform the services you will be receiving.

> "Working at a startup, you have to wear a lot of hats. You're either a team of one or part of a small team. You should have some knowledge of HTML, you actually do need to be good at numbers. You need to understand how AdWords works, how advertising on social works ... Sometimes you just have to go and Photoshop something, or you have to create the visual for a campaign you're doing."
>
> Anadelia Fadeev

Variability

It is common for services to be created through an interaction between the service provider and the customer. If the service provider is a human being (as opposed to an ATM machine), consistency is going to be an issue. This sets up a little bit of a paradox. If consistency is an important element of product quality and if human beings are inherently inconsistent, how can we provide a quality service experience? There are a couple of ways to deal with this issue of **variability**. One way to increase consistency is through business systems and training. By specifying in advance what you want the customer experience to be, you can develop training programs to increase the likelihood of achieving that experience. This is one reason business franchises are successful. When you buy a franchise, you get the business systems and training programs developed by the franchisor in addition to other benefits of being associated with the brand.

Another approach is to create the appearance of consistency with uniforms. From a customer perspective, uniforms minimize the service provider's individuality, allowing the customer to focus on the service rather than on the person. If you want to see the power of uniforms in a service environment, try wearing a solid red shirt into a Target Store and see how many people approach you for help. Solid red shirts and khaki pants are the employee uniform at Target. As a rule, employees dislike uniforms for the same reason customers appreciate uniforms. In many informal surveys over the years, people say they don't like to wear uniforms. It minimizes their individuality and encourages people to treat them as a store fixture rather than as a human being. The exception to the rule is for people who have to earn the right to wear a uniform. Military personnel, law enforcement officers, firefighters, and other first responders wear their uniforms with pride.

Inseparability

There are many situations where both the service provider and the customer have to be physically present to perform the service. A barber can't cut a person's hair unless they are both in the same place at the same time. This **inseparability** issue recognizes that the capacity to provide a service is limited to the capacity of the individuals providing the service. One way to deal with the inseparability issue is to maximize the efficiency of the service provider by having people specialize in specific tasks much as an assembly line does in manufacturing. For example, if you go to see the dentist for a checkup, you will first stop by the reception window where a person will handle insurance/payment information and make sure your files are up to date. Then, a technician will take an x-ray and clean your teeth and check for any abnormalities. Finally, the dentist will come in to check your teeth and recommend any necessary treatments. In a one-hour appointment, you might spend 15 minutes with the dentist. This allows the dentist to see more patients in a day.

Another way to increase the efficiency of service providers is to automate routine transactions allowing service personnel to focus on unusual situations. Retail banks encourage you to handle routine transactions (deposit, withdrawal, check balances) through an ATM or online. That increases the efficiency of the tellers who are now dealing with issues more complicated than what can be handled automatically. Many airport restaurants provide a "grab 'n go" window where frequently ordered menu items are prepared in advance so busy travelers can quickly purchase a meal without working with a service provider to take the order.

Price rationing is a way to maximize the efficiency of a service provider by using price to encourage customers to choose the level of service they desire. The idea is to charge a higher price to work with a highly skilled service provider and a lower price to work with a lower-skilled provider. In the legal arena, if you need advice on something like a simple will, you might choose to work with a paralegal under the supervision of an attorney. If your need is more complicated, you may choose to work with an attorney at a higher rate. If you need the best legal advice you can find, you might choose to work with a senior partner of a law firm although you will pay a very high fee to do so. This approach ensures that the highest-skilled service providers are only used in situations where a lesser-skilled provider won't do.

Perishability

The **perishability** issue recognizes services can't be stored or put in inventory to be sold at a later time. If an airplane leaves the airport with an empty seat, the opportunity to sell that seat is gone forever. You can't put the unsold seats on the next scheduled flight. If a television show airs with unsold advertising time, you can't put that time back in a later show. This is especially critical for services with a high fixed cost component. Just as the approach to the inseparability issue is to maximize the efficiency of the service provider, the approach to the perishability issue is to maximize capacity utilization.

Price rationing can be an effective tool to maximize capacity utilization. In the hospitality industry, it is common for resort hotels to offer discounted rates during the off-season and for restaurants to offer early bird specials as a way to encourage patrons to visit at times when there is excess capacity. **Dynamic pricing** uses a highly flexible pricing structure that fluctuates depending on various demand factors in an attempt to maximize revenue from the available capacity.

The airline industry uses dynamic pricing by continuously monitoring the number of seats sold on a given flight and adjusting prices accordingly. Because airlines have a very high fixed cost associated with airplanes, terminal fees, and maintenance facilities, it is critical to make as much money from each seat on the plane as possible. The basic premise is that some people are unable to make travel plans until the last minute and would be willing to pay a high price for a seat on a flight if it were available. People planning vacations are very sensitive to price and have the ability to make reservations far in advance of the trip. The goal of the dynamic pricing algorithm is to allow vacationers to book early at a discount while still maintaining an inventory of unsold seats available for last minute travelers.

As the day of the flight grows nearer, if there are fewer seats sold than is normal for that particular time, the airline will offer some seats at a lower price. If more seats than normal have been sold, the airline will raise the price on the remaining seats. Just in case there are unsold seats as the plane is ready to depart, the airline may sell standby tickets—offering a very low fare to passengers who are willing to be present in case there is an available seat. It is better to charge a very low fare for standby travelers than it would be to allow the plane to leave with empty seats. Because of dynamic pricing, there may be several hundred price changes from the first day a flight is available for booking until the moment of departure.

Another way to manage capacity is through scheduling. For service situations where the time required to perform the service is fairly consistent, such as a medical checkup, scheduling can increase the efficiency of capacity utilization. This is why you make an appointment to see the doctor even though the doctor might be running behind schedule if there are unusual circumstances. For situations where the time required to perform the service is highly variable, scheduling can decrease the efficiency of capacity utilization. In these situations, "first come, first served" or asking customers to wait in line will maximize capacity utilization. This is why many fine restaurants refuse to accept reservations during peak dining hours. Because the amount of time a diner will spend during a meal will vary a lot, in order to accept reservations, the restaurant needs to under schedule the dining room to be sure one party has finished before the next party's reserved time.

There is a tradeoff with the "first come, first served" approach to scheduling. While it minimizes unsold inventory, it can annoy customers. When the service is a discretionary purchase, such as dining at a fine restaurant, some providers will accept reservations to improve customer relationships even if it means there is unused capacity. On the other hand, when the service is required, there is no incentive to accommodate customers who desire reservations. This is why you will stand in line at the DMV (Department of Motor Vehicles) when it is time to renew your driver's license. Even if you have a reservation at the DMV, you will stand in the "reservations" line.

10.3 MANAGING SERVICES

Because there is so much variety in the kinds of services offered, there is no "one size fits all" approach to managing services. As a starting point, we'll talk about internal marketing, the service encounter, and service quality (Chapter 10.4).

Internal Marketing

One of the differences between a good and a service is that for many services, the service provider and the customer work together to create the service. This means that in order for your employees to deliver a quality service experience, the employees need to believe in the service. The concept of **internal marketing** recognizes that before you can sell the service to customers, you need to sell the service to the people working with customers. For example, many retailers have adopted the convention of referring to customers as "guests." The idea is that if you treat someone as a guest rather than as a customer, the store experience becomes a relationship building opportunity rather than a sales transaction. However, to successfully implement this strategy, the company needs to determine what to do differently to serve a guest, and the employees need to be trained on how to treat a guest and to believe that this is something more than a name change. For example, some retailers welcome their guests with a beverage and provide areas for the guest to relax while enjoying the shopping experience. On the other hand, if employees don't believe that being a guest is anything different than a customer, they may become cynical. At one major retailer, managers use the euphemism "promoted to guest" as a way of saying "you're fired."

In addition to buying into the service experience, it is important for employees to believe that they are well treated. If your people aren't happy, how do you expect them to make your customers happy? Have you ever been in a restaurant where the server was obviously unhappy? Did you enjoy the experience?

The Service Encounter

It may be useful to draw an analogy between managing services and theater. It is management's job to write the script (design the service experience), to build the set (the space where the service encounter will take place), and to hire the cast (service employees). First impressions are important. Customers will experience the setting before any interaction with your people. The space should be consistent with the service provided. A restaurant should be clean with an appropriate atmosphere. A law office should be well furnished and quiet. A huge steel vault door tells you your money will be safe in the bank.

The role of the service provider is to direct the customer through the service experience. Because of internal marketing, your employees will believe in the service and will know the script. The service provider also has to make sure the customer understands his or her role in creating the service.

The role of the customer is to participate in the service creation by communicating his or her expectations and offering feedback during the process. The customer needs to be willing to share the information needed for the service provider to perform the service.

10.4 SERVICE QUALITY

Service quality involves meeting or exceeding customer expectations or, as the conventional wisdom goes, "delighting the customer." There are some practical issues associated with delighting the customer that make understanding service quality challenging. First, you need to know what your customers' expectations are in order to meet or exceed them. Second, if you exceed customer expectations, you run the risk of setting up increased customer expectations for the next time. Customers are more likely to punish you for bad service than they are to reward you for exceptional service.[2]

Service Attributes

One issue in managing customer expectations is that it is easier for people to evaluate physical products than it is to evaluate intangible products. There are three levels of attributes people use to evaluate service products: search attributes, experiential attributes, and credence attributes.

Search attributes are characteristics a customer can evaluate before buying the service. Things like price or hours of operation are easy to understand and can be used to encourage a customer to try the service. Search attributes can be featured in advertising as a way to differentiate your offerings from you competitors' offerings.

Experiential attributes are factors the customer can evaluate only after using the service. Disneyland claims to be the "Happiest Place on Earth," but a visitor to the park can only say whether it is true after he or she has visited the park. Experiential attributes can be used to create customer expectations (that you can meet or exceed). They are a promise of what the customer can expect from your service. Because you have control over what you are promising, experiential attributes are useful in managing expectations. It is a good idea to under promise and over deliver.

Credence attributes are factors a customer might not be able to evaluate even after receiving the service. This is the situation for many professional services. Do you know whether or not your doctor did a good job the last time you had a physical examination? Because customers are unable to evaluate credence attributes, documentation or certification can help assure customers that you are doing a good job. You might not know whether your doctor did a good job, but you can assume that the people granting the license could tell whether or not they were a good doctor.

Customer Perceptions of Service Quality

In addition to evaluating the service product, there are five dimensions customers use to evaluate the quality of the service as delivered: reliability, assurance, empathy, responsiveness, and tangibles.[3] The most important factor is reliability. This is consistent with the concept of product quality being related to the benefits received and consistency. Because customers are personally involved in creating the service, interpersonal factors such as assurance and empathy play an important role in the perception of service quality. This is especially important for service products with credence attributes. Patients may not be able to evaluate the quality of a medical procedure, but patients are able to evaluate how they were treated. As you might expect, tangibles are the least important dimension of service quality. Perhaps this is because tangibles are associated with search attributes, and the customer can evaluate them before purchasing the service.

Measuring Service Quality

How do you know whether or not you are providing a quality service? First, you need to understand what customer expectations of the service are. These might be expectations you have created through promises you made to your customers, or you might have surveyed your customers to determine what they expect from you.

Gap Analysis

In any case, once you understand your customer's expectations, you need a way to determine if you are meeting them. **Gap analysis** is a common approach to measuring service quality. Gap analysis is research to determine if there is a difference between customer expectations and what is actually happening—sort of a reality check. Typical areas for gap analysis include differences between customer expectations and service quality standards, differences between expected service and perceived service, differences between service quality standards and service delivery, etc.

One approach to measuring service quality in a retail setting is to use a **secret shopper** service. A secret shopper is an agent trained to understand the service quality standards who, unknown to the staff, poses as a customer. The secret shopper can observe what is actually happening and report it to management. Sometimes, the secret shopper is asked to test the limits of the service by asking for services not allowed in the store or by being obnoxious to see how the staff handles a difficult customer. Properly used, secret shoppers can help evaluate the quality of your service. Improperly used, secret shoppers can hurt employee morale.

Service Failure

Another approach to measuring service quality is to pay attention when things go wrong. A service failure can help identify areas where the service could be improved. The first thing to do when a customer complains is to take care of the customer. The conventional wisdom is that only one out of ten customers will complain when he or she has a problem (but you can bet he or she will be talking about the experience on Facebook®). While not all problems can be resolved to the customer's satisfaction, the way you handle the complaint can make a big difference. This is where empathy can help turn the situation around.

After dealing with the customer, it is time to step back and ask, "Was this a one-time issue, or is there something that needs to be fixed with the way we do business?"

10.5 NOT-FOR-PROFIT MARKETING

A **not-for-profit organization** (also referred to as nonprofit or nonbusiness organization) is an organization created to provide a public or mutual benefit other than the pursuit or accumulation of profits for owners or investors. In exchange for providing this benefit, the organization may be tax-supported or given tax-exempt status. The two major types of not-for-profits are government (federal, state, municipal, military, public education), which include tax dollars as a major source of support, and nongovernment organizations or NGO's (private education, arts, health and human services), which are supported by fees and individual contributions, many of them tax deductible.

As corporations are becoming more focused on social issues, there has been movement toward creating a hybrid between a profit and a not-for-profit organization. These benefit corporations, or B Corps, have a corporate charter that allows the corporation to have dual goals of achieving a return for the investors and providing a public or mutual benefit. Currently, 34 states have enacted legislation allowing benefit corporations.[4]

The reality is that a not-for-profit organization needs to be run like a business. While making a profit may be a secondary goal, unless the organization's revenue exceeds its expenses, it will have to cease operations.

> "Someone can move into the non-profit world from the for-profit world and vice versa, as long as they recognize the principles—whether it's marketing or finance—are very similar"
>
> Steve Pollyea

Characteristics of Not-for-Profits

There are some unique characteristics of not-for-profit organizations that have an impact on their marketing programs. The first question we ask in marketing is: "Who is the customer?" For a not-for-profit, the answer isn't that simple. There are multiple constituencies that might be considered customers.

Take for example, a public university. Who is the customer? Obviously, students are the customer; aren't they the ones paying for their education? But a public university is supported by the state, so wouldn't the state legislature be a customer because it is also paying for the education? Some students may also receive scholarships from other not-for-profit organizations, so would they be customers as well? And how about the people who hire the university's graduates? For a prospective employer, the student is the product, not the customer of a university. And we haven't even begun talking about the research universities conduct. You see how complicated this answer can become.

A not-for-profit has many customers: clients, individual donors, corporate and foundation donors, government, news media, and the general public. Sometimes the needs of one set of customers may be at odds with the needs of another set of customers. The not-for-profit has to balance these competing needs.

Another issue for not-for-profits is the scope of the problems they address. If the solution to the problem could generate a profit, the for-profit sector would handle it. So the problems in the not-for-profit sector tend to be bigger than any one organization could handle on its own. As a result, it is common for a not-for profit to be one element in a network of organizations focusing on the solution to a problem. Rather than using market positioning to differentiate itself from the competition (Chapter 6), some not-for-profits use complementary positioning to emphasize their role in the network. In the case of higher education, it is in society's interest for talented people to attend university even if they don't have the financial resources to do so. In response to this problem, many organizations contribute to the solution. Individuals contribute to the best of their abilities; government subsidies to the university and grants to students help make college affordable. Student loans, private scholarships, and part-time jobs make up the difference.

Not-for-Profits and the Marketing Mix

These unique features of not-for-profits have an impact on the marketing mix. Here are some of the issues around product, place, promotion, and price faced by the not-for-profit sector.

Product

Because the problems addressed by not-for-profits are complex, the benefit to the customer may not be clear. While it is easy to understand how a contribution to a homeless shelter can help feed a hungry person, it is less clear how one might make a difference in preventing sexually transmitted diseases with a financial contribution. Donors want to see that their contributions make a difference, but sometimes the benefit may be weak or indirect. Sometimes NGOs with good public relations are better at attracting support than other worthy causes that are harder to explain. Indoor air pollution by black carbon causes some 4.3 million deaths worldwide every year, which is more than HIV, malaria, and tuberculosis combined. Most of those deaths happen in poor countries where people unable to afford cleaner stoves use kerosene or even cow dung as cooking fuels.[5]

Place

For not-for-profits, the issue of place depends on the services provided and access to donors and volunteers. An organization providing shelter to homeless people needs to have a physical facility located near to where homeless people gather. An advocacy organization whose primary mission is to increase awareness around an issue can locate its facilities where costs are lower or where it is convenient for employees and volunteers to gather.

Promotion

One of the biggest differences between a for-profit business and a not-for-profit organization is the use of volunteers. Not only do volunteers help defray the cost of providing services, but volunteers are great ambassadors in their communities for the organization. People are proud of the work they do with a not-for-profit and will speak highly of the organization to their friends and families. The principle of cognitive dissonance suggests that people who work for an organization for free need to believe that what they are doing has value. An active network of volunteers is a valuable asset to any not-for-profit organization.

Corporate sponsorships and promotions are another way not-for-profits can increase their communication effectiveness. Corporations seeking to be associated with the good work of the organization can donate money, time, and publicity to a not-for-profit in exchange for being publicly associated with the organization. Many times in-kind donations can be as important as cash contributions for certain activities. Having a media company (television, radio, news) as a partner increases the chances of success for fundraising events. Many media outlets will offer airtime for public service announcements (PSAs) to not-for-profits as community service. The Ad Council (adcouncil.org) helps provide not-for-profit organizations professionally produced PSAs to make the most of these opportunities.

Price

If clients could afford to pay the cost of benefits provided by not-for-profit organization by themselves, the problems would be addressed in the for-profit sector. Therefore, pricing strategies in the not-for-profit sector seek to find ways to extend services to those who need them the most while stretching the resources to serve as many people as possible. Many not-for-profits providing direct services to people use a **sliding scale fee** structure. With a sliding scale fee, those who can afford to pay the full cost of the service are asked to pay the full cost; those who are not able to pay the full cost of the service pay a lower fee based on their ability to pay.

Sometimes there is separation between the people receiving the service and the people paying for the service. For example, a city may allocate tax dollars to address the homeless issue but use the funds to pay independent not-for-profit organizations that actually work with the homeless population. These **third-party payer** systems can create tension because the people receiving the service may not be aware of the cost of providing the service, and the people paying for the service are looking for the service provider to minimize the cost of providing the service. This is an issue in the health care system. Since the passage of the Affordable Care Act, more people have access to health insurance. When you visit the doctor, you, as a patient, can insist on the highest quality of care because you are paying only a fraction of the cost. The insurance company paying for the cost of your care is encouraging your doctor to keep the costs as low as possible.

Many times there is a nonfinancial cost to receiving services. For example, a person in need of treatment for substance abuse may be unwilling to admit there is a problem or be too embarrassed to ask for help. Some organizations ask potential beneficiaries to contribute "sweat equity" to help defray the cost of providing the services. Habitat for Humanity® (habitat.org) is a not-for-profit that provides low-cost housing. Potential recipients of a Habitat house are asked to work 300–500 hours building houses for others before they can receive their own.

The Not-for-Profit Sector Is a Great Place to Start a Career

People embarking on a professional career face a dilemma. Many employers want you to have meaningful work experience before they will hire you. But unless you get hired, how can you get any meaningful work experience?

The good news is that the not-for-profit sector offers many opportunities to launch a career. According to the 2017 Nonprofit Employment Practices Survey,™[i] 51% of not-for-profit organizations were looking to add staff compared to 31% of private companies looking to hire. In the not-for-profit sector, you are likely to get a broader view of how an organization runs, have more access to strategic decision making, and are challenged to take initiative.[ii] Add to that the opportunity to build your personal network working with the organization's volunteers, it makes the not-for-profit sector a great place to start a career. In fact, many people find working in the not-for-profit sector personally satisfying and choose to make it a career.

i   file:///C:/Users/900014~1/AppData/Local/Temp/2017-Nonprofit-Employment-Practices-Infographic-FULL-1.pdf. Accessed May 24, 2018.

ii   http://commongoodcareers.org/articles/detail/movin-on-up-nonprofit-career-paths Accessed October 12, 2016.

(ENDNOTES)

1. http://www.statisticbrain.com/golf-player-demographic-statistics/. Accessed April 6, 2015.

2. Dixon, Matthew, Karen Freeman, and Nicholas Toman, 2010, "Stop Trying to Delight Your Customers," *Harvard Business Review,* July/August.

3. Parasuraman, A., Valarie A. Zeithaml, and Leonard L. Berry, 1994a, "Reassessment of Expectations as a Comparison Standard in Measuring Service Quality: Implication for Further Research," *Journal of Marketing,* 58 (January), 111–124.

4. http://www.benefitcorp.net/state-by-state-legislative-status. Accessed May 24, 2018.

5. http://www.pressreader.com/usa/san-francisco-chronicle/20150409/281621008854546/ TextView. Accessed April 10, 2015.

PRICE BASICS

CH11

The reason we are in business is to make money. Lots of money. Money with a capital "M." More money than we could possibly spend. Now do I have your attention? Price is the element of the marketing mix that deals directly with how much money you are going to make. As a result, the prices we charge and the prices we pay are an important part of any business conversation. Are our prices too high? We're driving business away. Are our prices too low? We're giving our product away. While it is natural to focus on the money, there is more to price than the dollars that change hands. Understanding how price interacts with the other elements of the marketing mix can increase customer satisfaction at the same time that it improves your bottom line.

11.1 WHAT IS A PRICE?

Merriam-Webster defines price as the cost at which something is obtained.[1] This is a good place to begin discussing what price means. It might help to clarify three of the words in the dictionary definition: cost, something, and obtained. The cost could be money, it could be a substitute for money (such as in a barter situation), it could be the time and effort expended in the process, or it could even be the opportunity cost of more productive ways you might have invested those resources. The something you pay for is usually a product, but it could be some other desired outcome such as to change someone's behavior or opinion. The word, obtained, recognizes that price is something offered in exchange for something as in a transaction. You can see that price is one of those concepts that extends beyond a business setting. Understanding what people are willing to exchange for what they want and the circumstances needed for the exchange to happen allows you to increase the likelihood of success in your personal life as well as in business.

However, this is a business book, so let's think of what price means in a business setting. From a business perspective, **price** is the amount of money or other consideration, which is exchanged or offered for a product or other desired outcome. There are two implications of this definition. First, a price does not always lead to an exchange. This means there may be other uses for price than directly obtaining money from someone else. Second, there is no such thing as setting your prices too high. This may sound immoral but it is not. When participation is voluntary, a customer is free to accept or to reject your price. No human being will voluntarily pay more for something than it is worth. If someone pays your price, that someone believes the cost is worth it. There may be reasons to ask for something lower than the highest possible price (for instance, to increase the number of people who believe the cost is worth it), but there is no such thing as a price that's too high when participation is voluntary.

So what does price mean? The obvious answer is that price is the element of the marketing mix that determines how much money you make. The definition of profit is revenue minus cost ($\pi = r - c$) and the definition of revenue is price times quantity ($r = p \times q$), so the price you charge will have a direct impact on your bottom line.

Price and Value

Price means more to a customer than the money exchanged for a product. Price is an important determinant of value. If you remember from Chapter 1.1, value is a function of perceived benefits and perceived costs. The lower the perceived cost, the higher the perceived value. In the next chapter, we'll talk about strategies to lower the perceived price to the customer.

In addition to being a component of the value equation, price is a signal of value in and of itself. Many people use price as a mental shortcut in decision-making. The price/value heuristic suggests that if a product has a higher price, it must be a better product otherwise people wouldn't be able to charge more for it. This is especially true for products where we might not be able to judge the quality of the product easily through observation. Take, for example, a fine wine. We all know that some wines are much better than others, but we might not be able to tell the difference between a good wine and a very good wine by reading the label. However, we can easily tell that one bottle of wine costs more than another bottle of wine. If it costs more, it must be better. If it costs a lot more, it must be a lot better.

Price and Positioning

Because price is a signal of value, price can be an effective positioning tool. Your price compared to your competitors' prices is a signal of the relative quality of your product. If the price is higher, a customer would naturally assume it is a better product. If the price is lower, a customer would assume it is lower quality. With luxury goods, a high price tag is part of what makes the product successful. The status associated with luxury products comes from everyone knowing that you could afford to buy such expensive products.

Price as a Promotional Tool

One way to increase demand for a product is to offer a discount off of the original price. The original price is a signal of the quality of the product, and the discount increases the perception of value to the customer. Weber's law, or the concept of a just noticeable difference (JND), plays an important role in discounting. In order to be effective, a price discount needs to be big enough to be noticed, usually a 20–25% difference, although the actual threshold will vary. Discounts below the JND threshold are unlikely to generate the attention to which the promotional discount was intended. Discounts much larger than the JND threshold will reduce your revenue unnecessarily. On the other hand, price increases should be kept below the JND threshold to minimize negative attention.

On a related note, when offering discounts, you can describe the discount in terms of dollars or as a percentage. You want to make the choice that has the most impact on the customer. In general, use percentage discounts when the dollar amounts are small. Selling a $1 item at 20% off is much more effective than saving 20 cents. On the other hand, saving $1,000 on a car is more impressive than a 3% discount.

List Price vs. Actual Price

Many times, the advertised price or list price is different than what the customer actually pays. The actual price is the list price, plus any extra fees, minus any discounts. In industries where price shopping is common, it is not unusual for sellers to set the list price as low as possible and require additional fees in order to conclude the transaction. Take a look at your mobile communications bill and compare what you are actually paying to what you were promised when you signed up. On the other hand, some sellers set list prices relatively high to increase the perception of value and then offer discounts off the list price as described above. The point is that a lot is riding on the price you set for your products, including the revenue you will receive through selling the product.

So what should the price of your product be? It depends. It depends on the nature of demand in your industry. It depends on your company's objectives. It depends on the constraints your company faces, it depends on your cost structure. And that's just for starters.

11.2 NATURE OF DEMAND

One of the factors influencing price is the nature of demand in your industry. Your approach to pricing will vary dramatically depending on the demand structure.

Law of Demand

In microeconomics, the law of demand talks about the quantity of a product your customers will buy at a given price. If the price increases, the quantity demanded decreases. If the price decreases, the quantity demanded increases. This is usually expressed with a demand curve that looks something like Figure 11.1.

The price is on the vertical axis and increases as you go higher. Quantity demanded is on the horizontal axis and increases as you go further right. As you can see, when the price is high, the quantity demanded is low and vice versa. If the goal is to sell more units, lowering the price is usually an effective way to do it.

Price Sensitivity

How sensitive customers are to changes in price is a function of **price elasticity**. Price elasticity is defined as % change in quantity demanded ÷ % change in price. Because this is usually a negative number, we use the absolute value instead of the actual number when talking about elasticity. An **elastic price** (price elasticity greater than 1) means a small change in price will lead to a big change in demand. With a price elasticity of 2, a 1% increase in demand will lead to a

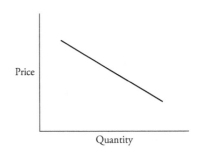

FIGURE 11.1 Normal demand curve

2% decrease in sales. An **inelastic price** (price elasticity less than 1) means a large increase in price will lead to a smaller decrease in demand. With a price elasticity of 0.5, a 10% increase in price will lead to a 5% decrease in the quantity demanded.

FIGURE 11.2   Elastic demand curve

Figures 11.2 and 11.3 show the slopes of an elastic and an inelastic demand curve. When demand is elastic, you can increase revenue by decreasing prices. The amount of revenue you lose on each unit will be more than made up by the increased sales. This is where the saying "we can make it up on volume" comes from. When demand is inelastic, you increase revenue by increasing prices. The higher price per unit more than makes up for the loss in unit sales.

Cross elasticity refers to two or more products whose price elasticity is related to each other. For **complementary products**, an increase in demand for one product will lead to an increase in demand for the other product. For example,

FIGURE 11.3   Inelastic demand curve

Keurig® coffee makers and K-Cups® are complementary products. A decrease in price for Keurig coffee makers will lead to an increase in demand for K-Cups even if there was no change in the price of the K-Cups. For **substitute products**, a decrease in demand for one product will lead to an increase in demand for the other. Butter and margarine are substitute products. A price increase for butter will lead to an increase in the demand for margarine as some people will switch to the (now even lower) lower-priced substitute.

Luxury Products

In our culture, wealth is an important component of status, so the fact that you can afford to pay a lot of money for a product that everyone can see is an important status symbol. This is why luxury products and status goods follow an inverted demand curve— implying that the law of supply and demand has been revoked. In Figure 11.4, the part of the demand curve below the horizontal line is the inverted demand curve. In this region, an increase in price will lead to an increase in the quantity demanded. For example, Rolex® watches start at $3–5,000, and the most popular models go for more than $10k. Add a little bling, and the price

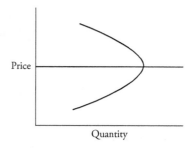

FIGURE 11.4   Inverted demand curve

can easily end up in the high five figures. The point is, when you wear a Rolex watch, you are saying to the world, "I can afford to buy a very expensive watch." If the price were cut in half, the company would sell fewer watches because at the lower price, they are less exclusive.

However, there is a limit even for luxury goods. At some point, if the price gets too high, the quantity demanded will decrease. This is represented by the part of the demand curve above the horizontal line.

Oligopoly Markets

An oligopoly is a market in which a small number of companies dominate the market. Because of this, demand in oligopoly situations is both elastic and inelastic as suggested by the kinked demand curve illustrated in Figure 11.5 below.

The horizontal line represents the current market price for the product. Above the market price, demand is highly elastic. If one of the players chose to raise prices and the others did not, customers would quickly switch to the lower-priced competitors, and the company would lose market share. The result would be that the company retracts the price increase in order to maintain market share. Below the market price, demand is highly inelastic. If one of the competitors lowered prices and the others did not, customers would switch to the lower-priced product, and everybody else would lose market share. But once the other companies noticed they were losing market share, they would match the price cut in order to retain customers. In this scenario, everybody (except the customer) loses. Demand for the product is the same; the market price has decreased, so everyone is making less money.

Given this situation, it would make sense for businesses in an oligopoly to get together and set a price that allows everyone to make a nice profit. If all of the players raised their prices at the same time, customers would have no choice but to pay the higher price. Fortunately, this is called collusion and is against the law in the United States. Instead, prices are managed through an informal **price signaling** process. One company (usually the largest player in the market) will publicly announce a price increase to be effective at a future date. This gives the other companies a chance to respond before the price increase goes into effect. If the other companies also announce a similar price increase, the price increase will stick. On the other hand, if none of the other companies follow the increase, the original company will retract the offer—either by canceling the price increase or by offering a rebate or discount to bring prices back to the market price.

Because the market price tends to be stable in oligopoly situations, cutting costs is an important way to boost profits.

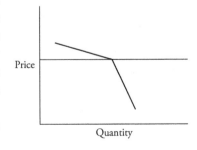

FIGURE 11.5 Kinked demand curve

11.3 BUSINESS OBJECTIVES AND CONSTRAINTS

Marketing may not be the only functional area of a business to be involved in pricing decisions. The business objectives of the company and the constraints the company face have a significant impact on the prices it can charge. Generally speaking, the business objectives are to increase profitability, and the constraints are limitations on the ability to charge higher prices.

Business Objectives

The most important business objective is to make a profit. In the long run, revenue has to exceed expenses, or the business will cease to exist. Most companies are looking to do more than break even, so some sort of profit objective or internal rate of return on investment is part of the equation. Publicly traded companies are required to publish earnings every quarter. Investors like to see a steady increase in revenue and profitability, so positive quarterly results are important to corporations.

Assuming revenue exceeds expenses, there may be other objectives you want to achieve through your pricing. For many businesses, simply surviving is the price objective. If you have the luxury of flexibility in setting your prices, you may want to keep prices as low as possible to increase market share or to pump up unit sales to achieve economies of scale in production. On the other hand, a desire for corporate responsibility or other socially conscious goals may cause you to charge a higher price to cover the cost of these activities.

Organizational Constraints

In addition to your cost structure, which we will cover shortly, there may be other external influences that limit your ability to charge high prices for your product. These include demand issues, product issues, competitive issues, and profit structure.

Demand Issues

Obviously, the higher the demand for your product, the higher the prices you can charge for it. In addition, price elasticity has an effect on the impact of price changes. The market structure of your industry plays a role in the ability to set prices. In a monopoly situation, there are no short-run constraints on pricing. In an oligopoly situation, or monopolistic competition (the situation for many maturity stage industries), the price is set by the market leader. In pure competition, prices are set by the market as with commodities such as corn or gold.

Product Issues

Although we cover each element of the marketing mix individually, the reality is that they are interrelated. Where you are in the product life cycle has an impact on your ability to set prices. In the introductory and decline stages, you have a lot of flexibility. In the growth stage, pricing decisions will encourage differentiation and the development of profitable market segments. In the maturity stage, the smaller number of competitors leads to monopolistic competition, and pricing is similar to an oligopoly situation.

Also, you will need to consider the impact of a pricing decision for one product on the other products in your product mix. What are the cross elasticities? Will a change in price for one product increase or decrease demand for other products in your mix?

Finally, if you are selling your product through an intermediary such as a retailer or a wholesaler, you will need to allow room for your channel partners to make a profit from the price charged to the end user.

"In marketing, or in any business, having a strong understanding of the numbers is crucial. With so much data we're able to collect today, and so many decisions being made from data; it's really important to have familiarity with Excel, basic financials. To understand the cost of customer acquisition and to be able to measure whether a campaign was successful."

Marketing Professional

Competitive Issues

While there is no such thing as a price that is too high if a customer is willing to pay it, nobody will buy your product if a competitor is offering something comparable at a lower price. So knowing what competitors are charging is an important consideration in pricing. Also, your competitors' response to a price change is a significant constraint on pricing.

Many products have an "expected" or "customary" price where the consumer knows what the price of the product should be. Knowing the expected price for a product will help you use price as a positioning tool. Setting your price above the expected price is a signal of quality while setting your price below the expected price is a signal of value.

People perceive prices relative to the expected price, but there are limits. A price too far above or too far below the expected price will not be believable. For example, the average price of a smart phone without a subsidy from a wireless carrier is around $525.[2] You would expect a smartphone selling for $600 or $700 dollars to be a high-end device such as the most recent version of the iPhone® or the Galaxy®.

For $400, you would expect an older model or one with fewer features than the high-end phones. Would you buy a smartphone that only cost $25? Probably not. The price is too low to be believable, and you would suspect there is something wrong with the phone. Similarly, you probably wouldn't pay $1,500 for a high-end smartphone (unless the case was made of gold). It's too far above what you would expect to pay for a smartphone.

Profit Structure

If the goal is to make a profit, you need to understand "the numbers." It may be helpful to review some of the basic revenue and cost concepts before applying them with breakeven analysis. We'll look at some issues related to revenue and costs as well as some basic marginal analysis. These concepts will be important when we move into breakeven analysis in the following section. Table 11.1 expresses these concepts in equation form.

Table 11.1 Cost Structure

	PROFIT
1	Profit = Revenue − Cost
2	Marginal Profit = ΔProfit ÷ ΔQuantity Sold
	REVENUE
3	Total Revenue = Unit Price × Quantity Sold
4	Average revenue = Total revenue ÷ Quantity Sold
5	Marginal Revenue = ΔTotal Revenue ÷ Quantity Sold
	COSTS
6	Total Cost = Fixed Cost + Variable Cost
7	Variable Cost = Unit variable Cost × Units Sold
8	Average Fixed Cost = Fixed Cost ÷ Quantity Sold
	BREAKEVEN
9	Unit Contribution = Unit Price − Unit Variable Cost
10	Unit Breakeven Point = Fixed Cost ÷ Unit Contribution
11	Dollar Breakeven Point = Unit Breakeven Point × Unit Price

Profit. The definition of profit is total revenue minus total costs (Equation 1). There are only two ways to increase profits: you can increase revenue, or you can decrease costs. When it comes to pricing decisions, it can be helpful to look at marginal profits as well. Marginal profit is the change in profit associated with the last unit sold (Equation 2). As sales and production levels increase, cost and revenue structures can fluctuate. For example, you may find yourself reducing prices or offering discounts to high-volume customers in order to increase unit sales. As long as the marginal profit associated with the next unit is positive, it makes sense to offer the discount. You may not be making as much profit as you had been making on earlier sales, but you are still making money when marginal profit is positive. When marginal profit is zero, you have maximized your profits. Revenue may increase with additional units, but you won't be making any additional profit on them. If marginal profit is less than zero, you are bleeding money. Its time to increase prices or cut back on production costs to restore profitability.

Revenue. Revenue is the amount of money you take in. Total revenue is simply the number of units sold times the price per unit (Equation 3). Because prices will fluctuate over time, it is sometimes useful to think in terms of average revenue (Equation 4) to get a sense of revenue per unit for planning purposes.

Marginal revenue, or the incremental revenue you get the last unit you sell (Equation 5), is an important consideration in pricing decisions as well. Suppose you were considering a price cut to stimulate sales. If marginal revenue is positive, a price cut will cause unit sales to increase and total revenue to increase, but average revenue will decrease. You are selling the additional units at a lower price, which is why average revenue decreases at the same time total revenue increases. Is the price cut a good idea? Maybe. We'd still need to look at costs to see the impact on the profit picture. On the other hand, if marginal revenue is negative, a price cut is probably a bad idea. Unit sales will increase, but average revenue and total revenue will decrease.

Cost. The final piece of the profit picture is cost, or expenses. Total cost is the combination of fixed and variable costs (Equation 6). Variable costs are tied to production and increase as production increases. Raw materials, sales commissions, or a retailer's merchandise are usually considered variable costs. Unit variable costs are relatively stable, so total variable cost increases with an increase in units sold.

Fixed costs, on the other hand, are related to things that don't change with units sold. Rent, salaries, and advertising expenses are typical examples of fixed costs. Total fixed costs remain constant, therefore, average fixed cost will decrease with an increase in production (Equation 8).

The difference between fixed cost and variable cost has important implications for profit and pricing decisions. In the long run, total revenue has to exceed total cost for the business to remain profitable. In the short run, it is possible to set prices below total cost but above your variable cost. As long as unit revenue exceeds unit variable costs, you will have to be able to make some contribution to covering your fixed expenses. If unit revenue is less than variable costs, there is no short run. You will quickly go out of business.

11.4 BREAKEVEN ANALYSIS

Breakeven analysis is a simple yet powerful tool that applies some of these cost concepts in a variety of contexts. You may remember from the discussion of the product life cycle in Chapter 8.1 that how quickly you need to recover your product development costs determines whether you choose a skimming or a penetration pricing strategy. That was an example of a breakeven analysis question.

At its most basic, the breakeven point is the number of units you need to sell in order to pay for your fixed costs. This takes into account the idea that average fixed costs decrease with volume while unit variable costs remain constant. The difference between the price and unit variable costs is the unit contribution (Equation 9), or the amount you have left over after paying the variable cost to help pay for the fixed cost. You simply divide your fixed cost by the unit contribution (Equation 10) to find out how many units you need to sell to cover your fixed costs.

Examples of Breakeven Analysis

Example 1

A simple example might help. Let's suppose you were planning to open a coffee shop. You found a location that you can rent for $15,000 per year, and it will cost you another $15,000 to furnish the shop and purchase the equipment. You plan on charging $5 for a cup of coffee, and it will cost you $2 per cup for coffee, paper goods, and condiments. How many cups of coffee do you need to sell to get your investment back? Fixed costs are $30,000 (rent and furnishings), variable costs are $2, and your unit price is $5.

Your unit contribution is $3 ($5 price minus $2 variable cost). Breakeven volume = $30,000 ÷ $3 = 10,000. This means you will have to sell at least 10,000 cups or $50,000 in revenue (Equation 11) to cover your cost in the first year. Is that a realistic number? If it seems reasonable, you may want to proceed with the plan. If not, then don't. This is known as a "go/no go" decision.

Example 2

Now let's look at how that same principle can help with more complex issues. Perhaps you don't want to work for free. Maybe you'd like to pay yourself a salary. How does $30,000 a year sound? How many cups of coffee would you need to sell in order to pay yourself a salary? You would treat the salary as a fixed cost. Now your fixed costs are $60,000. Breakeven point = $60,000 ÷ $3 = 20,000 cups or $100,000. Is it reasonable to believe you can sell 20,000 cups?

Example 3

Suppose you believe that you can double your sales if you cut your price to $3. Should you cut your price? Your unit contribution is now $1. Breakeven point = $60,000 ÷ $1 = 60,000 cups or $180,000. If you doubled your sales, you would sell 40,000 units; but you would need to sell 60,000 units to break even at that price. This price cut is not a good idea.

Example 4

OK, you won't cut the price, but a salesperson came by and offered you an advertising package for $15,000. How many additional cups of coffee would you have to sell to make the advertising deal worthwhile? In this case, we just look at the advertising as the fixed cost. Breakeven = $15,000 ÷ $3 = 5,000. You would need to sell an additional 5,000 cups of coffee to pay for the advertising. But wait, what if you don't just want to break even on the advertising? What if you want to earn an additional $15,000 in profit if you are going to go through the hassle of developing an ad campaign? In this case, you would consider the required profit a fixed cost. Breakeven = $30,000 ÷ $3 = 10,000 cups or $50,000. You would need to sell an additional 10,000 cups to pay for the ad campaign and make it worth your while. That means you would need to be able to sell 30,000 cups of coffee. Is that a reasonable expectation?

You can begin to see how this tool can be used in a variety of situations.

11.5 PRICING FRAMEWORK

As you can see, there are a lot of issues to consider when setting prices. It may be helpful to establish a basic framework as a summary (Figure 11.6). The highest possible price you would ever be able to charge for a product is what it is worth to your customer. As long as there is value—benefits received greater than the cost of acquiring them—people will pay. This is called charging what the market will bear. At the other end of the scale, the lowest possible price you could charge would be just slightly higher than your direct variable costs. Although this is not a sound long-term strategy, there may be situations where it is appropriate for short periods of time. This is the theoretical range for pricing decisions.

However, in the real world, we don't deal with theoretical maximums. You probably have some profit objective that would have you set your price not only above direct variable costs but well above total average costs. On the other side, while customers may be willing to pay the theoretical maximum for your product, there are probably competitors offering a similar product. You would have a hard time selling anything if your prices are way higher than the competition. So competitive pressure lowers the maximum price you can charge.

That leaves you with the practical range you have for making pricing decisions. The size of the practical range will vary from product to product, from industry to

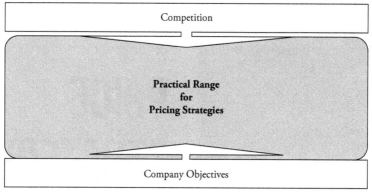

Theoretical Maximum: Value to Customer

Competition

**Practical Range
for
Pricing Strategies**

Company Objectives

Theoretical Minimum: Unit variable Cost

FIGURE 11.6   Pricing framework

industry, and over time. All of the strategies we'll discuss in the next chapter take place within this range.

(ENDNOTES)

1. http://www.merriam-webster.com/dictionary/price. Definition 4. Accessed April 13, 2015.
2. Louis, Tristan, "The Real Price of a Smartphone," *Forbes.com, September 14, 2013,* http://www.forbes.com/sites/tristanlouis/2013/09/14/the-real-cost-of-a-smartphone/. Accessed July 3, 2015.

PRICE STRATEGY

CH 12

Because prices are expressed as numbers, they are the easiest element of the marketing mix for customers to use to compare products. This means your pricing decisions will come under a lot of scrutiny from customers and competitors, as well as government regulatory bodies. As marketers, we have the responsibility to set prices in order to maximize revenue. As consumers, we have the desire to pay as little as possible for the products we use. Understanding the specific tactics used to set prices and understanding when and why they can be effective will help you in both of these roles.

12.1 LEGAL ISSUES

Setting prices is an art as well as a science. In Chapter 11, we described the practical range for setting prices with a ceiling based on competitive pressure and a floor based on business requirements. Within that range, there are many different approaches to setting prices. In this chapter we will look at demand-based strategies, cost-based strategies, and competition-based strategies, as well as some specific tactics used to make prices more palatable.

Before talking about specific pricing strategies, it is important to look at some of the legal constraints on your pricing decisions. In the United States, commerce is regulated at the federal, state, and local level. This means specific regulations may vary, depending on where your business is located. In general, the government favors things that increase competition and discourages things that limit competition or create monopolies. The Sherman Antitrust Act (1890) and the Clayton Antitrust Act (1914) are two landmark laws implementing this pro-competitive approach. There are four pricing strategies that can get you in trouble: price fixing, price discrimination, deceptive pricing, and predatory pricing.

Price Fixing

The intent of federal regulation is that prices are determined by supply and demand rather than arbitrarily dictated by an agreement among manufacturers. There are two types of price fixing. **Horizontal price fixing** is an agreement between competitors in the same industry to fix prices. **Vertical price fixing** is an agreement between businesses at different levels of the channel of distribution (Chapter 13) to fix prices.

Horizontal Price Fixing

In the last chapter, we talked about the kinked demand curve faced by companies in an oligopoly situation. If one company alone raises prices, it will lose market share to others in the industry. If one company alone lowers prices, competitors will likely match the price cut in order to preserve market share. The ideal (from an industry perspective) would be for everybody to agree in advance what prices will be. That way, everybody wins. This is horizontal price fixing and is against the law.

While it is illegal to get together to set prices, highly concentrated industries use **price signaling** as a way to communicate pricing actions (Chapter 11.2). Usually the largest company in the industry takes the lead by publicly announcing a price change (usually a price increase) that will become effective at some future date. After making the announcement, it will wait to see what other companies in the industry will do. If other companies also make announcements that their prices will rise, the price change sticks. If other companies do not follow, the leader may rescind the price change.

Vertical Price Fixing

Vertical price fixing usually involves a manufacturer trying to dictate the prices a retailer can charge its customers for the product. The most common situation is where a manufacturer doesn't want one retailer to sell the product at a lower price than others and sets a minimum retail price for the product. Up until 2006, this was always illegal. The idea is that when a retailer takes title to the manufacturer's products, the retailer then owns the product and can dispose of it however the retailer desires. The only way for a manufacturer to encourage minimum retail prices would be to stop selling to retailers who discount too heavily.

However, a recent Supreme Court decision (*Leegin Creative Leather Products, Inc. v. PSKS, Inc.*) determined that there may be circumstances where an agreement to fix retail prices might not be illegal. If the effect of the minimum retail price is to encourage, rather than to discourage competition, vertical price fixing is allowed. For example, if your product has a small market share, a minimum retail price might encourage more retailers to carry the product, which would increase competition against more established brands.

Price Discrimination

Have you ever been on an airplane and checked to see what other people had paid for their tickets? You are all on the same flight, yet there was a huge difference between the highest price and the lowest price paid for the trip. **Price discrimination** is the practice of charging different customers different prices for the same product. It happens all the time in consumer marketing and is usually perfectly legal.

Under the Robinson-Patman Act (1936), price discrimination becomes illegal in interstate commerce (so it is usually a B2B issue) when it gives favored customers a competitive advantage over others for no economic reason. If you owned a chain of skate shops, you would expect to pay the same prices for skateboards as your competitor does. It would be unfair for the manufacturer to charge you a higher price for skateboards in order to help out your competitor.

If there is a legitimate economic reason for the price difference, then there is no crime. For example, if your competitor orders 1,000 skateboards every week, while you order 100 skateboards every month, the transaction costs for your skateboard would be higher than your competitor's cost as it is more efficient to process and ship large orders than it is to process and ship small orders. In this case, the manufacturer would be justified in charging you a higher price.

Deceptive Pricing

As a consumer, it is frustrating to go into a store thinking you are going to pay one price for a product and end up paying a lot more. In many cases, this is due to excellent salesmanship (Chapter 18). In some cases, it is because the retailer used deceptive pricing practices such as bait and switch or reference pricing.

Bait and Switch

Bait and switch tactics usually happen with expensive, discretionary purchases such as electronics or furniture. Typically, a product is heavily advertised at a very low price (let's say a 70-inch-wide screen TV for $499) in order to generate traffic (get people to come into the store). Once you are in the store, you are told by a salesperson that the store sold all of the featured TVs, and then, they try to sell you a different, more expensive product. There is nothing illegal about attracting you to the store with the "bait" and then trying to sell you something else. It is only illegal when you are unable to purchase the "bait" should you choose to do so. While the Federal Trade Commission (FTC) has guidelines about bait and switch tactics, most regulation occurs at the state and local levels.

A reputable retailer has a couple of approaches to dealing with bait and switch concerns. One approach is to offer a limited amount of the product and make the limit clear in the advertising. This is common among retailers offering super-deep discounts, or "door busters," on the day after Thanksgiving. As a customer, you know that you have to be there early to have a chance at that $499 TV. Another approach is simply to offer a "rain check," which will allow the customer to purchase the product at the advertised price when the product is back in stock, or, if that is too inconvenient, to allow the customer to substitute a comparable product at the sale price.

> "When I worked at CISCO where I was on a sales enablement team, one of the vice presidents, Chuck Robbins, (who is actually now the CEO) said to our team, 'You guys need to understand there are 20,000 salespeople here at CISCO, so every time you send an email out to my sales team, you are wasting 20,000 minutes of the company's time.' That reinforced that when we connect with the sales team, we need to be clear, concise, and correct so that we are only wasting 20,000 minutes; not 40,000 minutes or 80,000 minutes."
>
> **Julie Clarke**

Reference Pricing

Reference pricing is where a retailer promotes a price for a product that is higher than the actual price. The most common example is to put a product on sale at a percentage discount, or markdown, from the regular price. This works on the principle of anchoring and adjustment (Chapter 13) where the reference price serves as the anchor and makes the actual price seem much lower by comparison. This becomes illegal when the reference price has no basis in reality. For example, if you claim to be selling a product at 30% off, you need to be able to document that you have actually sold the product at the full price.

The defense against illegal reference pricing is to document the source of the reference. If, for example, the reference price is the manufacturer's suggested retail price (MSRP), then you could claim 30% off MSRP but not 30% off regular prices.

Or, suppose you were able to purchase a shipment of televisions at half of the cost you would usually pay. It would be illegal to advertise them at 50% off regular prices because you didn't sell any of them at the regular price. To document the reference, you might say "special purchase" and compare the price to a competitive brand.

Predatory Pricing

Is there such a thing as setting your prices too low for the consumer? In general, no. The lower the better. It is not uncommon for businesses to set prices below their cost of production (but, hopefully, higher than direct variable costs) in order to gain market share. The idea is to will recover your investment in low prices from the new customers you gained when prices go back to normal. **Predatory pricing** is when a company sets its price below the cost of production in order to put a competitor out of business or to prevent a competitor from entering the market. A consumer is only harmed—and below-cost pricing becomes predatory—when a dominant competitor uses low prices to knock a competitor out of the market and then raises prices to above the previous market price for an extended period of time.

12.2 NEW PRODUCT PRICING

In Chapter 8, we talked about two basic pricing strategies for the introductory stage of the product life cycle. A **penetration** strategy sets initial prices low in order to gain market share quickly and to discourage competitors from entering the market. A **skimming** approach sets initial prices high in order to recover development costs quickly and then lowers prices as economies of scale and competitive pressure set in.

A short-term strategy for new product pricing is to use a very low introductory price, or **trial pricing**. This approach can be used with either a penetration or a skimming strategy. When used with a penetration strategy, the trial price might take the form of a coupon for the new product to stimulate demand. Or it might take the form of a free sample in order to generate awareness of the new product, especially when it is easy to see the benefits of the new product compared to the one it is intended to replace.

When used with a skimming strategy, the goal is to get the product into the hands of influential early adopters. This might involve offering a free upgrade to current users or making a special offer to influential bloggers who write about the product category. Another approach would be to offer a pre-introduction price to attendees of a convention or other product-related gathering. Getting the new product into the hands of influential users can work against you if they do not like the product. Good marketing will make a bad product fail faster.

A variation of the trial pricing approach that works well with shopping goods is to offer a free trial period. This takes advantage of the loss aversion principle: people will work harder to avoid a loss than they will work for a comparable gain. What this means in practice is that a product becomes more valuable to a person when it is taken home. Because the person had temporary ownership during the free trial, they will pay more money not to have to give it back than they would have paid for it up front.

12.3 DEMAND-BASED PRICING

With demand-based pricing strategies, the focus is on the customer's perception of value. The goal is to capture as much of that value as possible for your company. Demand-based pricing strategies include prestige pricing, price line strategies, target profit pricing, price bundling, captive pricing, and yield-management pricing.

Prestige Pricing

Prestige pricing is used for high-status, socially consumed luxury products. For these customers, the fact that the product is too expensive for others to purchase is an important component of the value proposition. These products follow an inverted demand curve where (up to a point) you can actually increase demand for the product by raising the price.

Because you can copyright a logo, but not a design, there are two kinds of luxury products. Entry-level status goods feature recognizable logos of well-known companies so that it will be obvious to others that the person buys Gucci® or Coach™ products. This makes it easier to pursue counterfeiters. Ultra-status products feature very small, almost indistinguishable logos. The people who are likely to recognize these ultra-luxury products are other high-status insiders who would recognize a counterfeit product on sight.

Price Line Strategy

A **price line strategy** involves offering at least three similar products in a product line. Sometimes called the "good, better, best" strategy, one product will be the high-priced option, one product will be the low-priced option, and the other will be somewhere in the middle. There are a couple of principles at work here. The first involves anchoring and adjustment. For people unfamiliar with the product, the price line sets the anchor in the middle and defines the extremes of the range. The second is it allows you to differentiate the products based on specific features or attributes.

This practice is widely used in selling mattresses. A typical mattress store will have a number of options starting with the very plain basic model and several choices leading up to the deluxe model. Because people don't always understand what goes on inside a mattress, the ticking (or outside fabric) and the display will be more attractive for the higher-priced models than for the lower-priced models. Attributes, such as the layers of padding or the number of springs, are used to differentiate between the models.

As you might imagine, while some people will always choose the cheapest option, and some will always choose the most expensive option, most people will choose one of the middle options. It is important to have a high-priced option even if very few people actually purchase it. The high-priced option makes the middle choices seem like more of a bargain. In fact, you can increase the sales of the high-priced option by adding an even higher-priced product to the line. While very few people will buy the new higher-priced item, more people will buy the "old" high-priced option because it is now one of the middle choices.

Target Profit Pricing

Target profit pricing involves identifying an attractive price point for your product and then designing a product that you can sell profitably at that price. When I was working in the furniture industry in the '90s, the goal was to develop a promotional sofa that a retailer could sell for less than $600 and still make money. That was an attractive low end to the price line for sofas, and such a product would allow the retailer to advertise the $600 sofa to attract customers to the store yet still make a profit if it was unable to persuade the customer to buy a more expensive option.

The advantage to this approach is that it is market driven. You know what the customer wants to pay for a product, and if you can deliver it, you will make money. The disadvantage is that it is easily imitated. Once you've shown that it can be profitable to produce a product at that price point, competitors will follow.

Price Bundling

Price bundling involves selling multiple products for a single price in order to increase the perception of value to the customer. There are several ways price bundling can increase value. Multipacks bundle several identical items together. This saves customers money for a bulk purchase. Bonus packs include a little extra product as an alternative to a price discount. Including a sample of a new product as a bonus for purchasing an existing product is a technique for introducing incremental innovations for mature stage products (Chapter 8). Complementary packaging makes it convenient for a customer to purchase related products. The s'mores kits sold in grocery stores in the summer are an example complementary packaging. Everything you need to make this campfire favorite (marshmallows, chocolate, graham crackers, and roasting sticks) is in one convenient package at a single price.

Captive Pricing

Captive pricing works well when you have two products that have to work together to deliver the core benefit to the customer. You price one of the products very low in order to encourage people to buy the system and then set a high price for the other "captive" product. In order for this strategy to be successful, you need to discourage customers from choosing a lower-cost substitute for the captive product.

The classic example of captive pricing is ink jet printers. You can buy a very nice ink jet printer for a very low price. Many times, the printer is bundled with a computer purchase. Replacement cartridges for the printer are relatively expensive. Once you have the printer, you are encouraged to use only brand-name replacement cartridges to avoid damaging the printer. As a convenience for you, the manufacturer may include a postage-paid envelope to allow you to dispose of the used cartridges responsibly. (This also makes it impossible to reuse the cartridges by refilling them with less expensive ink.)

Yield-Management Pricing

Yield-management pricing charges different prices to different market segments based on the relative value of the product (usually a service) to the customer. This works best in service industries with a high fixed cost component such as airlines or television advertising (Chapter 10). The advantage to yield management pricing is that it maximizes revenue for a given amount of inventory. The disadvantage is that customers perceive it as unfair, especially when they end up paying some of the higher prices.

Subscription Pricing

With **subscription pricing**, the customer pays for access to a product or service for a specified period of time. Pioneered in the periodical media (newspapers, magazines) this approach is being adopted by software companies and other businesses. Rather than purchasing a video game, gamers can buy a one-month or three-month subscription to Sony's PlayStation® Now and have access to a library of video games. A subscription box model sends you regular shipments of candy, flowers, wine, gifts ... there is even a "sock of the month" program for those looking for excitement in their footwear.

Subscription pricing reduces the perceived total cost of the product because the price is a low monthly fee rather than a large purchase amount. Rather than paying $59.99 to own a video game, PlayStation Now customers pay $19.99 a month.

The key to a successful subscription model is renewal. The marketing emphasis shifts from customer acquisition to customer retention. Every time the subscription period ends, the customer needs to sign up for another period. To minimize customer loss through attrition, many companies are moving to an "opt out" or automatic renewal procedure. With opt out renewal, the subscription is automatically renewed unless the customer acts to end it. Typically, the customer is notified that the subscription is coming up for renewal and is billed for the next subscription period. Ideally, you would ask for credit card information when the customer subscribes. This makes renewal much easier.

Many online businesses use a "freemium" pricing model where an introductory tier of service is available for free but a subscription is required to have full access.

For example, music streaming company, Spotify®, offers a limited free service which includes advertising and limited functionality; and a premium subscription service that eliminates ads and provides additional functionality to users.

12.4 COST-BASED PRICING

With cost-based pricing strategies, the focus is on the lower end of the practical range for setting prices. The goal is to make sure revenue exceeds expenses. Cost-based strategies include standard markup pricing, cost-plus pricing, and geographic pricing.

Standard Markup Pricing

Standard markup pricing sets prices by considering the total cost for the product as well as the desired profit margin. This is usually expressed as a percentage markup over cost of goods sold. For example, a retailer desiring a 50% gross margin would have to markup products 100% (sometimes called a "keystone"). There is no "typical" markup as each retail operation will have a unique cost structure and profit objective.

The advantage of standard markup pricing is that is easy to apply when your product mix includes lots of individual items. This is why it is used in many retail operations. For example, according to the Food Marketing Institute, the average grocery store carried around 44,000 individual items in 2013[1]. It would be impractical for the grocer to take time to consider each item individually to determine the optimal price. In addition, customers perceive standard markup pricing to be fair because every product is priced using the same formula, and they don't have to negotiate each purchase.

The disadvantage of standard markup pricing is that it ignores what customers are willing to pay for each individual item. You can observe this for yourself simply by walking through any grocery store. When you see empty spaces on the store shelves, you know the item in question was priced below what people are willing to pay, and, as a result, it sold out very quickly. On the other hand, you may see a "bargain bin" for products that are being discontinued or are close to their sell-by date. These are products that were priced higher than customers were willing to pay and, as a result, didn't sell.

Cost-Plus Pricing

Cost-plus pricing is used for products where it is impossible to determine what the final cost of the product will be. This is used with regulated utilities such as the gas or electric companies as well as with large, one-of-a-kind projects. In the case of utilities, rates are determined by taking into account the utility's investment in infrastructure, or rate base, and then allowing a reasonable profit margin on top of it. The classic example of a one-of-a-kind project would be the space race in the 1960s. Each new rocket was built for a specific mission, and there was no way to anticipate what the final cost of the product was going to be. Cost-plus pricing is sometimes used in military procurement, especially with the development of a new weapons system such as the F-117 stealth fighter. It is impossible to know in advance how much it will cost to develop the plane, so manufacturers would be reluctant to submit competitive bids for the project. Instead, the contract negotiates the profit level based on what the eventual cost of the project will be.

> "When I first started, social media was big, a lot of sharing content and scheduling tweets and [I thought] that's how marketing works. Through this experience, [I] got to work on the numbers side and [see] how marketing actually impacts the running of a company."
>
> Anadelia Fadeev

Geographic Pricing

In situations where transportation costs are a significant component of the total cost of a product, there are four approaches to **geographic pricing** commonly used: FOB, CIF, uniform delivered price, and zone pricing. With FOB (free on board) and CIF (cost, insurance, and freight) pricing, the issue is whether the buyer or the seller pays for shipping costs. With FOB pricing, the customer is responsible for transportation costs. This is used in B2B situations where the customer may have better access to transportation than the seller. For example, WalMart® now asks manufacturers to use the company's high-efficiency trucks for shipping in order to help meet environmental goals. With CIF, or delivered pricing, the cost of shipping is built into the purchase price.

Uniform delivered pricing and zone pricing come into play for delivery and personal transportation when transportation costs are the primary component of the service. With uniform delivered pricing, the cost is the same no matter the destination. The best example of uniform delivered pricing is mailing a first class letter in the United States. One postage stamp will send the letter anywhere in the country. Many cities use uniform pricing for bus transportation. One fare will take you anywhere in the city.

Zone delivered pricing is a variant of uniform delivered pricing. Rather than negotiating a price for every individual trip as you would when taking a taxi, zone delivered pricing creates tiers of uniform prices. For example, UPS® uses eight zones to determine shipping rates in the continental United States. The price would be the same for any destination in a given zone.

12.5 COMPETITION-BASED PRICING

Competition-based pricing strategies come into play in highly competitive industries. In these situations, your ability to set prices is limited by the actions of your competitors. Competition-based strategies include customary pricing, price positioning, price leadership, below cost pricing, and non-price pricing.

Customary Pricing

In mature markets as well as in oligopoly situations, there are typically a handful of competitors in each product category. As a result, there is frequently a customary price, or prevailing price, for the product. Take the candy bar industry, for example. The price of a standard candy bar is the same regardless of the maker. In these situations, it is important to price your product in line with the customary price.

Price Positioning

When there is a customary price for your product, you can use the price/value heuristic as a way to position your product relative to the competition. A candy bar that costs more than the customary price is a signal of higher quality. A candy bar priced lower than the customary price is a signal of a lesser quality value offering. Anchoring and adjustment effects kick in with customary pricing. A price that is too high or too low compared to the customary price will not be believable. If the candy bar is priced too low, there must be something wrong with it.

Price Leadership

As we discussed earlier, anticipating the competition's response to a price change is critical in an oligopoly situation. It is illegal to meet with your competitors to work out a price everyone (except the customer) can live with, so price changes are usually announced in advance, allowing others in the industry to react before the change becomes effective. Typically, the dominant firm in the industry, as the price leader, makes the first move.

Below Cost Pricing

There are a couple of times when it may be tempting to lower your prices below your total cost. As we discussed in the section on predatory pricing, lowering your prices for a short period in order to gain market share can pay off if the increased volume from the new customers makes up for the lost revenue while prices were low.

This is a risky strategy because it assumes your competitors will be unwilling or unable to match the price cut. If your competitors are willing to match the price cut, you can get into a price war. In a worst-case scenario, the competitive response may be so intense that you are unable to raise prices back up to a profitable level.

Another time when it makes sense to set prices below your total cost is when you have excess manufacturing capacity and are looking to expand into a new market or territory. Because your overhead costs will have been covered serving your existing customers, the marginal cost of producing new units will be very close to your direct variable costs. This would allow you to sell these extra units at a lower price and still be profitable. As you build a position in the new market, prices would have to gradually increase to cover the full cost.

While this strategy makes economic sense, it might not make political sense. Selling a product in another country below your cost of production could be considered "dumping" and trigger a regulatory response.

Non-Price Pricing

In some consumer markets where customers are particularly sensitive about price, price changes are made indirectly by manipulating the product offering. For example, a "quart" of ice cream now comes in a 28-ounce container rather than 32 ounces. On the freezer shelf, it looks about the same as the half gallon you remember buying in the past and you are paying the same price as the half gallon you remember buying, but the effect is to increase the cost of the ice cream by 14%. One industry representative defended the change by observing that research showed people don't eat the last little bit of ice cream in the container and end up throwing it out. They just saved them time by throwing that last little bit out before they purchase it.

This works for price cuts as well. Apple® works hard to maintain minimum retail prices for its products. If you have shopped for an Apple product, you may have had a hard time finding a retailer selling at a significantly lower price than others. And while the list price is pretty consistent, the offer that goes along with the product might vary considerably. One retailer might offer a store gift card with every purchase. Another might offer a free accessory kit with your purchase. These are all non-price pricing tactics.

12.6 RETAIL PRICE TACTICS

In this section, we'll talk about some specific tactics retailers use to make prices more attractive to customers. You will probably recognize many of these tactics. By understanding single vs. multiple prices, fixed vs. flexible prices, EDLP, negotiated prices, dynamic pricing, high-low pricing, and price adjustments, you will be both a better marketer and a better shopper.

Single vs. Multiple Prices

What is the price? We expect the answer to that question to be a number. Preferably a single number. It is an important number because price is a search attribute people use to compare one product against another. Most of our retail transactions—groceries, gasoline, shoes—involve paying the price we see on the shelf. However, splitting the price into multiple parts can make the price appear to be significantly lower.

One approach is to charge two separate prices for the product in order to compare favorably to your competitors on price. The list price is the one publicized. The additional prices—initiation, surcharge, franchise fee ... the list goes on—come into play after the customer is seriously considering your product. What is the cost of a gym membership? Only $29.95 a month? That's way cheaper than the other guy at $35.95 a month. But what about the initiation fee? Or how about one of those amazing bargains "As Seen on TV" where shipping and handling charges that cost more than the product? The second one is free - as long as you pay additional shipping and handling.

The travel industry is notorious for having a low list price and lots of hidden costs. Check into a resort hotel, and you might be asked to pay an additional resort fee, a security fee, and even a fuel surcharge, none of which is negotiable. Fortunately, many travel websites now include these hidden fees so you can make your decision by comparing the actual price.

Another approach is to take a very expensive purchase and break it down into several smaller segments to make it easier for the customer to accept. Breaking the price down to monthly payments can be effective because people pay their bills monthly. It is much easier to sell you a $299 a month lease payment than it is to sell you a $30,000 car. You can see how well $299 will fit into your budget. Salespeople are trained to break prices down into smaller chunks that customers can relate to. Rather than saying something will cost $100 a month, say it's about the cost of a Starbucks® coffee each day. That's not very expensive at all.

Fixed vs. Flexible Prices

Again, the norm in this country is that the price on the label is the price you pay. When you go into a retail store, you expect to see the price clearly displayed. Dollar-type stores take this to an extreme and price every item in the store at the same price: one dollar.

EDLP (Every Day Low Prices)

EDLP is another tactic retailers use to communicate fixed prices to customers. The EDLP promise is that not only are prices fixed but products never go on sale, so you don't have to worry about whether or not you are getting a deal. While many retailers have attempted EDLP, it is challenging to maintain in the long run. Some customers enjoy occasional discounts, so the EDLP might be modified by offering temporary price reductions (not to be confused with putting a product on sale). Also, once you have announced your fixed prices, your competitors can undercut you. The dollar store concept has become popular enough for a competitor to open a chain of 99-cent stores.

Negotiated Prices

Not all sales in this country are based on fixed prices. In retail, the higher the price, the more likely some negotiation is involved. In some industries, for example, the automotive industry, retail negotiations are the norm rather than the exception. You come into the car dealership armed with facts and figures to help you get the best deal possible on your car. In B2B settings, negotiations are the rule rather than the exception. The printed price list is the starting point for the negotiation.

Speaking of which, it is a good idea to have your prices printed by a machine. This accomplishes a couple of things. First, when the numbers are printed, people are more likely to perceive them as fixed and less likely to ask for a discount. On the other hand, a handwritten price looks like it was something you came up with off of the top of your head and is an invitation to negotiation. Second, if there is to be a negotiation, the printed price becomes the starting point.

Everything's Negotiable

You'd be surprised by how many things are negotiable. Even in a retail setting, if you ask for a discount, you just might get one. If you don't get a discount, you still might get a "nibble."

In negotiations, a nibble is when you ask for a small concession after the deal has been made, for example, free delivery or gift wrapping.

Dynamic Pricing

Dynamic pricing is a highly flexible pricing strategy usually supported by technology. Prices can change in real time in response to changes in market conditions. The yield management pricing structure used by airlines is one example of dynamic pricing. Dynamic pricing is used in e-commerce to help optimize prices.

Many retailers do A/B testing to fine tune elements of the marketing mix, including price. In an A/B test, the retailer would offer the same product at two different prices to see which price converted more shoppers to buyers. Because of the high volume of transactions, you can get hundreds or even thousands of responses in a very short time. This allows you to test several different price levels to find the optimal level of pricing and to help estimate price elasticity for the product.

The downside of dynamic pricing is that it can be perceived as unfair. A customer might be distressed to check an online price at work and log in later from a home computer only to see a different price for the same product.

High-Low Pricing

With **high-low pricing,** a retailer sets overall prices high and then puts many items on sale. This creates a perception of overall low prices because a customer entering the store would see lots of big signs saying things like "50% off" or "sale" located near the little signs showing the regular price. The payoff is when the customer enters the store to seek out these bargains and ends up purchasing additional, full-priced merchandise during the expedition.

The items put on sale change periodically, usually once a week, although "flash sales," where selected items are put on sale for a very short time, are becoming more common. This approach generates excitement as shoppers hunt for and find bargains. Advertising selected sale items can help generate traffic by enticing customers to include your store on their next shopping trip.

A **loss leader** is an extreme example of high-low pricing. With a loss leader, the retailer will take a frequently purchased item and put it on sale at a very low price, sometimes, below its cost. By advertising these super bargains on products people know they will have to purchase anyway, the retailer can generate traffic for the store. Don't look for loss leaders at the checkout stand. Part of the strategy is for you to wander past tempting full-price items on your way to pick up the bargain product.

The downside of high-low pricing is that it trains your customers to only buy things when they are on sale. You may have been shopping at a department store, found an item you really like, and rather than buying it, asked the salesperson when it will go on sale. Also, it is expensive to reprice the affected items each week. When JC Penney® eliminated high-low pricing in 2012, there were significant savings in personnel costs because it no longer needed people to change prices every week. However, its core customers had been trained to shop for sales and were less interested in shopping there because the thrill of the hunt was gone. Eventually, Penney's returned to high-low pricing.

Odd-Even Pricing

Odd-even pricing sets a price ending in an odd number (1,3,5,7,9) just below a larger even number. From a psychological perspective, $99.99 is perceived to be significantly lower than $100. A similar effect can be achieved with a non-round even number just below a larger round number. For example, if a product is priced at $9.86, it is perceived as less expensive than $10.

Price Adjustments

Discounts and allowances are used to reduce the final selling price at the time of purchase and are used for a variety of reasons such as encouraging customers to buy in larger quantities or to reduce transaction costs. Table 12.1 lists some commonly used price adjustments and how they are used. You may be familiar with many of these.

Table 12.1 Price Adjustments

PRICE ADJUSTMENT	DESCRIPTION	PURPOSE
Quantity Discount	A reduced price for purchases of multiple items.	Encourage larger transactions, reduce transaction costs
Trade Discount	A reduced price for channel partners who will be re-selling the product to their customers	Allows consistent retail pricing with multiple channel outlets
Seasonal Discount	A reduced price for a purchase at a specific time of year	Allows more efficient production scheduling for seasonal products
Cash Discount	A reduced price for a cash sale	Avoids costs associated with credit transactions
Cash Rebate	Returning a portion of the purchase price to the customer after the purchase. Usually for a limited period of time	Encourages immediate purchase decision for products that can be postponed. Increases customer's available cash after a large purchase
Trade-in Allowance	Purchasing the old product when the customer replaces it with a new one	Reduces the cost of the transaction for the customer, can be used as a negotiating tactic
Promotional Allowance	A discount offered to retail partners with the understanding the savings will be used to promote the product	Support channel partners, encourage local sales promotions.

12.7 PRICE CHANGES

We live in an inflationary environment. This means that for long-term success, a business will periodically have to raise prices. Putting through a price increase is a tense situation, especially for small businesses because it makes the product more expensive for the customer. This causes your customers to re-evaluate your value proposition in light of the changed circumstances. Most businesses will temporarily reduce prices, usually to increase sales or market share. In rare instances, it may be appropriate to implement a permanent price cut.

Price Increases

There are three variables you want to keep in mind when planning a price increase: perceived cost, perceived value, and switching costs. In Chapter 1, we defined value as a function of perceived benefits and the perceived cost of acquiring those benefits. While the actual cost will increase, it is important to remember that customers base their decisions on perceived cost. The goal is to minimize the perceived cost of the increase and emphasize the perceived value of the product.

Switching costs are an important factor in price changes because the easier it is for the customer to switch to an alternative product, the more likely it is the customer will switch to another provider. For example, switching costs for a grocery store are very low. If a person is unhappy with one store, there are usually several others nearby selling essentially the same products. On the other hand, switching costs for a retail bank relationship are very high. A person unhappy with a retail bank would have to close out the accounts, wait for all of the outstanding transactions to clear, replace the ATM and credit cards linked to the account, and change the automated deposits and withdrawals from the account. In addition, there may be other accounts such as a mortgage, car loan, or investment account bundled with the checking account. That's a lot of work.

Switching costs are critical for two types of customers: price sensitive customers and dissatisfied customers. Price-sensitive customers are likely to leave you when switching costs are low. This isn't the end of the world. Price-sensitive customers tend to be less profitable over the life of the relationship than loyal customers. Dissatisfied customers are the nine out of ten people unhappy with your product who choose not to complain about it. They continue to buy from you because switching to a competitor is too much of a bother. A price increase will cause them to re-evaluate the relationship and just might be enough to nudge them into action. The good news is that because they are re-evaluating the relationship, you have an opportunity to remind them of the benefits of doing business with you.

The time to increase prices is when you are no longer meeting your profit objectives. Duh! But it is a little more complicated than that. It is important to re-evaluate the marketing mix to assess whether there are alternative ways to increase profitability (i.e., reduce cost or increase unit sales). Those actions are invisible to the customer, so they won't trigger an evaluation of the relationship.

Three scenarios for increasing prices include inflationary pressure, a new and improved product, and the competitive environment. The most common scenario is that inflationary pressure has increased your production cost, and you need to increase prices to cover your costs. Your customers are facing the same inflationary pressure, so they will accept the need for a price change. Another scenario is when you introduce a new or improved version of your product. The cost of the added features and increased perceived benefits could justify a higher price. Finally, it may be time to raise prices because everybody else is doing it. Most mature stage (Chapter 8.1) consumer products are in a monopolistic competition environment where the demand curve is similar to that of an oligopoly (Chapter 11.2). If your competitors raise their prices, your choices are to maintain a lower price in order to increase market share or to follow with your own price increase.

How to Increase Prices

The tactics used to implement the price increase are intended to minimize the perceived cost and maximize the perceived benefit. With that in mind, it is better to have regular incremental price increases than to wait as long as you can and then have a large catch-up price increase. Many businesses evaluate their pricing annually and adjust prices accordingly.

The way you explain the price increase to the customers is also important. First, thank them for their past business and remind them of the benefits of doing business with you. Then explain the circumstances that led you to increase prices. Close with another thank you and leave a way for your customers to give feedback about the change. This should be done far enough in advance of the price increase that customers will be able to factor the new pricing into their budgets. This also gives you a window to change course if customer resistance to the change is stronger than anticipated.

Consumer packaged goods companies frequently minimize the perceived cost of a price increase by simultaneously raising the price and putting the product on sale. At the time of the increase, customers focus on the sale price. After the sale is over, they are less likely to remember that the price is now higher.

Price Cuts

Permanent price cuts are the exception to the rule. Temporary price cuts are the norm in business. Two scenarios that might justify a permanent price cut are achieving economies of scale and competitive pressure. With the skimming approach to new product pricing, the idea is to set initial prices high to recover development costs and then lower the price as economies of scale reduce your costs. This is the norm with consumer electronics. Prices for the latest gadget start out high and then decrease over time. Prices only increase with the introduction of the next big thing.

Temporary price cuts should be looked at as an investment. As with any business decision, there should be a clear outcome the investment is intended to achieve combined with an evaluation of the investment against alternative uses for the money. The two most common objectives of a temporary price cut are to stimulate new business or to increase unit sales. Think about it. A 10% price cut is the same thing as investing 10% of your sales in sales promotion. How much money is 10% of sales for the duration of the promotion? Are there other ways you could invest that amount of money to achieve the desired result?

(ENDNOTE)

1. http://www.fmi.org/research-resources/supermarket-facts. Accessed July 24, 2015.

DISTRIBUTION BASICS

CH13

Distribution, or physical distribution, is the unknown soldier of the marketing mix. Everybody has a favorite brand, a favorite commercial, or even a story to tell about how they got a great price on a purchase; but most people have never even heard of distribution. This is because when it is done well, distribution is invisible to the consumer. We don't think about how the cranberry sauce got to the grocery store in time for the Thanksgiving feast. In fact, as consumers, the only time we do think about distribution is when it doesn't work. We are annoyed that those cranberries were out of stock the day before Thanksgiving.

Business people, on the other hand, understand that getting distribution for your product is critical. Very few businesses have the resources to make the product available to the customer on their own. They rely on a network of specialists and resellers to make purchasing convenient for the customer.

13.1 WHAT IS DISTRIBUTION?

Physical distribution, or distribution, deals with managing the finished goods inventory of a firm. From a marketing perspective, this involves creating one or more marketing channels, or channels of distribution, as a way to get the finished product from the manufacturer into the hands of the consumer. A **marketing channel** is all of the organizations and activities associated with moving the finished product from the producer to the end user. This is how we create place utility.

A **supply network** is all of the organizations and activities associated with moving raw materials and components from their point of origin to the producer.

It might be helpful to think of marketing channels and supply networks in the context of a **value chain**. A value chain is all of the activities involved with taking a raw material and turning it into a finished product and getting it into the hands of the customer. Typically, there will be multiple organizations involved in the process, with each organization adding value to the product. Figure 13.1 shows how a marketing channel fits into a simplified value chain for a can of peas.

At the beginning, you have a farmer who uses seeds and fertilizer as raw materials and creates ripe peas as a finished product. The farmer uses a broker to sell the ripe peas to a canning plant. The broker adds value by having relationships with several farmers in order to source enough peas for the canning plant. The canning plant uses the ripe peas and empty cans as raw materials to create cans of peas as a finished product. The canning plant sells truckloads of canned peas to a distributor or grocery store that adds value by combining the peas with other products for the convenience of the end user.

The farmer's marketing channel involves the activities associated with getting the ripe peas from the farm to the canning plant. From the perspective of the canning plant (marked "you are here"), the marketing channel involves the activities associated with getting the cans of peas from the canning plant into the hands of

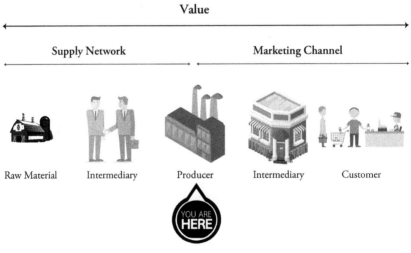

FIGURE 13.1 Value Chain (Copyright © Depositphotos/bigredlink; Copyright © Depositphotos/venimo.; Copyright © Depositphotos/petitelili.; Copyright © Depositphotos/sukmaraga.; Copyright © Depositphotos/macrovector.; Copyright © Depositphotos/porjai.)

the end user. Getting adequate supplies of ripe peas and cans involves the canning plant's supplier network.

Traditionally, marketers have focused on the marketing channel, or downstream logistics, while the supply network, or upstream logistics, has been the focus of operations or manufacturing. Many of the activities in the value chain are the same regardless of whether you are buying or selling, and your perspective will change depending on where in the value chain your firm is located. The point is to recognize that the marketing channel is part of a larger effort to serve the customer, and coordinating your efforts with the rest of the value chain will improve your marketing efforts.

We will take a closer look at the activities and organizations before discussing specific channel issues.

13.2 CHANNEL FLOWS

Stern, El-Ansary, and Coughlin[1] describe the activities associated with moving the product from producer to consumer in terms of **channel flows,** or a set of functions performed in sequence. There are eight basic functions that have to be performed in order for a transaction to occur: physical possession, ownership, risking, negotiation, ordering, payment, financing, and promotion. Figure 13.2 shows these functions and the direction of their flow.

The first three functions: physical possession, ownership, and risking involve the transfer of the product from producer to consumer. Physical possession deals with the tangible aspects of the transfer while ownership and risking deal with the intangible aspects of the transfer. When talking about ownership, we ask, "At what point does the customer take title to the product?" Many people driving new cars

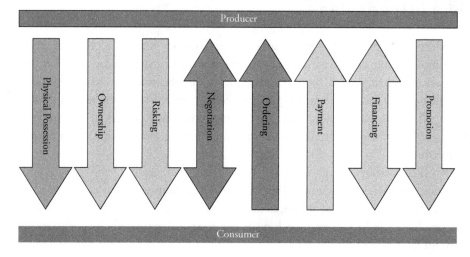

FIGURE 13.2   Channel flows (Adapted from: Louis W. Stern, Adel I. El-Ansary, and Anne T. Coughlin, *Marketing Channels,* pp. 10, Prentice Hall, 1996.)

have physical possession of the car but don't own it. The finance company owns it until the loan is paid off. When talking about risking, we ask, "Who is responsible for damage to the product or caused by the product during the transfer process?"

The flow for physical possession has a solid outline in figure 13.2, while the rest of the channel flows have a dotted line outline. This is because, unlike movement of the physical product, the rest of the channel flows deal with intangibles such as information or communication. This distinction is important to understand because advances in information technology are having and will continue to have have a profound impact on marketing channels and supply networks. In fact, in industries such as publishing or entertainment, where the product itself can be digital; the entire distribution process can me managed with information technology. How many people do you know that actually get a physical copy of a newspaper (a bundle of information) delivered to their door each day?

Negotiation and ordering deal with communication between producer and consumer while creating the transaction. Negotiation flows both ways while the actual order flows from the customer to the producer.

Payment and financing deal with the financial aspects of the transfer. The payment goes from consumer to producer as a result of the negotiations. If the customer is unable to make full payment at the time of the order, a financing company might get involved as in the case of a new car purchase described earlier. On the other hand, the producer might need financing to cover the costs of raw materials and finished goods inventory.

Finally, promotion deals with the communication from producer to consumer to make the customer aware of the great deal to be had.

The key to understanding channels of distribution is that all of these functions have to take place, but one company doesn't have to do all of them.

13.3 INTERMEDIARIES

A marketing channel always includes at least two members—a producer and a consumer. If you don't have at least two parties, you can't have a transaction and marketing can't happen. The goal of a channel of distribution is to move the product as efficiently as possible from producer to consumer. If the producer isn't good at doing all of the channel functions, the channel might be more efficient if someone else handled some of them. This is the reason for having intermediaries in a channel of distribution.

An **intermediary** (or go-between) is an entity that assists in the movement of products through the channel. There are three ways intermediaries create value: specialization, economy of transactions, and providing value-added functions. An intermediary will be successful as long as the channel is more efficient with it than without it.

Specialization

One way for an intermediary to increase the efficiency of the channel is to specialize in one or more of the channel functions. In today's lean business environment, many companies focus their resources on the things they do well and rely on other companies for everything else. For example, very few manufacturers are good at selling their products to individual consumers. They rely on retailers to sell the products for them. Even Apple®, which has its own retail stores, gets more than 80% of retail sales through intermediaries.[2]

Thus, you have insurance companies that specialize in managing risk, retail stores specializing in generating orders, agents and brokers specializing in negotiations, advertising agencies specializing in promotion ... you get the idea.

Economy of Transactions

Sometimes, adding an intermediary to a channel of distribution can make communication more efficient. At first glance, that doesn't seem to make sense. Won't it take more effort to communicate with everybody if you add another business to the channel? The answer is no. Because the intermediary specializes in communication, the channel becomes more efficient. This is best illustrated with this simple example using a market with three producers (Goodco, Betterco, and Bestco) and

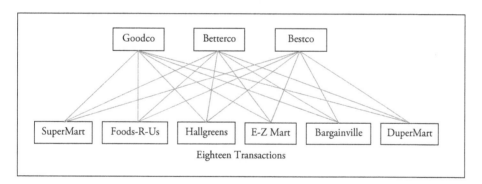

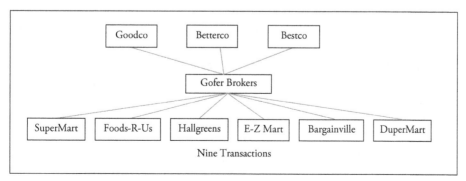

FIGURE 13.3   Economy of Transactions

six retailers (SuperMart, Foods-R-Us, Hallgreens, E–Z Mart, Bargainville, and DuperMart).

For every producer to communicate with every retailer requires, it requires 18 sales conversations as each producer needs to talk to all six retailers. However, when you add an intermediary (Gofer Brokers), the number of sales calls needed is cut in half. Each producer now only has to talk with the broker. The broker then represents all three producers when calling on the six retailers. To be effective, the broker would need to have relationships with all three producers and with all six retailers. It is in everyone's interest to work with the broker.

Value-Added Functions

Some of the ways intermediaries can add value to the product include creating assortment, breaking bulk, storing, transportation, and grading. *Creating assortment* and *breaking bulk* (buying from manufacturers in large quantities and selling to consumers in smaller quantities) add value because it is in the interest of the manufacturer to have long production runs of a small number of products to increase economies of scale. Consumers, on the other hand, want to spend as little time shopping as possible and want to buy in household quantities rather than by the truckload. A distributor or retailer will buy in bulk from a number of different manufacturers. This allows the shopper to select small quantities of a variety of products in one trip.

Storing and *transportation* help with the physical flow of the product. By holding inventory in warehouses, the intermediary can help the manufacturer schedule production efficiently, especially for seasonal products. *Grading* is when a third party certifies the quality of a product as an assurance to the customer. For example, the US Department of Agriculture assures us the eggs you purchase in the store are Grade A.

13.4 CHANNEL STRATEGY

The first consideration in developing marketing channels is to determine what role distribution plays in your overall business plan. From a "levels of the product" perspective (Chapter 7.1), you must consider if distribution is your core product, as with a trucking company, or if it is part of the augmented product. Amazon Prime®, which provides free two-day shipping for an annual fee, uses distribution as part of the augmented product. The major issues addressed through distribution are service level, market coverage, and inventory, which we will cover in Chapter 14.1.

Service Level

The level of service required to support your distribution strategy will vary from product to product. Expensive shopping products, such as smart phones or automobiles, require high levels of sales support and customer support after the purchase. Because high levels of support add to the cost of delivering the benefit, you'll need to determine where in the marketing channel to provide it. In the case of smart phones, most manufacturers rely on retailers to provide salespeople and after-sale service. The manufacturer may support the retailer's effort with sales training and sharing the cost of warranty claims. In addition, the manufacturer may offer customer support through a company website or Facebook® page.

Inexpensive convenience products don't require a lot of in-person selling or customer service. The package will do most of the selling. The service issue for convenience products is the in-stock levels. This is the part of distribution that is invisible to most people. A customer will not be willing to wait a week for a fresh shipment of laundry detergent to come in. If you go to the store for Tide® laundry detergent, and the shelf is empty at the store, you will either switch to another brand or go to a different store. If the product is out of stock because it is on sale, you might ask for a rain check. This would allow you to buy it later at the sale price; but you still need detergent today and will buy it somewhere else.

There are several costs associated with an out of stock item, or stock out. First, you have annoyed your customers and forced them to expend more mental effort in acquiring the product than they had planned. Second, you invite customers to try a competitor's product. It may turn out that the customers are happier with the substitute product and are lost to you. To the retailer, a stock out means you have forced the customers to find an alternative way of acquiring the product. If they go to another store or simply purchase the product online, they may never come back.

The way to avoid stock outs is to have sufficient backup inventory, or safety stock, on hand. The cost of a possible stock out has to be weighed against the cost of the inventory needed to ensure the desired level of service.

Market Coverage

Another issue addressed through distribution is: "How available do you want your product to be to your customers?" Market coverage looks at how many outlets there are for your product in a given market area. This is also called distribution intensity. It may be helpful to think of market coverage as a continuum with intensive distribution at one end, exclusive distribution at the other end, and selective distribution as you approach the middle.

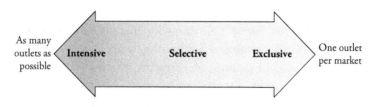

FIGURE 13.4   Market Coverage

Intensive Distribution

Intensive distribution is where you try to saturate the market by having as many outlets for your product as possible. You will sell to any intermediary that meets your credit standards. This is the approach you see with convenience products, consumer package goods, and impulse items. The Coca Cola® Company never wants you to be more than a few minutes away from an outlet for a refreshing Coke® when you realize you are thirsty.

The disadvantage to intensive distribution is that it doesn't give your channel partners an incentive to push your product. Because these well-known products are available everywhere, a retailer won't be able to attract customers by featuring the product. Also, because consumers are able to compare prices for products with intensive distribution, retailers find it harder to charge premium prices for the product.

Exclusive Distribution

At the other end of the continuum, **exclusive distribution** is where you would have only one outlet for your product in a given market area. This gives you the ability to choose who will be your channel partner in a given market. It also makes you more attractive to potential channel partners because there are no direct competitors in the market area. This approach is used for high-value products that require high levels of service after the sale; for example, "How many outlets for the Tesla Motors™ electric car do you need in a given city?"

The disadvantage of an exclusive distribution strategy is that it makes it more difficult for the customer to find the product.

> "I'm sort of mixed minds about whether you should go for it and try to get a job at a startup, or go to a great established company and learn something for three years. One or the other. Taking a job at a company that is middling and meandering, and is not world class. I think that is a mistake."
>
> **Andy Wiedlin**

Selective Distribution

Selective distribution falls somewhere in the middle. You have multiple outlets in a market area, but the number is limited. This approach has benefits for both the manufacturer and for the channel partner. By limiting the number of outlets, you increase the importance of your product line to your channel partner and can ask for more service and selling support. Giving your channel partner limited exclusivity allows using your product line as a positioning factor.

In the 1970s, the La-Z-Boy® furniture company switched from an intensive distribution strategy to a selective distribution strategy. There were two forces driving the change. First, because anyone could carry La-Z-Boy products, many furniture retailers would "cherry pick" the line—only purchase the most popular items—and then feature the recliners at a low price in order to encourage traffic to their stores. At the same time, the La-Z-Boy company was expanding its product line to include more than reclining chairs.

The solution was to change to a "gallery" format. Rather than selling to anybody, the company worked with a limited number of dealers to open a limited number of La-Z-Boy showcase stores in a given market. Showcase operators had to agree to carry only La-Z-Boy products and to carry the entire line of furniture. Because they had exclusive access to La-Z-Boy products, this encouraged them to promote the brand through their shops. The result was a short-term decrease in sales volume, as the number of outlets was reduced, but an increase in profitability for both the manufacturer and its channel partners.

13.5 CHANNEL STRUCTURE

There are two issues in developing marketing channels: the number of intermediaries in the channel and the number of channels.

Number of Intermediaries

A marketing channel will always have at least two parties—the producer and the consumer. This is called a **direct channel,** and there are many instances where a direct channel is enough to get the job done. For example, in B2B marketing, it is common for large suppliers to sell directly to large customers. When the Ford® Motor Company buys tires to put on its new cars, it deals directly with Firestone®. Because the quantities involved are so large, it is most efficient for them to work together.

An **indirect channel** uses one or more intermediaries to help reach the customer. As a rule, channels for consumer products tend to involve more intermediaries than in business markets. In consumer markets, an indirect channel frequently includes retailers, wholesalers, and agents, as well as other intermediaries providing support services. In B2B settings, indirect channels frequently involve distributors and agents. The number of intermediaries to use in an indirect channel will vary from one situation to another.

Number of Channels

Most businesses of any size will have more than one channel of distribution. There are many reasons for this. Having alternative channels avoids becoming dependent on a single channel partner. Also, different market segments may have different distribution requirements. For example, in the automobile parts industry, there are two major segments: OEM (original equipment manufacturing) and the aftermarket (replacement parts for cars on the road). OEM involves shipping parts by the train-load directly to the manufacturer. The aftermarket requires an indirect channel for shipping individually packaged replacement parts to a variety of repair shops, auto parts stores, and dealerships, who will then sell the part to the end user.

Other reasons for having multiple channels of distribution? Different products in your product line may have different shipping requirements. Shipping ice cream requires different treatment than shipping ground coffee. Different geographic locations or international distribution may have unique needs. In the North, some products need to be protected from freezing during the winter months. The needs of large customers compared to smaller customers may require different marketing channels. You simply cannot have a personal relationship with thousands or even millions of smaller customers.

Many large retailers are using blended distribution channels (AKA "bricks and clicks," or **omni-channel marketing**) to better serve customers. The most common model is to blend physical and online stores. The physical store offers customers the opportunity to enjoy the social aspects of shopping while, at the same time, serving as a local distribution center. The online channel offers 24/7 access and convenience. Customers can search for and order a product online and then arrange to pick it up at the local store. Similarly, if a product is out of stock, customers can check the retailer's website using computer kiosks situated on the sales floor. Best Buy® has adapted to online competition re-purposing the large storage areas in its physical stores. At one time, this space was needed to keep an inventory of bulky CRT televisions in stock for local customers. As the physical size of televisions had decreased, Best Buy is using the space as local distribution centers to serve online customers.[3]

So what is the optimal channel structure? It depends. It depends on market factors such as market structure, customer segments, geographic concentration, and order size. It depends on product factors such as unit value, perishability, and the technical nature of the product. It depends on what added value your channel partners will be providing your customers as well as what it takes to support your channel partners. It depends on company factors such as the need for control over the channel, service requirements, and the internal and financial ability to provide channel functions. It depends on what is going on in the larger business environment.

It's Not That Easy

It may seem from reading this book that putting together a marketing channel is easy. Simply choose the intermediaries that best fit your needs. In practice, it is difficult. We'd all like to have WalMart® carry our products. The reality is that you need to be able to show what's in it for WalMart. They have a lot more potential suppliers than you have potential distributors. To get distribution, you need to prove your product will be a good fit for the retailer. In other words, "show them the money!"

13.6 CHANNEL RELATIONSHIPS

Because channels of distribution involve independent businesses allied to deliver value to the end user, there is a need for these businesses to work together over time. This involves developing means of cooperation as well as dealing with conflict within the channel. The Clayton Act and the Sherman Antitrust Act (Chapter 11.1) discourage channel partners from cooperating in ways that reduce competition or that give a company monopoly powers.

Cooperation

While each business in a marketing channel may be independent of the others, all of the businesses in the channel are part of the value chain leading to a satisfied end user. Thus, when problems occur between channel members or with the final product, it is in the interest of everyone involved to resolve the problem in a way that has the least impact on the relationship with the final customer. For example, when a manufacturing defect in an automobile requires a recall, the manufacturer and the dealers work together to serve the customers. Even though the dealers were not responsible for the manufacturing defect, the reputation of the brand is important to their customer relationships (thanks to selective distribution), so they share in the effort to repair the affected cars.

A **channel captain** is the member of the channel that coordinates the activities of the rest of the channel. Usually the channel captain is the largest/strongest member of the channel. This gives the channel captain the ability to control, or regulate, other members of the channel. Thus, WalMart can insist that manufacturers use WalMart's trucks to ship its products.

One of the key issues in channel control is how the efficiencies created by the channel are distributed among channel members. If the channel is more efficient than alternative configurations, then each channel member is adding value to the process. Obviously, some of the efficiency has to affect the end user, or customers wouldn't perceive the channel as the most efficient way to obtain the product. How the remaining savings are distributed is a channel control issue. Historically, manufacturers were the dominant channel members. Currently, large retailers such as WalMart or Target® dominate the channel. In the future, the efficiencies in communication created by the internet and the widespread use of social media may lead consumers to dominate the channel.

Conflict

Channel conflict occurs when one member of the channel perceives that another member of the channel is keeping it from achieving its goals. **Horizontal conflict** occurs when there are too many outlets in a market area or too many intermediaries at the same level of the channel. While an intensive distribution strategy will create convenience for customers, saturating a market area with outlets can cause conflict between outlets. The Starbucks® on one end a strip mall may feel conflict when a new Starbucks opens at the other end of the same strip mall. **Vertical conflict** occurs between members at different levels of the channel. For example, a manufacturer may feel that the distributor doesn't provide a level of service that justifies the cost of working with that distributor. On the other side, the distributor may feel the manufacturer doesn't understand how much it costs to develop and maintain good customer relationships.

(ENDNOTES)

1. Stern, Louis W., Adel I. El-Ansary, and Anne T. Coughlin, 1996, *Marketing Channels 5th Ed.,* Upper Saddle River, NJ: Prentice Hall, Inc., 10.
2. http://www.sfchronicle.com/business/article/To-help-sell-its-new-watch-Apple-turns-to-old-6408654.php. Accessed July 30, 2015.
3. Lee, Thomas, 2014, *Rebuilding Empires: How Best Buy and other Retailers are Transforming and Competing in the Digital Age of Retailing*, New York: Palgrave Macmillan.

LOGISTICS AND WHOLESALING

CH 14

Most elements of the marketing have a direct interface with the customer. Product, pricing, and promotion need the active engagement of the customer to succeed. Logistics and wholesaling are the "backstage" of marketing. The activities involved with moving the product from point of origin to point of purchase take place "behind the scenes." Have you ever made the connection between all of those semitrailers on the interstate highways and the availability of laundry detergent at your local store? Transporting detergent is just one of the activities needed for you to have a successful shopping expedition.

14.1 WHAT IS LOGISTICS?

The Council of Supply Chain Management Professionals defines logistics management in part as:

> "That part of supply chain management that plans, implements, and controls the efficient, effective forward and reverse flow and storage of goods, services, and related information between the point of origin and the point of consumption in order to meet customers' requirements. Logistics management activities typically include inbound and outbound transportation management, fleet management, warehousing, materials handling, order fulfillment, logistics network design, inventory management, supply/demand planning, and management of third-party logistics services providers ..."[1]

In other words, **logistics** deals with the flow of physical goods and related information through the value chain. While logistics is usually associated with supply chain management, the issues associated with physical products also apply to marketing channels and the flow of finished products. We can think of the supply chain as "upstream" logistics, and the marketing channel as "downstream" logistics.

The Logistics Concept

The big issue in logistics is finding a balance between the cost of moving the product and the desired service level. There is a tradeoff between the efficiency of the channel and its ability to respond to customers. Responsiveness, or service level, deals with the time in transit, dependability, and convenience. It is important to specify the service commitment you want for your customers as part of your marketing strategy. That way, you can support it with the appropriate systems.

Efficiency deals with the costs of providing the logistic functions such as order processing, transportation, materials handling, warehousing, inventory, and third-party providers. There is also the cost of a stock out to consider. In Chapter 13, we looked at the consequences of a stock out from a consumer perspective. In supply chain management, the cost of a stock out is lost production due to a shortage of raw materials.

Information technology plays a major role in creating a smooth flow of goods from point of origin to point of consumption. Much of the information associated with logistics is automated, so the ability to share information between channel members is critical. The risk of having another company with access to your internal systems is offset by the increased efficiency of the channel. A perfect example of this is the tracking number you receive when you order a product online. The tracking number allows you access to the delivery company's internal systems, so you can follow the progress of your package.

14.2 LOGISTICS FUNCTIONS

Each of the logistic functions, order processing, transportation, materials handling, inventory management, and dealing with third-party providers, has its own set of issues related to responsiveness versus efficiency. Here are some of the major issues and their associated tradeoffs.

Order Processing and Production Scheduling

Order processing deals with the information flows associated with moving the product. The tradeoff is between transaction costs and inventory levels. Economic order quantity, or EOQ, considers the cost of placing an order, lead time (the time it takes to receive the order after placing it), inventory costs, and the risk of a stock out to optimize the ordering quantity. The trend in order processing is to move to automated systems such as the ERP (enterprise resource planning) packages offered by SAP® or Oracle®.

The tradeoff in production scheduling is between economies of scale and customer responsiveness. From an operations perspective, long production runs of the same product are desirable as the cost per unit decreases with volume production. On the other hand, customers are asking for more choices in the products they buy. Each additional option increases production costs.

Some industries are able to minimize this tradeoff through mass customization using flexible manufacturing techniques or three-dimensional printing technology. These allow for efficiency in very small production runs.

Transportation

In transportation, the tradeoff is between speed and cost. The faster the delivery mode, the higher the cost. There are five basic modes of transportation: air, truck, rail, water, and pipeline; the mode you select depends on the nature of the product and your desired responsiveness.

Air transportation is the fastest and most expensive mode of transportation. The advantage is that you can ship a product anywhere there is an airport in a day or two. Because of the expense, products requiring air transportation tend to be time sensitive or perishable products, such as fresh flowers; or high-value items, such as jewelry, which are less sensitive to transportation costs.

Shipping by truck is less expensive and slower than shipping by air. In the continental United States, it may take a few days to ship a product coast to coast. The advantage with trucks is that they can go anywhere there is a road. This allows for door-to-door shipping if desired. Less than truckload (LTL) carriers allow you to make smaller shipments economically by sharing a trailer with other shippers. The limitation is that there are size and weight limits for what you can put on a truck. Most consumer packaged goods will spend at least part of the journey on a truck.

Railroads have a very high ton-miles/gallon ratio, which means shipping by rail is both economical and has a smaller carbon footprint than other land-based modes. And besides, railroads are just cool. The big limitation with rail shipping is that trains can only load and unload at a station equipped for cargo handling. This means that rail shipping is used to send large quantities of products a long distance, with the balance of the journey completed by truck; or bulk commodities such as coal or fertilizer that are sensitive to transportation costs.

The slowest and least expensive form of flexible transportation is water. River barges transport bulk commodities within the United States, and most products made overseas are shipped by water. Because water shipping is slow, the lead time required to get a shipment delivered is an important consideration. The limitation of water transportation is that you can only ship to or from a port located on the water.

The least expensive form of transportation is by pipeline. Pipelines are used to transport bulk fluid commodities such as oil or natural gas inexpensively over long distances. Rather than time in transit, the capacity of the pipeline determines how much of the product will be available at the terminal. There is a high fixed cost associated with pipelines, so they are only used where there is consistent high demand for the product, for example, moving water from the Sierra Mountains to San Francisco.

"We track all of our design work in the cloud and I can communicate with my teams from any device at any time. I was just Skyping with one of our factories in Bangladesh, and they happened to be in Seoul at the time."

Ted Church

Intermodal Transportation

It is not uncommon for a product to use more than one mode of transportation while going from producer to consumer. Take, for example, a shipment of toys intended for the holiday season in Denver, Colorado. The toys will start their journey in July moving from Asia to the US by ship. The ship will unload at a West Coast port, and the toys will be put on a train for shipment to Denver. In Denver, the train will be unloaded, and the toys will move by truck to a warehouse or a retailer in time for the holiday shopping season.

In the 1950s, Malcolm McClean, an American transport entrepreneur, developed the standardized shipping container, which has revolutionized cargo handling.[2] Before the container was developed, intermodal transportation required manually unloading the cargo from a truck and then loading it on another platform such as a boat or train. McClean's idea was to build a container the same size as a semitrailer, which could be moved without having to unload it. Now, intermodal transportation involves moving the loaded container from one mode to another. The basic container is the size of a semitrailer and can be pulled by a truck. Two of them can be loaded on a flatbed rail car (piggyback) for shipment by rail. The containers can also be shipped by water (fishyback) or air (birdyback).

There are several advantages to using a shipping container. First, the standard dimensions allow manufacturers to design products and packaging to fit the container. This reduces waste and the shifting of contents in transit. Second, there are significant labor savings because the container is loaded and unloaded once. There is less chance of product being damaged or going missing during the loading process. Finally, containers allow for special handling. The containers can be sealed for security. You can also include sensors in the container to monitor shaking or temperature that may affect the goods being shipped.

Materials Handling

Materials handling involves moving physical goods from point A to point B. This could involve loading and unloading trucks, shifting products from one point to another in a warehouse, or moving the product from inventory to where it will be used or consumed. The tradeoff is between speed and loss of control. The faster the material is moved, the less time in transit. However, you don't want to move so fast that you sacrifice the accuracy of the shipment. There are also concerns over damage or breakage while products are being moved. As a rule, the less handling of a product in transit, the better.

There are a variety of tools used in materials handling. Forklifts and conveyor belts help with the heavy lifting. Many tracking systems use bar code scanners or RFID (radio frequency identification) labels to keep track of where goods are in the process. These are the midpoints you see when you track a package on UPS® or FedEx®.

Storage

A **warehouse** is a physical facility used primarily for the storage of goods held in anticipation of sale or transfer within the marketing channel. The tradeoff with warehouses is between inventory costs and responsiveness. A storage warehouse holds goods in inventory for eventual shipment to a retailer or other end user. The facility is designed to meet the needs of the products being stored. For example, some products need refrigerated storage while others may need additional security.

A distribution center is a facility designed for transshipment of a product. For a distribution center serving a retail chain, one side of the facility is for unloading truckloads of product from the various manufacturers. The other side of the facility is for loading delivery trucks to be sent to each store. Using materials-handling tools for breaking bulk and creating assortment, the goods are sorted so that each store gets the product it needs to replenish its inventory.

Inventory

The decision to carry inventory is a straight cost-benefit analysis. The benefits are many. Inventory supports better responsiveness and customer service. The more inventory available, the less the chance of a stock out. There can be financial benefits to carrying inventory such as being able get a volume discount or, in the case of commodities, as a hedge against inflation.

Inventory can also be used to increase production efficiency. Producing products for inventory enables longer production runs and economies of scale. Safety stock can be a buffer against supply interruptions. The 2004 Indian Ocean earthquake and tsunami affected automobile production in the United States as many Asian parts suppliers were unable to ship, and domestic inventories were so lean that production shut down.

The obvious cost of carrying inventory is the financial cost. In addition to requiring capital to finance the inventory, service costs, taxes, and storage costs all have a financial impact. In addition, there are risk-related costs to carrying inventory. Loss, damage, obsolescence, and spoilage can reduce the amount of effective inventory.

Inventory Management

One of the ways a channel can be more efficient is through effective inventory management. Recognizing that intermediaries at each level of the distribution channel may need to carry inventory, the cost of carrying inventory is spread among the channel partners. Using material requirements planning software to help coordinate the flow of physical inventory through the channel and just in time (JIT) delivery can reduce the amount of inventory needed at all levels of the marketing channel.

Third-Party Providers

The tradeoff in working with third-party providers is between the cost of providing the function and control over how the function is performed. For example, a manufacturer working with independent sales representatives has less control over how the product is presented to prospective customers than it would using employees as salespeople. There are third-party providers for virtually every logistic function, allowing a business to determine which functions to handle internally and which can be best performed by others.

Having decided that an independent company can provide a function more efficiently than you can, the issue is how closely you work together. One big consideration is how important the function/intermediary is to your business. If on-time delivery is critical to the company's strategy, then a close relationship such as a contractual or partnership agreement would be appropriate. Even though an outside company is providing the function, there needs to be internal management attention monitoring the process.

Reverse-Logistics

Reverse logistics is the process of returning products from the customer to the manufacturer. For products that require warranty repairs, reverse logistics would involve moving the product from the consumer to a repair facility (which could be the manufacturer, or a third-party provider) and then back to the customer. In the case of a product recall, arrangements need to be made to return the product for repair or for disposal. Samsung's effort to recall the Galaxy Note 7 after reports of the battery overheating were complicated by third party carriers such as Fedex® and UPS® requiring special packaging for the returned phones and limiting them to ground transportation. Finally, as businesses adopt more environmentally friendly policies, reverse logistics are needed to support recycling. This could involve returning old products for reconditioning, or disposing of products that are no longer useful. The State of California imposes an electronic waste fee on certain electronic products to help pay for the cost of recycling these products.

14.3 WHOLESALERS

Perhaps you've heard the saying "I can get it for you wholesale," implying a great bargain is to be had. This is because wholesalers are the archetype of an intermediary, and most people understand that things cost less at wholesale than they do at retail. **Wholesalers** are firms that assist in the flow of products from the manufacturer to the retailer. In consumer markets, they are called wholesalers. In B2B markets, distributors serve a similar function, handling the flow of components and raw materials from the source to the end user.

There are many different names for wholesalers, and this is an area where there is a lot of change happening as the internet and social media disrupt traditional distributor models. For example, an electronic parts distributor may have served a specific geographical area by providing quick delivery of replacement components to manufacturers. Maintaining a building, staff, and inventory to provide service is expensive. An online parts distributor can serve the entire country, making it feasible to carry a wider selection of parts. Online ordering and FedEx delivery satisfy the quick-service requirement of customers. As a result, a local distributorship is no longer the most efficient way to move goods through the channel.

This suggests that a listing of the types of wholesalers would be out of date very quickly. Having said that, there are two basic types of wholesalers: merchant wholesalers and agents.

Merchant Wholesalers

Merchant wholesalers take title to the goods and resell them to retailers or other businesses. In addition to reselling the goods, wholesalers provide additional services to their customers. A **full-service wholesaler** acts as a partner, providing backup inventory and other services to a number of retail outlets in the geographic service area. For example, one small retail drugstore has a relationship with the wholesaler where each day the sales data from the drugstore was transmitted to the wholesaler. The next morning, there would be a number of bins containing replacements for everything that was sold. With this arrangement, the druggist only has to carry two of each item in inventory, greatly reducing inventory expense. Having two of each item in stock at the beginning of each day was the druggist's answer to the cost/responsiveness tradeoff associated with inventory. There would only be a stock out if three people wanted to purchase the same item in a single day.

A **limited service wholesaler** provides backup inventory at a minimum and may provide other services as determined by the needs of the channel. The most basic limited service wholesaler would be a cash and carry like Costco®. Costco makes inventory available for small businesses at wholesale prices; however, the business has to select, pick up, pay for, and transport the merchandise. A truck jobber (a jobber is someone who deals in smaller quantities) is a limited-service wholesaler that sells a limited variety of goods from a truck. Snap-On® tools is an example of a truck jobber. Franchisees visit automotive-related businesses weekly, carrying an inventory of tools and supplies to provide convenience as well as inventory.

Agents

Agents and brokers are intermediaries who facilitate transactions without taking title to the goods. Agents represent a manufacturer while calling on a number of customers. Brokers emphasize making transactions happen and may represent a different buyer and seller for each transaction. Although primarily sales oriented, agents can also provide other services such as customer service or arranging transportation. While agents don't own the merchandise, they need to have access to it in order to represent it to customers. Some agents maintain a showroom where customers can view the merchandise; others carry samples with them when working with customers. It is not uncommon for independent agents to represent more than one manufacturer as a way of leveraging their relationships with the customers.

Some companies hire manufacturers' representatives (reps) rather than working with an independent agent. While not technically an intermediary because the reps are not independent, the functions they perform are essentially the same. The advantages of a manufacturer's rep are that you have more control over their activity, and you can ask them to represent your company exclusively.

(ENDNOTES)

1. https://cscmp.org/research/glossary-terms. Accessed August 7, 2015.
2. https://en.wikipedia.org/wiki/Malcom_McLean. Accessed August 8, 2015.

RETAILING

CH 15

There are a lot of reasons to talk about retailing in a "Marketing Fundamentals" book. For consumer products, retailers are the members of the distribution channel who deal directly with the customer. Regardless of where your business fits in the value chain, understanding retailing will help you design offerings your retail partners will be able to sell. And we sell a lot at retail—over $4 trillion annually in the United The structure of retailing is rapidly evolving as e-commerce becomes more important to the economy. More than 14 million people work in retail,[1] roughly 10% of the workforce. If you haven't already worked for a retail store, there is a one in ten chance you will at some point in your career. Understanding retailing can help jump-start your career. Finally, all of us have shopped at retail stores. Understanding retailing can help make you a better shopper.

15.1 WHAT IS RETAILING?

Retailing is the process of selling goods and services to individuals or households for their personal use. Retailing is also an important hurdle for new products to overcome in order to reach a mass market. The retail market is highly concentrated and works on relatively low margins.

A concentrated market is one in which a small number of businesses control a majority of the market. For example, in the grocery business, the top 50 firms in the US control 70% of the market. As an even more extreme example of concentration, the top four grocery chains control over 30% of the market.[2]

This concentrated structure suggests a two-pronged approach to gaining distribution. Obviously, you would want to sell through the major chains as that would give you access to the majority of the market. As you would imagine, competition for access is intense, and the process will involve extensive preparation and negotiations. The payoff is high volume of sales to a relatively small number of big customers. This is sometimes called getting distribution wholesale.

While it is important to sell to the majors, you can't afford to simply write off the vast majority of retailers who account for 30% of the market. However, it is more expensive to reach the smaller retailers as you will need to make lots of contacts, and the sales volume per account will be much lower. This is sometimes called buying distribution at retail.

Margins are relatively low in retail. Nationally, retailers have an average operating margin of 27% and net profit margin of 2.7%.[3] Because of this, the key to success is inventory turnover, or velocity. If a store sells out of everything in a year, it will net a 2.7% profit. If it can turn over the inventory four times, its annual profit becomes more than 10%. There is a relationship between retail velocity and operating margins.

A "keystone," or 100% markup, is a benchmark used in retailing. Stores with relatively low turnover such as clothing or furniture stores will need to work on a keystone margin or higher to achieve profitability targets. Furniture stores average 200–400% markups, and clothing stores, 100–350% markup, with fashion boutiques at the higher end of the range. Stores with high retail velocity such as grocery stores can be profitable with an average markup of 5–25%.

15.2 EVOLUTION OF RETAILING

Have you ever heard of a greengrocer? Today most people would guess it is some kind of an environmentally conscious grocery store. In fact, greengrocer is an archaic term for a shop where you would buy fresh fruits and vegetables. The reason you have never heard of a greengrocer is because it disappeared with the advent of modern supermarkets. Today, you don't go to a butcher for your meat, a greengrocer for your vegetables, a bakery for your bread; these are all departments in a supermarket.

While the retail scene has always been changing, the pace of evolution has picked up, especially with the opportunities available through internet, social, and mobile marketing. Two theories are widely used to help understand how retail evolves: the wheel of retailing hypothesis and the retail life cycle.

Wheel of Retailing

The **wheel of retailing** hypothesis proposes that new retail operations start out at the low end of the price spectrum and gradually move upscale. Someone may come up with a way to reduce costs or to be profitable with a lower operating margin and take a low price market position. This gives them a toehold in the market. As the operation scales up, he or she may no longer be satisfied with rock-bottom pricing and gradually add more upscale and higher margin products to the lineup. We are seeing this in both WalMart® and Target® stores. Both chains started out as deep discount department stores and have been gradually moving upscale. For example, Target has experimented with name designer products, and WalMart has moved into higher-end electronics. As the established retailers move up in prices, it creates an opportunity for a new player to enter the market with very low prices, and the cycle starts all over again.

Retail Life Cycle

The **retail life cycle** theory looks at retail concepts more so than at individual stores. The thought is that retail concepts go through a life cycle similar to the product life cycle with an introductory stage (early growth), a growth stage (accelerated growth), a maturity stage, and a decline stage.

In the introductory stage, an innovator introduces a novel retail concept, usually by emphasizing one or more elements of the marketing mix. Thus, Amazon® was an innovator in what is now called e-commerce by taking advantage of a new technology (the internet) to build a bookstore that could offer a greater selection (product) at a lower price and allowed customers to place their orders 24/7 (distribution).

In the accelerated growth stage, more and more customers are responding to the new concept, which attracts new entrants to the market. In the case of e-commerce, think of the dot-com boom when any business could get funded by putting a small "e" in front of its name or ".com" at the end of its name. Remember Pets.com®?

As the market matures, and the number of new customers begins to stabilize, smaller, less successful businesses die off, leaving a few strong survivors. After the dot-com bust in 2001, many online stores folded, while, at the same time, traditional retailers like Target and WalMart entered the market as a defensive maneuver.

Eventually, the retail concept falls out of favor as customers abandon it for more productive ways to shop.

> "You can't expect to read a book and think that you understand how to fill a marketing team, or build an e-commerce site."
>
> **Felicia Terwilliger**

Factors That Affect Retail Evolution

Three major factors that affect retail evolution are changes in demographics, changes in technology, and globalization. Changes in demographics deal with the evolution of your customer base. If you are targeting the teenage market, teenagers grow up. Do you remain focused on teenagers and build relationships with a new set of customers, or do you change your operation to meet the changing needs of your market? Maybe tone down the loud music and add a line of "comfortable fit" jeans to appeal to an older audience.

Technology is a major driver of change, and the widespread availability of the internet and social media has disrupted the way retailers do business. As with any business, management needs to be aware of emerging technologies to avoid "Marketing Myopia," which we'll discuss more in Chapter 20. It may be hard to estimate the impact of an emerging technology on your business. For example, what would you consider to be the most significant technological innovation in shopping in the twentieth century? The *Harvard Design School Guide to Shopping*[4] named air conditioning (or manufactured weather as it was called at the time) as the most significant innovation. With a controlled environment, stores can get bigger, windows can be eliminated, and people can shop comfortably at any time of year and in any weather.

Globalization impacts retailing with the transfer of both retail concepts and product ideas across borders. For example, the concept of a **hypermarket**—a gigantic store, including a discount store, supermarket, and warehouse under one roof, was originally developed in Europe by Carrefour and introduced in the United States by Meijer® in the Midwest. Both WalMart and Target have been experimenting with versions of a hypermarket in the US.

15.3 CLASSIFYING RETAILERS

There are a number of different taxonomies (classification systems) you can use to classify retailers. Ownership structure, service level, merchandise mix, and nonstore retailing each offer a different perspective to a manufacturer looking to gain distribution for a product.

Ownership

There are three basic ownership structures for retail operations: corporate chains, independent stores, and vertical marketing systems. A corporate chain consists of two or more stores owned by the same company. There usually is a centralized management structure and a consistent format across stores. Independent stores are usually smaller and have a higher cost structure. Because of this, they are frequently service oriented or specialize in order to support higher retail prices.

Vertical marketing systems such as cooperative chains and franchises are groups of independent businesses that are vertically aligned and professionally managed. **Cooperative chains** are groups of retailers who join together in order to achieve economies of scale in purchasing and advertising. Ace® Hardware stores is an example of a cooperative chain. With a cooperative agreement, the ultimate authority resides with the individual retailer. **Franchises** are contractual systems where the retailer is given the right to certain products or services subject to conditions specified in the franchise agreement. Typically, the agreement will require the franchisee to follow a specified business plan under the trade name of the franchisor. Both products (i.e., a Ford® dealership) and business formats (i.e., H&R Block®) can be franchised.

The ownership structure determines how you would approach the store to talk about getting placement for your product. In a corporate system, there may be a corporate buying office. There you will meet with a professional buyer by appointment and begin the negotiation. It may be productive to visit one or more of the chain's branches to develop an understanding of how your product might benefit the chain, but you won't be able to meet with a decision-maker while visiting the branch. For independent stores, decision-making authority rests with the owner or manager, who is usually on site. It is easier to gain access to a decision-maker at an independent store; however, you still need to develop a relationship to gain placement for your product. Because orders from a single store will be smaller than orders from a chain, selling costs are high. One approach for a new product is to work with smaller retailers to get initial placement for your product. The sales results from these stores can help demonstrate the viability of the product to a chain store buyer.

For vertical marketing systems, the key is to understand the agreement. Some decisions are reserved for the cooperative or franchisor while other decisions are made at the local store level.

Service Level

Another way of looking at retailers is by the level of service they provide. You will find a range of service levels with self-service at one extreme, full service at the other extreme, and a variety of limited service operations in between. The key in getting placement for your product is to match the service level required to sell your product with the service level provided by the retailer. At a self-service operation, the product needs to be self-explanatory. It can either be a well-known product, such as chewing gum, or a product whose packaging makes the benefit clear and easy to understand.

At a full-service retailer, personal attention from a salesperson is part of the package. The customer expects courteous service, free delivery, and gift wrapping. This all adds to the retailer's cost, which will make your product more expensive to the customer. The product needs to be perceived as high value in order to support the pricing. If the product is complicated, for example, a smart phone, you will need to make sure the retailer's sales staff is appropriately trained to sell the product.

In the middle, it is a matter of determining specifically the type and level of service needed to communicate the product benefit to the consumer and then looking for retailers that specialize in that area.

Merchandise Mix

The **merchandise mix** is simply the product mix from the retailer's perspective. It refers to the length and breadth of the product lines carried by the retailer. Traditionally, retail operations were organized around product categories, i.e., food vs. non-food stores or consumables vs. durable goods. Today, more stores are leaning toward a **scrambled merchandising** approach. Scrambled merchandising includes products not normally related to the retailer's primary lines. The idea is to develop an assortment to support the customer experience rather than to focus on one particular category. You will find a great example of scrambled merchandising in many large supermarkets. In addition to the expected produce, dairy, meats, bakery and canned goods; you might find a bank, a restaurant with take-away food, a video store, even a doctor's office. Each of these additional lines saves the customer a trip while running errands.

It is helpful to think of merchandise mix in terms of a 2 × 2 matrix when classifying stores (Figure 15.1). On the vertical axis we have line depth, which can be either shallow or deep. On horizontal axis we have line breadth, which can be either narrow or broad. This gives us four categories. In the upper left quadrant, you have stores whose merchandise mix is narrow and shallow. They don't carry many different lines and offer only a few choices within each line. This might be a mall kiosk selling sunglasses or cell phone accessories. In the lower left quadrant, you have stores whose merchandise mix is narrow and deep. They carry a limited number of lines but carry a lot of items in each line. This might be a specialty store such as a party supply store or a comic book store. You wouldn't expect to find

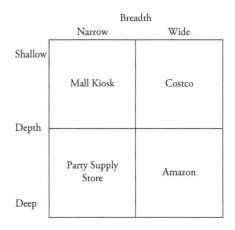

FIGURE 15.1   Merchandise Mix

much else than party supplies in a party supplies store, but you would expect to find everything you need to throw a party.

Moving to the other side, the upper right quadrant contains stores whose merchandise mix is broad but shallow. They carry a lot of different lines but only one or two items in each line. This is the mix you would find at a Costco® outlet. They carry everything from groceries to clothing, electronics, and cough syrup, but you only have one or two choices in each category. Finally, in the lower right quadrant, you have stores whose merchandise mix is both broad and deep. They carry a lot of different lines and have a lot of choices within each line. Probably the best example of this would be Amazon. No matter what the category, you will find dozens if not hundreds of choices within the category.

It is important for you to understand what position your product has in your category. If you are the category leader with a strong brand, all of these outlets would need to carry your product in order to have credibility in the category. A store that doesn't carry Tide® detergent doesn't carry detergent. If you are a relatively small player in the market, you will look for distribution from stores that both carry your product line and go deep in that line. It is in their interest to have as many choices in the category as feasible to support their strategy.

If you are introducing a new product, the sectors you pursue depend on your market entry strategy. If you are going for a penetration strategy, you would want placement in all stores that could carry your line. For stores that are shallow in your line, you might have to spend some money to get initial placement either through slotting fees or some other promotional allowance. For stores that are deep in your line, it is in the stores' interest as much as it is in yours to have them carry the product. If you are going for a skimming strategy, you would only seek placement with stores that are deep in your product. That is where the innovators and early adopters are likely to shop. Initially, you might offer exclusive distribution to a specialty store in exchange for prime placement in the store.

15.4 NON-STORE RETAILING

Nowhere in our definition of retailing does it state that selling has to occur from a fixed location. The reality is that there are many ways to sell products to customers outside of a store. For example, most B2B transactions are created through personal selling (Chapter 18) at the customer's place of business. In consumer marketing, there are several alternative ways to reach potential customers, including direct selling, telemarketing, vending, direct marketing, and e-tailing. More and more, these are used as part of an omni-channel strategy rather than as a stand-alone activity.

Direct Selling

Direct selling involves selling directly to the customer through an in-person explanation or demonstration, frequently at the customer's home or place of business. Most B2B transactions are created by direct selling. For consumer markets, the traditional direct selling approach has been door-to-door sales where a salesperson goes up and down the street knocking on doors to ask if the customer would like to buy a vacuum cleaner. Because people are less likely to be at home during the day, and even if they were, they would not like to speak to a stranger; many companies now work by setting appointments for the salesperson in advance. This is a common approach in the insurance industry.

Recently, party selling and multi-level marketing have added a social dimension to personal selling. In a **party selling** plan, such as a Tupperware® party, the salesperson arranges for a "host" to invite a group of friends to a product demonstration. While the primary goal is to sell product, there are games and refreshments involved to make it appear to be a social gathering.

In a **multi-level marketing** plan, such as Amway®, in addition to making presentations to customers, the salesperson recruits others to serve as distributors. The salesperson receives an additional commission (or override) on everything the distributor sells. The distributor, in turn, recruits more distributors and so on. The advantage to multi-level marketing is that the sales network grows organically through personal recruitment of distributors. The disadvantage is that, in some cases, the multi-level plan appears to be closer to a pyramid scheme where those who enter the system early make money, and those who enter the system last lose out.

Telemarketing

Telemarketing is a form of direct selling where the salesperson, located in a centralized call center, uses the telephone to make sales presentations to people in their homes. This is a somewhat controversial practice as most people dislike receiving unsolicited sales calls on what was perceived to be a personal communication channel. Efforts to limit telemarketing through the establishment of a "do not call list" and limiting the use of cellular networks for telemarketing and other regulations have had mixed success in resolving customer complaints. As more and more people cut the cord and give up their landline, the telemarketing industry has been contracting. However, in 2013, the industry still generated $18 billion in sales in the US.[5]

The advantage to telemarketing is that it an inexpensive means of creating a personal selling experience. Call centers can be located anywhere in the world, especially in areas where jobs are scarce. Because there is no customer relationship in telemarketing—usually it is a one-shot deal—there are no consequences for interrupting someone's dinner, such as loss of customer loyalty.

Vending

Vending machines are a form of non-store retailing growing in popularity. Traditionally, vending machines were coin operated and, thus, limited to inexpensive convenience products such as soft drinks, chewing gum, and cigarettes. With the development of magnetic stripe card readers and internet-connected vending machines, the range of products offered through vending machines has expanded greatly. Today, it is not uncommon to find moderately priced electronics or cosmetics sold through vending machines.

The advantage to a vending machine is that it is open for business 24/7 and can be placed in locations convenient to the customer. The disadvantage is that the machines need to be serviced regularly to replace inventory. Because they are located in high-traffic areas, they can be subject to vandalism.

Direct Marketing

With **direct marketing**, customers are exposed to products through an impersonal medium, such as an email, a catalog, or television show, and then purchase the merchandise by telephone or mail. With the widespread availability of the internet, direct marketers are moving from physical media to electronic media, such as email or social media. As this evolution continues, the role of the catalog has changed. In the golden age of direct marketing, when Montgomery Ward® and Sears® ruled, the catalog was the size of a telephone book and listed every product available to the customer by mail. It was the primary tool for generating sales. Today, the e-tailing website is the primary tool for generating sales. The catalog is smaller, uses full-color photographs to show the highlights of the line, and encourages the customer to visit the website where more options are available.

> "I've seen so many different things … I'm trying to understand it because I know my boss will ask about it because he saw it somewhere. He saw a post about predictive analytics, so he asked, 'Oh, are we doing predictive analytics?' I am expected to know all these things. The hardest part is staying current with the new, trendy thing in Marketing."
>
> **Anadelia Fadeev**

E-Tailing and Blended Channels

E-Tailing is the part of e-commerce that involves selling goods to consumers over the internet. As e-commerce moves from the growth stage to the maturity stage, we are seeing a smaller number of pure-play, or strictly online, e-tailers. Amazon has grown from an online bookstore and now dominates general merchandise e-tailing.

eBay® is the dominant player in the market for second-hand goods while Etsy® is making a name for itself in artisanal craft items.

While pure-play e-tailing is maturing, there is much activity in **omni-channel marketing**, or blended channels (Chapter 13.5). With a blended channel approach, a retailer will have both a physical presence and an online presence. The idea is to optimize the customer experience by providing a seamless customer experience regardless of the channel or device the customer uses to interact with the company. A physical retail presence gives the customer an opportunity to see, touch, and feel the products and adds a social dimension to the shopping experience. The physical location allows the customer to handle customer service issues in person and can serve as a warehouse for local inventory to support online sales. The online store provides 24/7 access allowing the customer to shop at their convenience. The online store also allows the retailer to take advantage of "the long tail" by being able to carry products online that wouldn't have enough sales volume to make it practical to stock them in the physical store. This greatly expands the range of products the retailer is able to offer. The mobile-friendly retailer allows customers to interact with the store whenever and wherever they want.

For direct marketing companies, the online presence is a much less expensive way to display the merchandise while the physical catalog is a way of generating interest in the website. For small businesses and for new products, an online presence is a way to expand the geographic scope of the customer base. Even the venerable Amazon is experimenting with blended channels by opening physical stores near some of its distribution centers.[6]

15.5 RETAIL POSITIONING

At the height of the dot-com boom, many were predicting traditional retailing would disappear. After all, why would anyone make the effort to visit a store when they could find a greater selection of products at a better price without leaving the comfort of home? While e-commerce has had an impact on retail shopping habits, people still choose to visit the store.

The reason is that shopping is more than negotiating a transaction. Shopping is a social experience where we see and can be seen. Shopping can be exciting, letting us discover products and ideas we would never have thought to search for online. Building on these strengths, retailers try to create an entertaining experience for shoppers. That is why the Mall of America®, the largest mall in the United States, includes an indoor amusement park and trendy nightclubs.

The psychology of entertainment retailing is that people use a different set of filters when paying for entertainment than when they are paying for groceries. A hot dog at a baseball game will cost you around five dollars. And it's worth it; it's part of the joy of experiencing America's pastime. On the other hand, at the grocery store, a pound of hot dogs will cost you a couple of dollars, unless you have a coupon, and you are likely to look for the ones on sale. The goal of experiential retailing is to put you in a ballpark frame of mind rather than in a grocery store frame of mind while shopping.

Creating a Brand Image

Retail positioning is all about creating a brand image around how you want the shopper to perceive the store. Is it a fun place to shop? Is it welcoming and friendly? (If you remember from Chapter 9.2, brands have an emotional as well as a cognitive component.) Or is it exclusive, conferring status on the people carrying big shopping bags emblazoned with the store's logo? The variables used to create the retail position include store design, merchandise mix, service level, pricing, location, and advertising.

Store Design

Store design involves the architecture, layout, and atmospherics that create the physical experience for the customer. Store architecture has remained remarkably stable through the years. The basic elements include an open, welcoming entryway; large open areas for customers to wander and explore; and smaller, side areas for closer inspection of the merchandise and for negotiations.[7] Virtually every shopping mall you visit will display these elements.

Store layout refers to the interior arrangement of aisles, shelves, and merchandise groupings throughout the store. The layout should provide maximum exposure to the merchandise and make it easy for the customer to navigate the store. Many stores use different colors or textures of flooring to indicate major aisles and side areas. The way the merchandise is displayed is a signal to what is in store for the shopper. For example, a crowded, messy display of merchandise suggests bargains are to be had for those willing to do some digging. On the other hand, high-end fashion stores will have the merchandise attractively displayed with lots of open space around.

Atmospherics refers to the lights, colors, noise, events, temperature, and other sensory stimulation used to attract attention and to generate excitement and create a mood for the store. For example, scent is a very powerful stimulant. Scent is processed in the primitive part of the brain associated with emotion and can invoke powerful memories. This is why you smell freshly baked bread when you walk through a grocery store or smell cinnamon and hear holiday music while shopping at Christmastime.

When you wander through a shopping mall, sometimes you "instinctively" feel that a particular store is calling to you. This means that (a) you are part of the retailer's target market and (b) store design is doing its job.

Merchandise Mix and Service Level

From a customer perspective, the merchandise mix and service level should support the customer experience you are trying to create. A specialty store should focus on one or two product lines but offer lots of choices within the line with knowledgeable sales people to help the customer find exactly the right thing. A convenience store should have a broad and shallow merchandise mix with products displayed in a way that makes it easy for the customer to find things without a lot of assistance.

Pricing

As discussed in Chapter 11.1, price is both an indicator of value and the product attribute that is easiest for customers to compare. Overall, prices should be consistent with the merchandise mix. Luxury stores will have higher prices while discount stores will have lower prices. How prominently prices are displayed has an impact on customer perceptions of the store. For example, with high-low pricing, sale prices are prominently displayed, creating an impression of overall lower prices. In an exclusive boutique, prices are disclosed by request only, if at all. The logic is "if you have to ask, you can't afford it."

Location

Ideally, you would want to locate your stores where your customers will shop. As a rule, people shop for convenience products, such as groceries or dry cleaning, close to where they live. For shopping goods, especially infrequently purchased goods such as automobiles or furniture, people are willing to visit a destination, but they want to be able to compare. This explains why there are so many shoe stores in a shopping mall.

Traditionally, retail stores are located in a central business district, in a shopping center, or as freestanding stores. Recently, there has been a trend for pop-up stores such as a Halloween store or a Christmas Store to open up for a short period of time in a nontraditional location or in a vacant store. The central business district, or "downtown," is located in the center of a city. Stores in the central business district tend to meet the needs of working people with office supplies, business services, and lunch-oriented restaurants as there is very little traffic in these areas at night or on weekends.

Shopping centers come in all sizes from the very large regional mall, such as the Mall of America, to small neighborhood strip malls featuring a grocery, a drugstore, a dry cleaner, a liquor store, a fast food restaurant, and one or two Starbucks. The regional mall is a destination and will offer a wide and deep assortment of shopping goods. The strip mall features an assortment of stores featuring convenience products. As variations on a theme, factory outlet malls are regional malls where manufacturers offer factory seconds or excess inventory at a discount.

Freestanding stores can be a challenge. To be successful, they have to be popular enough to generate traffic on their own. For example, outdoor enthusiasts will make a Cabelas® sporting goods store a destination. It is more common for freestanding stores to locate near each other to make it convenient for customers. While one store may not be popular enough to draw enough customers on its own, a grouping of stores is a stronger attraction. This explains big box centers where you will find a number of large, freestanding specialty stores such as Best Buy®, Office Depot®, Party City®, etc.

Ironically, this is also true for stores competing against each other in the same industry. This is why you will find clusters of car dealerships or furniture stores in the same area. Two freestanding furniture stores located next to each other will draw more customer traffic than the combined traffic they would have had from two separate stores.

Advertising

As we will see in the next two chapters, advertising is your opportunity to explain the store position and the experience a customer can expect when shopping there. The goal is generate traffic, or people who visit the store. You need to give potential new customers a reason to give the store a try and to give regular customers a reason to come back again and again. It is important that both the media and the message are consistent with the brand image you are creating for the store.

(ENDNOTES)

1. 2012 Economic Census. http://thedataweb.rm.census.gov/TheDataWeb_HotReport2/econsnapshot/2012/snapshot.hrml?STATE=ALL&COUNTY=ALL&x=23&y=5&IND=%3DCOMP%28C2%2FC3*1000%29&NAICS=44-45. Accessed August 10, 2015.

2. 2007 Economic Census. http://factfinder.census.gov/faces/tableservices/jsf/pages/productview.xhtml?pid=ECN_2007_US_44SSSZ6&prodType=table. Accessed August 10, 2015.

3. http://csimarket.com/Industry/industry_Profitability_Ratios.php?s=1300. Accessed August 10, 2015.

4. Leong, Sze Tsung, and Srdjan Jovanovich Weiss, "Air Conditioning," in Chuiha Judy Chung, Jeffrey Inaba, Rem Koolhas, and Sze Tsung Leong, eds., *Harvard Design School Guide to Shopping*, 2001, Köln: Taschen, 93–127.

5. http://www.statista.com/statistics/294189/revenue-telemarketing-and-call-centers-in-the-us/. Accessed August 12, 2015.

6. http://money.cnn.com/2015/02/04/technology/amazon-purdue/. Accessed August 13, 2015.

7. Chuiha Judy Chung, Jeffrey Inaba, Rem Koolhas, and Sze Tsung Leong, eds., *Harvard Design School Guide to Shopping*, 2001, Köln: Taschen.

PROMOTION BASICS

CH 16

There are lots of reasons people communicate with each other. We communicate to exchange information, we communicate to share feelings, we communicate in order to try to get other people to do what we want them to do, we talk to pass the time of day, others sometimes talk to hear the sound of their own voices.

Promotion is marketing communication. Businesses communicate with people for many of the same reasons people communicate with each other. We communicate to exchange information, we communicate to try to get other people to do what we want them to do, we communicate to develop customer relationships, we communicate to keep our products fresh in the customer's mind. However, there are two big differences between marketing communication and personal communication. Marketing communication costs money, and marketing communication is created to accomplish a specific goal. Rarely do businesses advertise simply to pass the time of day.

Understanding marketing communications will help you become a more effective communicator in general. Being an effective communicator will make it easier for employers and co-workers to see the value of what you do at work.

16.1 WHAT IS PROMOTION?

Promotion, or marketing communication, involves all of the communication activity to support the marketing program. Promotion plays many roles in implementing a marketing strategy. It can provide information about new or improved products to customers. It can help persuade people to buy your product or to change their attitude about an issue. It can help encourage two-way communication with customers to develop relationships and to improve our understanding of their needs. It can reinforce customer perceptions of your brand and keep your product fresh in their minds.

As you might guess, the objective of your promotion activity depends. It depends on what goal you are trying to achieve as well as what is going on with the other marketing mix variables. For example, the appropriate promotion strategy would change depending on where you are in the consumer buying process (Chapter 2.2). During the need recognition stage, the goal would be to inform or remind; during the decision stage, the goal would be to persuade; during the post-purchase stage, the goal would be to build relationships. Similarly, during the introductory stage of the product life cycle (Chapter 8.1), the goal of the promotion strategy would be to create awareness of the new product; during the growth stage, the goal would be to persuade customers that your version of the product is best. During the decline stage, no promotion goal is appropriate as spending money on communication would be a waste of resources.

16.2 BASIC COMMUNICATION MODEL

Before talking about the tools used to communicate and how to deploy them, it might be useful to take a closer look at how humans communicate. Wilber Schramm developed a basic communication model in the 1950s. This model is helpful in understanding why some attempts at communication work and some fail. Figure 16.1 is an adaptation of Schramm's communication model. This model works for all human communication, not just for business communication.

In order to communicate, you need to send a message to the recipient. Based on what the recipient interprets the message to be, there will be a response. Have you ever played the party game "telephone"? In this game, a group of people form a circle, and one person starts by whispering something into the ear of another person. That person whispers the saying to the next person and so on until the saying comes full circle, and the last person to receive it repeats it out loud. Usually what the last person says bears little resemblance to what started the chain. Marketing communications is like a game of "telephone." This model helps understand where distortions in the message are likely to originate, so you can control for them with your promotion strategy.

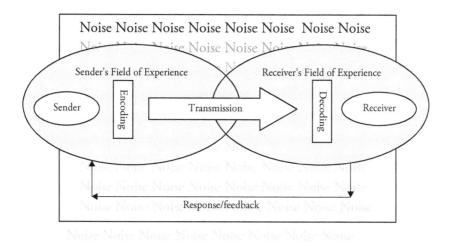

FIGURE 16.1 Schramm's Communication Model (Adapted from: http://commtheories.wikispaces .com/Wilbur+Schramm.)

Sending and Receiving

In marketing communication, you are the source of the message. You have something you want your audience to understand. Unfortunately, we do not yet communicate telepathically. This means that you will have to encode the message in order to transmit it. Encoding involves turning the thought into language and expressing the language through words, images, and actions.

Cues are the different ways we can encode information. For example, in this book we use words in the English language as a major cue. Headings and spacing help send the message, boldface and italics are used to highlight specific topics or words. In addition, the occasional figure or table helps make sense of complex thoughts. When meeting with someone in person, body language, how loudly or softly you speak, eye contact, etc., are all cues that help encode the message you are trying to send.

The way we encode messages is heavily influenced by our field of experience, or life experience. The vocabulary you use and the meanings attached to the vocabulary will change based on your experience. For example, many college professors have large vocabularies and tend to use words that carry a very precise meaning. We all have slang or technical jargon that allows us to communicate effectively within our field of experience. B2B is shorthand for business-to-business marketing, and we all want to get to the bottom line quickly.

In order to receive the message, the recipient needs to decode the message based on their field of experience. It is important that marketing messages be encoded using cues that are relevant to the recipient's field of experience. Thus, a college professor's precise language may be lost on a student who learned English as a second language and doesn't understand the words the professor is using. The differences can be even more subtle. For example, when medical professionals ask you about your diet, they want to know about the nutritional value of the foods you eat.

To the average person, a diet is a weight loss plan. Asking you about your diet implies that you are fat.

Metaphors Matter

In business, we draw heavily on sports and the military as metaphors to describe business activity (i.e., "somebody dropped the ball," "this is a full-out blitz," or "it's time to bring in the heavy artillery)." Because boys are more likely to be exposed to sports and military language in childhood, men are more likely to have these terms in their field of experience than women. This can put women at a disadvantage, especially early in their careers.

Having received and interpreted the message, the recipient will respond as seems appropriate. This response, compared to the desired response, provides feedback as to whether or not the message was effective.

212 Transmission

Once the message has been encoded, it has to be transmitted from sender to receiver. This involves selecting a **channel**, or medium, for transmitting information. For example, a printed book, an internet connection, meeting face-to-face are all communication channels. Different channels have different levels of **channel richness,** or the number of different cues a channel can carry. For example, print is generally considered to be the sparsest channel. The cues that can be transmitted through print are limited to words, color, pictures, italics, graphic layout. On the other hand, face-to-face communication is the richest channel. When speaking to another person, you can use words, gestures, movement, vocal tone, and music, plus you can interact with the recipient in real time. Video is somewhere in the middle in channel richness. You can transmit words, motion, sound, color, music, and graphics, but it doesn't have interactivity. In general, the richer the channel, the more expensive it is to transmit a message.

The internet is a major exception to this rule. The internet is a very rich medium—it has all of the cues you can transmit through video with the addition of interactivity and access to a computer at the time of transmission. Although it is very rich, the internet is an inexpensive medium. Access to the World Wide Web is essentially free. The cost is associated with finding an audience for your message. This is one reason why there is so much attention on social media marketing. A social network is one way of finding an audience for an online promotion.

It is important to choose a channel with sufficient richness to accomplish your objective. For example, many marketers believe that video has the minimum level of richness to be able to connect with a person on an emotional level.

Noise

Noise is a general term referring to anything that interferes with the successful completion of the communication process. It is much more than the level of sound in the room while you are talking. Noise could be a slow internet connection that makes a video keep buffering. It could be a coffee spill that smears some of the words on a written document. It could be the distraction from someone sitting near you playing a video game when you are trying to concentrate on your homework. It may be the thousands of other advertisements that have numbed your audience's brain to the point where they don't notice your advertisement.

In designing a promotion, it is important to anticipate potential sources of noise between you and your audience. One way to do this is to put yourself in the situation where the audience will be when designing the promotion. If your customers will be receiving your communication on their mobile devices, see how your message plays on a variety of devices with different levels of reception.

Persuasion

The **AIDA model**[1] is a template for communication intended to persuade—to change peoples' behavior or attitude. AIDA is not a reference to the famous opera by Guiseppe Verdi (see what we mean about fields of experience?), but an acronym for Attention, Interest, Desire, Action.

Before you can convince your potential customers of anything, you have to get their *attention*. Once you have their attention, you have to give them a reason to pay attention to your message. Now that you have them *interested* in what you are saying, you have to get them to want to do what you want them to do. And finally, when there is a *desire* to do what you ask, there has to be a call to *action*. Tell them how to do it. Better yet, give them a deadline.

All persuasive communication should follow this template.

16.3 PROMOTIONAL MIX

The **promotional mix** consists of the tools you will be using to communicate with customers: advertising, personal selling, public relations, and sales promotion. We will look at each of these more closely in the next two chapters. There are three major issues to keep in mind while determining which elements of the promotional mix to deploy: push vs. pull, control vs. influence, and mass appeal vs. personal appeal.

Push vs. Pull

Push vs. pull deals with the relationship between your distribution strategy and your promotional efforts. A **push strategy** works with channel partners to communicate with the consumer. For example, a manufacturer might offer a retailer a promotional allowance to encourage the retailer to put the product on sale or to give it prime display space. When you go into the grocery store and see people giving away free samples of various products, you are benefiting from a push strategy. The manufacturer is working with the retailer to entice you to buy the product.

A **pull strategy** focuses communication efforts directly on the consumer in order to generate demand for the product. For example, a manufacturer introducing a new brand of cereal might send you a coupon for a free box. You, as the consumer, will look for the new cereal the next time you are in the store to take advantage of the free product offer. If you don't find the product on the shelves, you might ask the manager of the store if it will be available. It is now in the manager's interest to stock the new product because customers are asking for it by name. In effect, you are communicating directly with the consumer to pull the product through the channel of distribution.

Control vs. Influence

If the purpose of marketing communication is to persuade the customer to do something (like buy your product), different elements of the marketing mix have different levels of effectiveness. If you remember from Chapter 2.3, people are more likely to believe personal communication than they are to believe marketing generated communication. This leads to an inverse relationship between the amount of control you have over the message and the influence the message will have on the customer. Table 16.1 summarizes these differences.

Table 16.1 Contol vs. Influence

ELEMENTS OF THE PROMOTIONAL MIX	
IN ORDER OF CONTROL	IN ORDER OF INFLUENCE
Advertising	Word of Mouth
Sales Promotion	Public Relations
Personal Selling	Personal Selling
Public Relations	Sales Promotion
Word of Mouth	Advertising

You have the most control over your advertising. You specify every aspect of the message as well as how, when, and where it appears. Sales promotion is also under your control although different sales promotion tactics may offer less control than others. For personal selling, you have control over the hiring and training of your salespeople, but you don't control the sales conversation with your customer. With public relations, you have control over the stimulus but not the response. For example, you can issue a press release but have no control over whether media outlets pick it up.

We've included word-of-mouth communication in this analysis. Word-of-mouth communication is the most influential form of communication. Marketers have no control over word-of-mouth communication, so it isn't considered an element of the promotional mix. However, much promotional activity is intended to stimulate word-of-mouth, or "buzz."

After word-of-mouth, public relations has the most influence. If a media outlet does pick up on your press release, to the consumer, it will appear to be news rather than advertising. Personal selling can be very influential. That is what salesmen are trained to do. Advertising is the least influential. Even if people notice your ad, they will discount it as one sided.

Mass Appeal vs. Personal Appeal

Some elements of the marketing mix work better for mass appeals while others are best for one-on-one personal appeals. With mass communication, you are sending the same message to multiple customers. Typically, customers will self-select whether they choose to receive the communication, so mass appeals are more effective for informing and reminding rather than developing a deep understanding of the message. Mass appeals are more expensive to create but much less expensive on a per-person basis because the cost of developing the appeal is spread out over many recipients.

With a personal appeal, the message is crafted to meet the needs of the individual receiving the message. Frequently, the personal appeal is two-way communication with the recipient. This makes personal appeals effective for persuasion and relationship building. Personal appeals are much more expensive on a per-person basis.

Figure 16.2 is a 2 × 2 matrix with mass vs. personal appeal on one axis and paid vs. unpaid on the other axis. Paid communication offers more control but less influence than unpaid communication.

Advertising and personal selling are paid communications. Advertising is intended for a mass audience while personal selling is conducted one-on-one. Public relations is mass communication that appears to be unpaid. Sales promotion doesn't fit neatly into any one of the quadrants although sales promotions are generally understood to be paid communication. Word-of-mouth is unpaid one-on-one communication.

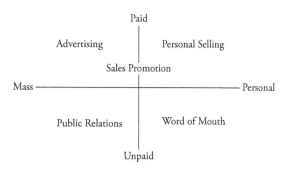

FIGURE 16.2   Mass vs. Personal Appeal

215

16.4 DEVELOPING A PROMOTIONAL PLAN

As with any component of the marketing mix, the first decision in developing a plan involves determining what role promotion plays in the overall marketing strategy. With that in mind, you will establish the objectives for the promotional activity, develop a budget in support of the plan, allocate the budget among the elements of the promotional mix, and, finally, evaluate the effectiveness of the promotion.

Establish Objectives

The first question to answer when setting the objective for promotion is: "What is the outcome we would like to see as a result of this activity?" Be specific. Who is the target audience and what change do we want to see as a result of our efforts? The objective needs to be quantifiable and measurable and completed within a defined time period. There needs to be a business reason to make the investment in promotion, and the objectives should relate to this objective. For example, a good objective might be: "We want to increase our market share among 18–35 year olds in the Midwest by 3% in the coming year. In order to do that, we need to increase awareness of our product from the current 10% to 40%." The promotional objective of increasing awareness in the target demographic ties into the larger goal of increasing market share.

A bad objective might be: "We want to run a television ad during the Super Bowl because it is the premier showcase for advertising and will put our product on the map." This is "art for art's sake," spending a lot of money with no specific objective in mind other than to be recognized for the quality of the promotion.

Determine the Budget

How much money should you allocate to the promotion? It depends. As a benchmark, 5% of revenue is a common starting point although the actual amount will vary by industry. In industries where most of the activity is B2B, the amount invested in promotion might be as little as 1%. In competitive, consumer product industries, the promotion budget might approach 10% or even more. In general, smaller companies will invest a larger percentage of revenue in promotion than larger companies. This is because for very large companies, the absolute dollar amount is bigger. Five percent of revenue for a business with $1 million in sales is $50,000. Five percent of revenue for a business with $1 billion in sales is $50,000,000. You can accomplish a lot with $50 million.

There are four commonly used techniques for setting the promotion budget. Three top-down approaches are budgeting on the percentage of sales, doing what the competition is doing, and limiting the budget to what you can afford; one bottom-up approach is using an objective task method. Top-down approaches start with a fixed budget amount and then allocate the budget to the various promotional activities. The percentage of sales approach is the most commonly used, as it is relatively easy to determine, and the budget will scale up or scale down in keeping with the overall business. The downside of the percentage of sales approach is that it is independent of what it will cost to achieve the promotional objectives.

Setting the promotional budget based on what the competition is doing or limiting the promotional budget to what you can afford are less optimal approaches to budgeting. If your competitor occupies the dominant position in your industry, simply matching the promotional spend (amount spent on promotion) will not help you gain ground. Similarly, limiting the promotional budget to what you can afford ignores the cost of achieving the promotional objectives. If the budget is not large enough to accomplish your goal, you may as well not spend it. You'd be better off investing the money elsewhere. If the budget is larger than you need (it could happen), you are wasting money if you use it all.

The bottom-up approach to developing the promotional budget starts by establishing the promotional objectives and determining the specific tasks needed to achieve the objectives. Then, an estimate of what it will cost for each activity is combined into the promotional budget. The advantage of this objective-task approach is that the budget reflects what it will take to achieve the goal. The disadvantage is that the process is cumbersome, and it requires a clear understanding of what tasks will be needed at the beginning of the planning process.

Allocate the Budget

The next step is to allocate the promotional budget among the various elements of the promotional mix. If the budget was developed using the objective-task method, this part is easier. If not, ask, "How do you invest the budget to achieve the greatest impact with the available resources?" The answer is: "It depends." It depends on who the target audience is, what your competencies are, where you are in the value chain, the nature of the product, the structure of the industry, etc., etc., etc.

In general, sales promotion is the largest expenditure followed by personal selling, advertising, and public relations. This surprises a lot of people because we all know that advertising is really expensive. Wouldn't you expect advertising to be the largest expenditure? If you think about it, a 5% off sales promotion is 5% of sales; you can see how expensive sales promotion can be. Similarly, while advertising is more expensive per message, personal selling is more expensive on a per-person basis. All companies have a sales force; even consumer packaged goods companies like Proctor and Gamble® have a sales force to call on retail customers. Not all companies need to advertise, especially in the B2B arena. Finally, public relations is the element with the most untapped potential. Currently the smallest part of the promotions budget, more companies are realizing the impact effective public relations can have.

Evaluate Effectiveness

John Wanamaker, of the Philadelphia Wanamaker's department store, is famously quoted as saying, "I know half of my advertising budget is wasted, I just don't know which half." This illustrates one of the frustrations in marketing—it is hard to measure a direct link between marketing actions and sales performance.

Many times, marketers will measure indirect or intermediate steps in the buying process as a measure of effectiveness. Thus, it is difficult to evaluate the effectiveness of an ad based on its impact on sales. There are just too many other variables that could come into play. Maybe it was a very cold winter and people stayed home while the ad was running. Maybe a competitor was running a sale at the same time the ad was running ... you get the idea. Instead, we might measure whether or not a person saw the ad as a measure of effectiveness, or if the person saw the ad, did it affect the intention to purchase the product?

Whatever the measure used to evaluate the effectiveness of your promotion, the measure and its interpretation should be established at the same time the objectives were set. If the objective was to increase awareness of our product from the current 10% to 40%, the measure of effectiveness should be how much awareness increased. If it was over 40%, the promotion was a success. If the objective was to run an ad during the Super Bowl, the measure of effectiveness would be: "Did the ad run?" It's just too easy.

16.5 INTEGRATED MARKETING COMMUNICATION

Before moving to a discussion of each element of the promotional mix, it is a good idea to think about the impact of them as a whole. The concept of **integrated marketing communication** (IMC) ties the marketing concept to the promotional mix. The marketing concept suggests that all of a business's activity should be focused on the customer. IMC takes this one step further by having all of the company's promotional activity focused on coordinated promotional objectives.

This is best illustrated by a laser analogy. If you remember from physics, white light consists of a number of different light wave frequencies all jumbled together. If you shine a flashlight, the white light will be seen a few feet away. A laser takes just one frequency of light and synchronizes it so that the light waves are all lined up together. When everything is moving in the same direction, you can shine a laser and see it on the moon. It is the same with IMC. You can have lots of different promotional activities, and the cumulative impact will be positive. But if you coordinate the activities so that no matter how a customer interacts with the company he or she is getting the same message. The impact is much more powerful.

One of the keys to IMC is to recognize customers have many different ways of interacting with the company. Think of a car customer. The customer is exposed to advertising from the manufacturer and the dealer sending one message. The customer comes into the showroom where the salespeople build on that message in order to make the sale. Then, after the purchase, the customer brings the car into the service side of the dealership to address a problem with the car. There is a good chance the service technician isn't on the same page as the sales force.

The Walt Disney Company® made just such an observation at the Disney amusement parks. It noticed that guests were reluctant to "bother" cast members with trivial questions but, instead, were more likely to ask the person sweeping the sidewalks. As a result, the sidewalk sweepers are given extra training on how to answer questions. The investment in training was important to give a consistent brand experience to all guests.

(ENDNOTE)

1. Starch, Daniel, 1923, *Principles of Advertising,* Chicago: A.W. Shaw Company.

ADVERTISING, PUBLIC RELATIONS, AND SALES PROMOTION

CH 17

From the time we were children, we have been bombarded with commercial messages every day. As a result, we love them. We all have our favorite advertisements and can't wait to tell our friends about a great new ad. In this chapter we will go "behind the scenes" to look at advertising and its near cousins, public relations and sales promotion, to understand the role these activities play in helping customers understand the value of our products.

17.1 WHAT IS ADVERTISING?

From Figure 16.2, we saw that **advertising** is mass, paid communication. To be more specific, advertising refers to paid messages placed in any of the mass media by an identified sponsor in order to inform or persuade members of a particular target market or audience about products, services, organizations, or ideas.

There are four criteria that distinguish advertising from other elements of the promotional mix: message, sponsor, medium, and payment. The biggest advantage of advertising is that you have complete control over the message. The sponsor is identified, so people will know they are looking at an advertisement and who is paying for the message. The media selected for transmission need to be appropriate for the message as well as for the audience. Again, because you are paying for the media, you have control over when and where the ad will run.

The Role of Advertising

Advertising is used to support the sale of products as well as for institutional purposes, and the objective will vary according to the situation. For product-related advertising, the objective might be to generate demand or to act as a call to action. For new products, pioneer ads inform potential customers about the value of the new product in order to generate **primary demand (Chapter 8.1)**, that is, demand for the product category rather than demand for a particular brand. Further on in the product life cycle, **comparative advertising** seeks to generate interest in your particular brand from among multiple competing products. Action ads may attempt to persuade customers to act immediately such as with a limited time offer or, perhaps, with reminder ads available to act as triggers. For example, when you are driving a long distance, you are never far away from a billboard or roadside sign advertising McDonald's®. The idea is that when you begin to notice you are hungry, you will be reminded that fast food might be the answer.

Institutional advertising has the primary purpose of promoting the name, image, personnel, or reputation of a company, organization, or industry. For example, following a disastrous accident, a West Coast utility company ran a series of institutional ads featuring company employees talking about how they care about the communities in which they live and work. **Advocacy advertising** is intended to communicate a viewpoint about a controversial issue. The Truth Initiative, funded by the 1998 Tobacco Master Settlement Agreement, ran a series of Truth® advocacy ads to discourage people from smoking tobacco. At the local level, retailers use advertising to generate **traffic**, or the number of people who visit the store during a specific period of time.

Working with Ad Agencies

Advertising agencies are intermediaries that provide advertising services to other businesses. When working with an agency, there is usually a professional associated with the company (client-side) who works with their counterpart in the ad agency (agency-side). It is not uncommon for an advertising professional to move from agency-side to client-side and vice versa over the course of a career.

A full-service agency works very closely with a client to provide a variety of services, including research, creative work, media buying, digital marketing, marketing communications (or marcom) … the list goes on. If the full-service agency doesn't have the in-house capability to provide a particular service, it will subcontract with other agencies to meet the client's needs.

Traditionally, a full-service agency charged a percentage commission on the media buy (the space in advertising media in which the ads will run) as a fee and provided the creative work as part of the package. The television show *Mad Men* portrayed life in a full-service advertising agency. Today, agencies are charging for creative services separately from the media buy. With digital marketing (internet, social, mobile) access to media is very low cost, so it is unrealistic to expect to cover creative costs as a percentage of the media buy.

In order to be effective, a full-service ad agency needs to understand the client's business thoroughly. This means that these outsiders from the agency need to know your business as well as the insiders do. In addition, the agency will bring insights learned by working with other clients over time. Because the agency is an independent contractor, you have the option of firing the agency and bringing in another if the relationship isn't working.

Limited-service agencies provide one or more promotional services but do not offer a complete solution as full-service agencies do. Freelance workers, or freelancers, are independent service providers who are available for contract work. Companies can work directly with limited-service agencies and freelancers or can work with a full-service agency that will subcontract with these providers as necessary.

Cutting Through the Clutter

Ad clutter refers to the ever-increasing number of ads competing for our limited attention. It is difficult to determine the number of ads you are exposed to in a typical day. Estimates range from 250 to 20,000 ad exposures per day depending on how you define an ad exposure. When talking about ad clutter, 250 ads per day or 3,500 ads per day are the most commonly used estimates.[1] At 3,500 ads per day, we are exposed to an ad every 24 seconds (assuming we don't sleep). Because of selective attention (Chapter 2.3), we don't even notice the vast majority of ads we see and respond to only a small fraction of the ads we notice.

The point is, with all that advertising going on, you will have to cut through the clutter before you can begin to communicate with your customers.

17.2 AD CAMPAIGNS

It is unusual for an ad to run in isolation because the influence generated by a single ad impression is very small. Instead, we think in terms of **advertising campaigns,** or a group of advertisements and related promotional activities conducted over a specific period of time in order to achieve a desired outcome. Frequently, paid advertising is the spearhead of an integrated marketing communication effort. Advertising in an information-rich medium such as television introduces the message while **collaterals**, or materials introduced later in the campaign, are used to support the message.

There are two costs incurred in developing an ad campaign: creative and media. Both costs vary widely depending on the scope of the campaign. Creative costs are the costs associated with developing the message such as research, photography, copywriting, video production, etc. The creative is usually the smaller of the two costs. Development costs for an online campaign start at a few thousand dollars[2] while production costs for a national television ad can run into the millions of dollars. The vast majority of the cost of an ad campaign goes to buying the media needed to get the message to the target audience. Media costs vary widely. For example, a 30-second television spot on local television may cost a couple of hundred dollars[3] while a 30-second ad on the Super Bowl football game costs upwards of $4 million.

Developing the Ad Campaign

There are six stages involved with developing an ad campaign: determine the target audience, establish the goals for the campaign, design the ad, choose the media, schedule the media, and evaluate the result.

Target Audience

In Chapters 6 and 7, we talked about segmenting, targeting, and positioning. The target audience and market position determine the overall direction of the ad campaign.

Establish Goals

The next step is to establish the goals and parameters of the campaign. What is the message you want your target audience to receive, and what is the desired outcome of the advertising campaign? Do you want to inform, persuade, remind, or build relationships? In marketing, you never spend money unless you have a clear understanding of how that investment will benefit the business. The goals should be specific and measurable. For example, the objective of a campaign for a new product might be to increase awareness of the product in the target market from 10% to 40%.

Once the objectives have been established, the budget and timeframe for the campaign need to be developed.

Design the Ad

There are two major issues in developing an advertising message: the appeal and production. The appeal deals with the central idea or theme of the campaign. The appeal is a way to catch the customer's interest and, thereby, cut through the clutter. Common appeals include unique selling proposition (USP), lifestyle appeals, emotional appeals, and jingles.

Appeals. The **unique selling proposition** focuses on a uniquely differentiating characteristic of the product that is important to customers and is a strength of your product when compared to competing products. **Comparative ads** show this characteristic in a side-by-side comparison with a competing product while *demonstration ads* show the characteristic without a direct comparison.

Lifestyle appeals show how the product will fit in with the customer's values, opinions, or way of living. *Slice of life* ads present a familiar vignette or scene where a person similar to a target customer's quality of life is improved by using the product. For example, in Hallmark's™ "Proud Mom" TV ad, a high school graduate finds a meaningful way to thank her hardworking mom for all she's done.[4] *Testimonial ads* feature people similar to the target audience explaining how the product improved their lives.

Emotional appeals tap into the customer's emotional and social needs to create a desire for the product. *Sex appeals* use attractive people to get our attention, and it works. Attractive people DO get our attention. *Fear appeals* scare us into buying the product by showing how miserable we will be if we don't purchase the product. *Humor appeals* provide entertainment along with the message. People are more likely to remember and less likely to fast forward through an ad that makes them laugh.

> "Not everybody claims to be an expert at product conversion, conversion rates of existing customers, that kind of business forecasting. But everybody, including our mothers, thinks that they are an expert on advertising. Everyone's got a position, a point of view on advertising."
>
> **Marketing Professional**

Jingles and slogans recognize that music and rhyme make things easier to remember. A *slogan*, or tag line, is a short, memorable phrase while a *jingle* is an advertising message set to music. Because our brains like to focus on patterns, we find rhyme and music both pleasant and easier to remember. We are predisposed to recognize rhyming from our early language development. In addition, recent brain scan studies suggest that the brain releases dopamine, a neurotransmitter associated with reward and pleasure, when we listen to music.[5] At its most effective,

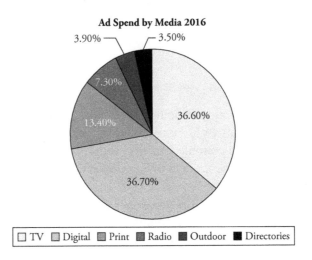

Ad Spend by Media 2016

3.90% — 3.50%

7.30%

13.40%

36.60%

36.70%

☐ TV ☐ Digital ☐ Print ☐ Radio ☐ Outdoor ☐ Directories

FIGURE 17.1   US Ad Spending by Media (Source: www.emarketer.com/Report/US-Ad-Spending-eMarketer-Forecast-2017/2001998, Accessed May 29, 2018.)

a memorable jingle can become an earworm—something that keeps playing in our heads long after the music has stopped.

Production. There are an infinite number of ways to craft an advertising message. This means there are lots of right answers to the question: "How do we turn this idea into a persuasive message?" Some answers are better than others. This is where creativity comes into play. Understanding the characteristics of the target audience will give you a better chance of crafting a message that connects with the customer.

Just to be sure, ad agencies put a lot of time and energy into pretesting ad messages. Before investing a lot of money in advertising media, it makes sense to have confidence that the message will be effective. The concept for the ad, ad copy (words used in the message), and especially the finished commercial can be tested before launching the campaign.

Choose the Media

The channel you choose to carry your message will be one of the mass media outlets. Each medium has differences in information richness, cost, and distribution. For example, television is an information rich medium and costs more than other communication media. Broadcast television covers the entire market area while addressable cable television allows you to focus your message on specific neighborhoods.

Television no longer dominates media spending in the US. Digital advertising accounted for 36.6% of the estimated $194 billion spent in 2016. Digital advertising overtook television in 2016 with accounting for 36.7% advertising spending led by strong growth in mobile media. Traditional media (TV, print, radio, outdoor, directories) have been steadily losing share to digital media (internet, mobile) for several years.[6] Figure 17.1 shows the proportion of ad spending by media in 2016.

In addition to choosing the medium to distribute your ad, you will need to select the specific vehicle within that medium. For example, if the medium is broadcast television, the vehicle would be the specific program(s) on which your ads will run. One tool used in allocating the ad spend, or advertising budget, among the various media alternatives is **CPM**, or cost per thousand impressions. This is calculated by taking the cost of placing an ad in a specific vehicle divided by the audience size and multiplied by 1,000.

There are a number of ways to reduce the cost of your media buy. For example, you will save money if you buy in bulk, especially for local media. You will pay a huge premium for spot (one-time) ads. Negotiating an annual contract with the media company will greatly reduce your CPM. Many manufacturers offer advertising support to their retail partners through co-op (or cooperative) advertising. This support can involve anything from sharing the cost of running ads on local media to providing production materials to assistance with media scheduling.

It is important to audit your ad expenditures to make sure that the vehicles selected delivered the audience that was promised. **Make-goods** are free ad space or airtime to compensate an advertiser for lower than expected audiences and missed or incorrect ads.

Schedule the Media

The media schedule, or continuity, is the plan that specifies when and where each ad will run over the course of the campaign. The goal is to maximize **exposures**, or the number of times each member of the target audience is exposed to the ad, while using tactics to minimize the cost of the campaign.

Gross Ratings Points. One way of measuring the impact of a campaign is by using **gross ratings points**. A gross ratings point is equivalent to one percent of the target audience having one exposure to the ad. It is calculated by multiplying the average **reach**, or percentage of the target audience covered by a vehicle, times average **frequency**, or the average number of exposures. Thus, if everyone in the target audience had one exposure to the ad, it would equal 100 gross ratings points (100% reach × 1 exposure = 100). It is possible, and even desirable, for gross ratings points to be higher than 100.

Gross ratings points are a way to measure the overall impact of a campaign rather than a tally of who has and who hasn't seen the ad. For example, 200 gross ratings points may mean that 100% of the target audience had two exposures to the ad, or it could mean that 10% of the target audience had 20 exposures to the ad. In the first case, everyone had a weak exposure to the ad while in the second case, a small percentage of the target audience had intensive exposure to the ad.

Scheduling Tactics. Advertising is subject to the law of diminishing returns. The term **advertising wearout** recognizes that an ad will lose its effectiveness after a number of exposures. People will get bored with an ad after a while. Ironically, advertisers can get bored with their ads more quickly than their audience and pull an ad that is still effective. This is because the advertiser may have been working with the ad for several months during the production period and will have seen it many, many times before it is available to the general public.

Three scheduling tactics, continuous, pulsing, and flighting, seek to maximize the impact of the ad campaign while minimizing the cost of the media. With a **continuous schedule**, the ads will run continuously over the course of the campaign. This is the most expensive approach and is most common with consumer packaged goods. To minimize ad wearout, a company may create a series of ads. As one ad begins to get old, another in the series can run. This way the consumer is constantly exposed to the product, but the specific ads will vary. GEICO® insurance is famous for saturating the airwaves with a variety of ad campaigns for auto insurance. When the gecko ads begin to get old, it runs the caveman ads. When the caveman ads get old, it runs the "good news, I just saved a bundle on car insurance" ads. The list goes on.

With a **pulsing** tactic, ads will run continuously over the period of the campaign, but the frequency will vary. They will run lots of ads for a while to generate interest and then reduce the number of ads for a while to minimize burnout and to stretch the advertising budget. With a **flighting** tactic, ads are run on a noncontinuous schedule. Ads are run for a period of time followed by a hiatus, or period when no ads are run. This approach is used for seasonal products or for when sales need a boost.

Evaluate Results

It is difficult to tie a sales response to a specific ad. There are a number of influences going on as a person goes through the buying process (Chapter 2.3) that may have a more powerful impact on the purchase decision than advertising. People develop attitudes towards brands over time, and it is the cumulative effect of many ad exposures that lays the foundation for a particular purchase. Even in the world of digital advertising, where you can follow the clickstream from ad to purchase, the response to a particular ad has many influences.

With that in mind, evaluating the results of an ad campaign involves research to measure recognition of the ad, attitude change, and behavioral measures where possible. In a **recall** test, members of the target audience are contacted sometime after the ad has run and are asked if they remember seeing the ad. In an unaided recall test, participants are simply asked to name the ads they remember seeing in a particular vehicle. In an aided recall test, participants are shown a list of ads that ran in the vehicle and asked if they remember seeing any them.

Measuring attitude change requires a longitudinal or pretest, post-test methodology. This approach is common in political campaigns where the candidate's standing in the polls is measured as a response to political ads.

While it is difficult to connect a purchase to a specific ad, there are circumstances where it is possible to measure behavioral responses to an ad. Behavioral measures are common in digital marketing as all of the customer's activity is online and, therefore, can be tracked. **Click-through rate** measures the percentage of people exposed to an online ad who clicked on it. With traditional media, marketers create a code for each channel in order to be able to track which advertisement generated the response. Some codes such as asking for a promo code when placing the order are explicit. Other codes can be more subtle. For example, the telephone number or URL for a website in the call to action may be different for each ad.

17.3 ADVERTISING MEDIA

Six mass communication media commonly used for distributing advertising messages are digital media, television, print, radio, and outdoor. Here is a brief description of each and where they might fit in an advertising campaign.

Digital Media

Digital media includes the internet, social media, and mobile media. This area is attractive for several reasons. First, it is the fastest growing advertising channel, coming from nowhere at the beginning of this century to the point where it may replace television as the dominant advertising channel in the near future. Second, it is a very rich medium. In addition to the information cues associated with video, digital media is interactive, allowing the customer to participate in the experience. Third, there is a lot of blurring of the lines between digital and other media. For example, many people choose to view television programming online through sites like Hulu® or Netflix® while 40% of smartphone and tablet owners use them at the same time they are watching TV.[13] This allows for cross-platform coordination of messages. Fourth, the cost of access to the internet is very low. Chapter 19 discusses digital marketing in more depth.

Television

Television is the most widely used medium for advertising for several reasons. First, it is a very rich medium enabling you to tell stories that can create an emotional connection to the brand. Second, lots of people watch TV, so it is a cost-effective way to reach a mass audience. Nielsen tells us that 289 million people in the US own at least one TV set, and the average person watches television for 144 hours each month.[7] Third, most television programming is entertainment or sports, so your ad will be paired with a positive experience. Finally, research firms measure the audience for each television program, allowing you to choose a vehicle whose audience fits your desired demographic profile.

There are three paths to placing ads on television: national network TV, local TV, and Cable. The national networks are a group of local market television affiliates who agree to carry a certain amount of programming (i.e., prime time) provided by the network. Each television program has an inventory of available ad space. Network programs average just over 14 minutes of advertising per hour while cable shows average just over 15 ½ minutes of advertising.[8] Some of this inventory is reserved for the network, and some of the inventory is made available to the local affiliate station to sell. This means that when you watch a network television show, you are seeing both national and local ads. A 30-second ad on national TV costs around $340,000 on average, while a 30-second spot on a local affiliate will run from $200 to $1500.[9] You have the option of running an ad on the national network or, if your company doesn't have national coverage, on the local affiliate stations in the areas you serve.

In addition to network programming, local affiliate stations also develop their own programming. Some of this programming, such as local news, sports and other features, are produced by the station. Syndicated shows such as reruns of prime time television shows or talk shows fill out the programming day. Long-format commercials, or "infomercials," may run during time slots with a small audience such as the early morning hours.

Cable offers more flexibility at the local level. The typical home has access to 189 channels, and viewers in the home watch 17 channels regularly.[10] Many of these channels, such as the Food Network®, cater to audiences with a particular lifestyle and can be a great way to reach these audiences. Addressable cable allows you to narrow the focus of the ad down to specific neighborhoods within the cable service area. In addition to buying ad time on specific programs, cable providers offer a "rotator package" where rather than buying time on a specific program, the ad will run at any time during a six- to 12-hour window.[11] This is a less expensive approach, but it makes it harder to be sure you are reaching the right audience.

Today's technology allows people to record television programming and watch the shows at a time more convenient to them. This also gives consumers the ability to skip through the ads. People viewing programming recorded on a DVR watch 45% of the ads.[12] One way advertisers are responding to this trend is to keep the brand information at the same place during the entire ad. This way, it will still be visible as the customer fast forwards through the ad.

Print

Print is the oldest mass communications medium and includes periodic publications such as magazines and newspaper. Print as a medium has been steadily losing ground to digital media, especially for younger people. Print is a relatively sparse communications medium, limited to printed words and pictures. Because of this, print is used for collateral material rather than as the spearhead for an advertising campaign.

Print has several advantages. First, customers subscribe to the print vehicle, so they are interested in its contents. Second, print allows you to deal with complicated issues at greater length than video. Third, unlike broadcast advertising—which is gone once it has aired—print is permanent. The ad exists in physical form and is available to more than one reader. Finally, readers expect their publications to include ads, and they are seen as less intrusive than ads in other media.

Newspaper subscriptions are declining and, of those who do subscribe to a newspaper, 56% read the physical paper exclusively while 44% of readers supplement the physical paper with digital media.[14] National newspapers have been hit the hardest while local newspapers still attract a loyal following because of local news and sports reporting. An average ad in a national newspaper runs upwards of $100,000 while a smaller ad in a local paper can be run for a few hundred dollars.[15]

Newspapers offer flexibility in your marketing communications. Because they are published daily and have very short lead times (the number of days before the publication date you need to have your advertising materials submitted to the newspaper), your message can be fine tuned as circumstances require.

Magazines offer a higher-quality user experience because they are printed on coated paper and offer full-color reproduction of photos. The average cost for an ad in a national magazine runs around $250,000.[16] With longer lead times of four to six weeks, magazine advertising is less responsive to changing circumstances.

There are three major categories of magazines: trade publications, national magazines, and specialty magazines. Trade publications are published by trade associations for the benefit of their members. These are suitable for B2B advertising targeting a specific industry. As with national newspapers, national magazines such as news magazines or celebrity gossip magazines are under the greatest pressure from digital alternatives. Specialty magazines allow you to reach an audience in a specific interest area such as home decor or cooking.

"Get really good at writing, be a really strong, effective communicator; and I'm not talking about writing long essays that only your professors are going to read. I'm talking about really learning how to communicate clearly. I call it the three C's: You need to be clear, your need to be concise, you need to be correct."

Julie Clarke

Radio

Radio is a broadcast medium that has been losing ground to digital media as well. It is a fairly sparse medium, limited to words and music, but its impact can be powerful. Ninety percent of the population listens to radio at least once a week.[17] Because people tend to listen to radio when they are alone—while driving or while working out—radio can be very intimate. Also, because it is an audio-only medium, people use their imaginations to create images.

Radio ads are typically 60 seconds in length and are bought locally as a package. A package of 60 radio spots on a top station can run anywhere from $4,000–8,000 in a major market such as New York or Chicago while the same package in a smaller market such as Green Bay, Wisconsin, or Topeka, Kansas, will run $500–1,500.

Outdoor

Outdoor advertising includes billboards, street displays such as ads in bus shelters, transit displays such as ads on buses or in airports, and alternative placements such as sporting events, shopping malls, and movie theaters.[18] Outdoor is an extremely sparse medium because in addition to being printed, the viewer only has a few seconds to see the billboard while driving by. Because of this, ad messages should be limited to six words or less and there should be a compelling graphic to draw attention to the ad.

Billboards come in three basic sizes: large (bulletin) 48' wide × 14' high; medium (30 sheet poster) 22' 8" wide × 10' 5" high; and small (8 sheet poster, junior billboard) 11' wide × 5' high. Billboards are rented by the month, and a large billboard can cost anywhere from $1,500–30,000 per month depending on market and location and is expected to generate 20,000–50,000 impressions per day. Lead times for billboards run about three weeks.[19]

The advantage of outdoor advertising is that it is intrusive—people will see it whether they want to or not. This makes it a solid choice for reminders and to create awareness around new or unsought products.

232

17.4 PUBLIC RELATIONS

The Public Relations Society of America defines **public relations** as a strategic communication process that builds mutually beneficial relationships between organizations and their publics.[20] This involves several management functions related to marketing, including managing public opinion, influencing public policy, and conducting programs to create an informed public necessary to the success of the organization's aims such as marketing objectives. Typical marketing objectives for public relations include introducing new products, influencing government legislation, and enhancing the image of the organization through community involvement, sponsorships, and crisis management.

Public relations (PR) recognizes that there are situations where the public wants information and will actively seek it out. For example, when it comes to new product introductions, the innovators and early adopters (Chapter 7.5) want to know what new products are coming out, so they can always have the newest gadget. From a negative perspective, when there is a serious problem with a company or its products, people will be looking for information about the problem. It would be better if the information came from the company responsible rather than from an outsider who may or may not have the company's best interest at heart.

As a result, PR communications appear unpaid in mass media channels. This gives the information greater credibility in the mind of the consumer as it looks more like news than like paid, sponsor-identified advertising. Mind you, it only appears to be unpaid. While we don't pay for the media exposure directly, there is an indirect cost. Creating the circumstances where unpaid media exposure will happen costs money. For example, inviting journalists to a press conference where refreshments are served and providing them with publication-ready collateral materials about a new product introduction will increase the chances that the new product introduction will be reported in the media. You have no control over where and how the product is reported.

PR has attracted increased attention in recent years as marketers realize that when the circumstances are appropriate, PR is a cost-effective means of achieving promotional objectives.

Public Relations Tools

Some of the tools marketers use to implement PR programs include publicity, media relations, and sponsorships. **Publicity** is any activity that results in unpaid mass communication. If the message being promoted is newsworthy, such as a new product introduction or even the launch of a new advertising campaign, a news release or press conference can make the information available to members of the media who will report it as they see fit. Understanding how each medium works will increase the chances of getting publicity. For example, local television news programs are always looking for compelling graphics that will look good on TV (this is why fires always get good local news coverage). Preparing a video news release with compelling video footage will make your announcement more attractive to local news editors. Even better, provide the video news release as a ready-to-run news story, and your announcement may be run as a news story without any editing.

Another approach to generating publicity is to hold a special event or "publicity stunt" designed to attract media attention. In one of the greatest publicity stunts of all time, on October 14, 2012, the Red Bull Stratos project had aeronaut Felix Baumgartner parachute to earth from 39 miles in the sky, becoming the first human to exceed the speed of sound in free fall as well as setting many other records.[21] All this on behalf of Red Bull® energy drink, whose slogan is: "Red Bull gives you wings."

The success of a publicity campaign is measured in terms of how much the coverage generated by publicity would have cost had it been in paid media. For example, if a special event gets coverage in the local newspaper and is a 30-second news story on local TV, how much would you have had to pay for a newspaper ad of similar size and a 30-second spot on local TV?

Media relations is the activities involved in working with the media to generate publicity for a product, service, or organization. This includes establishing contact with members of the media, providing publicity materials, and being available to answer any questions the media might have. There is an expectation today that a business will have information that might be of interest to a journalist or to the general public available online as part of the company's website. Company background should include such information as biographies of key people (people relate to other people, not to corporations), the company's history, product information, graphics and photos for use in stories, recent news releases, and a contact for further information. This way, the information is available 24/7 for journalists working under a deadline to get out a story.

Sponsorships are when a company makes a financial or in-kind contribution to an organization in exchange for public recognition of the company's association with the organization. Sponsored organizations could include sporting events, entertainment, not-for-profits, education, arts, and environmental causes, among others. The key to successful sponsorships is to have a good match between the organization sponsored and the objectives of the company. For example, Dick's® sporting goods sponsors local amateur athletic teams[22] while Microsoft® supports the ISTE® (International Society for Technology in Education).

17.5 GUERILLA MARKETING

Guerilla marketing is a term coined by Jay Levinson, an American business writer, in the 1980s. He defined the term as achieving conventional goals, such as profits and joy, with unconventional methods. In practice, that means investing creativity and energy instead of money. My own definition of guerilla marketing is 5¢ worth of money plus 95¢ worth of creativity equals $1 of impact. As such, it straddles the line between advertising and publicity and can be a powerful tool for small businesses or startups that are chronically short of money for promotion.

The typical guerilla marketing campaign identifies a location or a medium not normally considered for advertising and, therefore, available for a very low cost or even for free. Then a message is developed appropriate for that location. For example, Folger's® Coffee ran a guerilla campaign in New York City where it placed pictures of a cup of coffee over the city's manhole covers. People crossing the street would see big steaming cups of coffee in the street with the tagline: "Hey, city that never sleeps. Wake up. Folgers."[23] The image on the next page shows how the campaign creatively took advantage of the iconic steam that rises from New York City's district heating system

The downside of guerilla marketing is that it can actually be guerilla—unethical or even illegal. For example, hijacking is when an unauthorized company sets up a display near an event so as to appear to be a sponsor. The Olympics® has added measures to protect against hijacking after Samsung® set up a display in a parking lot outside of the Atlanta Olympic Games and generated more awareness than the official electronics sponsor whose display was set up inside the Olympic Park.[24] In another controversial guerilla campaign, the Cartoon Network® hung animated light boxes promoting characters from the show, *Aqua Teen Hunger Force*, from highway bridges in major cities.

FIGURE 17.2   Folger's Guerilla Ad (Source: http://www.puckett-associates.com/people/bill-puckett/.)

Drivers in Boston who didn't get the joke thought the blinking boxes were bombs, and traffic was shut down while the bomb squad investigated.[25] Some companies put advertising messages on sidewalks near major conventions. Although this is illegal, the companies believe the awareness created by the ads as well as the attendant publicity are worth the fines paid for cleaning up the graffiti.[26]

17.6 SALES PROMOTION

Sales promotion involves short-term marketing programs to stimulate trial, increase demand, or improve product availability. It is easier to define a sales promotion in terms of what it isn't rather than what it is. If it is a short-term program, and it isn't personal selling, advertising, or public relations then it is probably a sales promotion. Sales promotions can be targeted toward consumers as well as to the trade (B2B).

Consumer promotions center around deals and attention getters. **Deals** are discounts or other incentives designed to encourage customers to purchase the product. Deals would include coupons, online promo codes, sales, frequency or loyalty programs (i.e., buy ten, get one free), bonus packs or gifts, and rebates. Rebates are less expensive to offer than discounts because not everyone who purchases the product will follow through on the rebate. Attention getters are activities to increase awareness of the product. Common attention getters include premiums or promotional items (those giveaway trinkets with the company logo), sampling, contests, and in-store demonstrations, among others.

Trade promotions include everything used for consumer promotions as well as trade deals, sales incentives, and promotional support. Trade deals involve discounts or extra merchandise to make it attractive for the retailer to promote your product. The hope is that the retailer will use these concessions to increase consumer sales although some part will go to improving the retailer's bottom line. This is why sales promotions are frequently the largest part of a business's promotional budget. A five percent discount allocates five percent of sales to sales promotion.

Sales incentives are activities directed at a retailer's sales force to promote the sales of your product. Sales meetings, where a manufacturer's representative works with a retailer's sales, force increase awareness of the product and can provide training on the best ways to sell the product. Sales contests and incentive trips reward the salespeople who excel at moving your product. Push money, or "spiffs," are payments made by the manufacturer to the retailer's salespeople for selling the manufacturer's product on top of any compensation the salesperson has already received.

Promotional support is where the manufacturer works with the retailer to promote the product. Promotional support might include providing point of purchase displays or other display material, cooperative advertising, or other creative support. Slotting fees are paid by the manufacturer to get retail placement for the product. **Trade shows** are gatherings where manufacturers, distributors, and suppliers display their products and provide information to potential channel partners.

Product Placement, or embedded advertising, is the practice of using name brand products as props in entertainment vehicles, such as film or television. In some cases, the producer of the film will approach a manufacturer to allow the use of the brand in the film without any payment. In the film, *Castaway,* starring Tom Hanks, the crash of a FedEx® plane played a central role in the movie. FedEx agreed to allow the producers to use its name even though the product was involved in a disaster. More commonly, manufacturers will pay a producer to use their products in film. This has become an important source of financing for many film projects. Heineken® paid a reported $45 million to have James Bond drink beer rather than a martini in the film, *Skyfall* .[27]

The advantage of product placement is that the product is perceived as being used in a "natural" setting rather than in an advertisement. This bypasses the skepticism we use to filter messages when we know they are paid advertisements. In broadcast media subject to regulation by the Federal Communications Commission (FCC), payments for product placements fall under the sponsor identification rule which requires the sponsorship and the identity of the sponsor to be identified.[28]

Limitations

While sales promotions can be very effective at boosting sales over the short term, there is a downside to the practice. For one thing, customers can become "addicted" to sales promotions and learn not to buy from you unless there is a promotion in place. Many department store customers will ask if a particular product is going to be on sale in the near future before buying the product. In response, some retailers offer a low-price guarantee. If the product goes on sale after the purchase, the retailer will refund the difference to the customer.

There is also a concern that sales promotions encourage retailers to act in ways that aren't in the customer's best interest. Slotting fees limit the variety of new products available to customers. Push money encourages salespeople to steer customers toward the product with the biggest payment rather than helping the customer find the product that best meets his or her needs.

(ENDNOTES)

1. Othmar, James P., *Adland: Searching for the Meaning of Life on a Branded Planet,* New York: Anchor Books, 140.

2. http://www.webpagefx.com/blog/business-advice/the-cost-of-advertising-nationally-broken-down-by-medium/. Accessed September 7, 2015.

3. http://yourbusiness.azcentral.com/average-cost-national-advertising-campaigns-26091.html. Accessed September 7, 2015.

4. http://www.hallmark.com/commercials/. Accessed September 7, 2015.

5. Salimpoor, Valerie N., Mitchel Benovoy, Kevin Larcher, Alain Dagher, and Robert J. Zatorre, 2011, "Anatomically distinct dopamine release during anticipation and experience of peak emotion to music," *Nature Neuroscience* 14, 257–262.

6. McBair, Corey, 2017, *US Ad Spending: The eMarketer Forecast for 2017,* eMarketer Inc., www.emarketer.com.

7. http://www.nielsen.com/content/dam/corporate/us/en/newswire/uploads/2013/01/Consumer-Usage-Report-2012-FULL-SIZED.jpg. Accessed September 11, 2015.

8. http://www.tvweek.com/tvbizwire/2014/05/how-many-minutes-of-commercial/. Accessed September 11, 2015.

9. http://smallbusiness.chron.com/much-television-advertising-really-cost-58718.html. Accessed September 11, 2015.

10. http://www.latimes.com/entertainment/envelope/cotown/la-et-ct-17-channels-nielsen-20140506-story.html. Accessed September 11, 2015.

11. http://smallbusiness.chron.com/buy-ad-cable-tv-40549.html. Accessed September 11, 2015

12. http://www.nielsen.com/us/en/insights/news/2011/factsheet-the-u-s-media-universe.html. Accessed September 11, 2015.

13. http://www.nielsen.com/us/en/insights/news/2011/40-of-tablet-and-smartphone-owners-use-them-while-watching-tv.html.

14. http://www.journalism.org/2015/04/29/state-of-the-news-media-2015/. Accessed September 14, 2015.

15. http://www.webpagefx.com/blog/business-advice/the-cost-of-advertising-nationally-broken-down-by-medium/. Accessed September 14, 2015.

16. http://www.webpagefx.com/blog/business-advice/the-cost-of-advertising-nationally-broken-down-by-medium/. Accessed September 14, 2015.

17. http://www.nielsen.com/us/en/insights/reports/2014/state-of-the-media-audio-today-2014.html. Accessed September 14, 2015.

18. https://www.oaaa.org/Portals/0/Images/2015%20Number%20of%20Displays.jpg. Accessed September 14, 2015.

19. http://www.bluelinemedia.com/billboard-advertising. Accessed September 14, 2015.

20. http://www.prsa.org/aboutprsa/publicrelationsdefined/#.VfdcNJdEJ6I. Accessed September 16, 2015.
21. http://www.redbullstratos.com/. Accessed September 16, 2015.
22. http://dsgcommunity.sponsorport.com/. Accessed September 16, 2015.
23. http://www.puckett-associates.com/people/bill-puckett/. Accessed September 16, 2015.
24. http://www.performanceresearch.com/olympic-sponsorship-atlanta.htm. Accessed September 16, 2015.
25. http://www.washingtonpost.com/wp-dyn/content/article/2007/01/31/AR2007013101958.html. Accessed September 16, 2015.
26. http://www.sfgate.com/business/article/Blue-Wolf-defies-San-Francisco-graffiti-ban-at-6507124.php. Accessed September 16, 2015.
27. http://www.livescience.com/24957-james-bond-product-placement.html. Accessed September 16, 2015.
28. http://www.commlawcenter.com/2010/09/product-placement-and-the-fcc.html. Accessed September 16, 2015.

238

PERSONAL SELLING AND SALES MANAGEMENT

CH 18

Personal selling is the most important skill we will cover in this text. From a career perspective, personal selling skills are critical. It is estimated that 60% of all business majors and 80% of all marketing majors will spend at least part of their careers in a professional selling situation.[1]

From a personal perspective, selling skills are an important part of life. At its most basic, selling is persuading other people to do what you want them to do. Everybody is selling all the time. Are you trying to convince your boss you deserve a promotion and a raise? That's a selling situation. Did you promise your friend you would help move into a new apartment but no longer want to? Another selling situation. Are you thinking of asking someone out on a date? You guessed it, that's personal selling. Oh, yes, if you've been inside a car dealership trying to decide whether or not to buy a new car, that's a selling situation too.

18.1 TWO APPROACHES TO SELLING

Even though there are good career opportunities in personal selling, and even though most business majors will be involved with selling over the course of their careers, few business majors look forward to a career in selling. Why? Because for most of us, when we think of a salesperson, we think of someone who is greedy, pushy, fast-talking, aggressive, slick, egotistical, and generally annoying.

The good news is that this style of selling is not the norm. Most salespeople are decent human beings who take care of their families, are active in their community, and are kind to animals. **Personal selling** involves face-to-face interaction in order to assist and/or persuade a potential customer to buy a product or service. With rare exceptions, the goal is to create win-win situations where both the seller and the buyer benefit from the transaction.

With this in mind, there are two basic approaches to selling: high-pressure selling and consultative selling.

High-Pressure Selling

High-pressure selling, or the "hard sell," is the approach most likely to feed negative stereotypes of salespeople. With **high-pressure selling** the salesperson attempts to control the sales interaction and pressures the customer to make an immediate purchase. While this approach is becoming less and less common, there are still situations where the high-pressure approach is still used. Why? Because it works.

You are likely to find high-pressure tactics used with unsought goods (Chapter 8.3), in situations where there is a high information differential between the buyer and the seller, and with infrequent or postponable purchases. With unsought goods such as life insurance or magazine subscriptions, the assumption is that customers need to be convinced and if left to their own devices, would not buy the product or would not buy enough of the product. When there is a high information differential between buyer and seller, the push for an immediate sale limits the customer's ability to research the product. For example, when you buy a new car, you have a good sense of what a reasonable retail price for the car might be and what the dealer paid for the car. However, when you are buying a used car, you don't know how much the dealer paid for the car, and the retail price depends on mileage and condition of the specific car.

For infrequent purchases, say buying new furniture or getting new carpet, there is less of a chance for repeat purchases, so the lifetime value of the customer is limited to this one transaction. With no expectation of future business, the high-pressure salesperson knows that if the customer leaves, the opportunity to make the sale is gone forever. The customer will either buy somewhere else or simply decide not to buy. Similarly, with postponable purchases such as replacing kitchen appliances or an older car, the perception is that customers have already decided to buy, they just need help following through with the transaction.

When a salesperson has no expectation of future business, there is less of an incentive to treat the customer fairly.

Consultative Selling

Consultative selling (sometimes called need-satisfaction selling, relationship selling, or adaptive selling) is the "good" sales approach. With **consultative selling**, the salesperson acts as an expert consultant, working with the customer to develop the best solution to the customer's problem even if the best solution doesn't include the salesperson's product. When the customer realizes the salesperson is more interested in the customers' success than in "making the sale," they are more likely to trust the recommendation when the solution does include the salesperson's product. This approach is widely used in B2B markets and in consumer markets where there is an expectation of repeat business for a job well done. The rest of this chapter will focus on consultative selling.

18.2 SELLING AS A CAREER

A friend applying for a sales position wrote, "I like sales because at the end of each day, you know exactly where you stand. I wish life were more like that." He got the job. For many people, sales is a satisfying career because it calls on your people skills and because you have the ability to influence your earnings. The two distinguishing features of sales jobs are performance-based compensation and dealing with rejection.

Most sales jobs have performance-based compensation, meaning how much you earn depends on how much you sell. A **commission** is the payment made to a salesperson according to a fixed formula, usually a percentage of sales. At one extreme, 100% commission means you only get paid when you sell something. As selling situations become more complicated and the link between a single person's effort and the resulting sale are less clear, the compensation package may include a guaranteed minimum salary and an additional bonus or commission if performance targets are met. Many salespeople have a sales quota, or an expected level of performance, that relates to their compensation.

The other distinguishing characteristic is dealing with rejection. In field sales, 80% of sales are made after five or more contacts with the customer.[2] This means that if you hear four people say "no" for every person who says "yes," that would be a pretty good day. A significant part of selling and sales management is motivation. One sales manager chose to read the children's book *Green Eggs and Ham* by Dr. Seuss at a sales meeting to encourage salespeople to be persistent. In that book, the main character overcomes a series of objections in order to get the customer to realize that he likes the product.

The Role of the Salesperson

There are four basic roles of salespeople: transaction creation, new customer development, customer support, and market research. The primary role is to create transactions. The goal of a sales team is to have the salesperson spend as much time meeting with customers in order to generate new business and as little time as possible on administrative functions. Commissions are based on completed transactions, and in situations where commissions are a major part of the compensation package, it can be a challenge to get salespeople to invest their time in some of the other functions.

In some industries, such as pharmaceuticals, it is impossible for a salesperson to make a sale during the sales call. In these situations, the role of the salesperson or detail salesperson is to make "missionary" sales calls to keep the product fresh in the customer's mind. By calling on doctors to let them know the therapies available, there is a better chance the doctor will prescribe your product if a patient requires it.

New customer development is critical for the growth of a business. There will always be some customer attrition because of changing business circumstances or competitor activity. Before you can grow your business, you will need to replace lost sales with new customers. It takes more effort to generate sales from new customers than it does to renew sales from existing customers, so special attention needs to be paid to identifying and building relationships with potential customers.

Customer support is all about what happens after the sale. This includes working with the customer to make sure the product is performing as expected and resolving any problems that might arise. This is especially important in B2B selling where the relationship is more important than a specific transaction. In addition to making sure things are working out after the sale, salespeople working with the customer are in a good position to anticipate when future sales opportunities might open up.

Because they are continually calling on customers and dealing with competitor's attempts to win business from them, salespeople are a good source of market information. They are likely to be one of the first to hear about competitors' new products or marketing programs, as well as customers' response to those programs. By working closely with their customers, they have a sense of what general business conditions look like in an industry. Salespeople are unlikely to take time away from selling to report on market conditions unless this responsibility is built into the compensation package.

"Even though our current generation is really, really into social, they don't understand how to apply it toward business and get to know companies and flirt with them"

Neil Cohen

Inside vs. Outside Sales

There are two major types of sales jobs: inside sales and outside sales. With inside sales, the customer comes to your place of business (or is contacted by telephone), and with outside sales, you go to the customer's place of business.

Inside sales usually refers to outbound telemarking although store-based retail sales can considered inside selling. With inside sales, the transactions are smaller, and, therefore, the pay is less than with outside sales. The average retail salesperson earned just over $22,600 in 2016.[3] Inside sales operations will have on-site supervisors and clerical support to assist with the selling process. Because the customer comes to you, either in person or by phone, there is no travel involved other than the commute, and it is easier to have regular working hours. By regular, we mean predictable, not necessarily convenient. You will need to work at times the customer is available, so evening and weekend hours are par for the course.

With outside sales (or field sales), the salesperson travels to the customer. Transactions and compensation are larger for outside sales. The average cost of a field sales call in 2013 was just over $500. It takes an average of five sales calls to complete a sale, so we're talking around $2,500 to generate a sale.[4] This means the transaction has to have a potential profit well above $2,500 to justify the effort. As the transactions are larger, it is no surprise the pay is higher for outside sales, averaging more than $57,000 in 2016.[5]

Travel is required for outside sales. One thing to look for when considering an outside sales job is how many nights of travel are expected per week. Four nights of travel means you hit the road Monday morning and don't get back until Friday night. Because of the travel, there is less supervision of field sales reps. Recent developments in cloud computing and mobile communications allow for "digital" clerical support while traveling.

Team Selling

The common perception of selling is that of a "lone wolf" salesperson where one person manages the entire relationship with the customer. The problem is that very few people are good at everything. This is why many companies use a team approach to selling. Rather than having a single salesperson, a group of people work together to serve the customer. The sales process is unbundled to allow each person on the team to play to his or her strengths. For example, a person who is great at building relationships can generate leads but may not be very good at following up with the customer after the sale. A person who is very detail oriented can be good at follow-up service but may not be very good at generating new leads.

This approach has advantages for both sales managers and for prospective salespeople. From a manager's perspective, building a sales team increases the pool of qualified applicants. Rather than looking only for people good at everything, the manager can hire people with complementary talents to complete the team. From the applicant's point of view, you can focus on how your talents will strengthen the team rather than trying to pretend you are good at everything. One of the issues in team selling is developing a compensation package. It can be difficult to determine exactly how much each person on the team contributed to the sale, so it is a challenge to pay commissions to each individual on the team. Some combination of team-level incentive is appropriate.

In consumer marketing, sales teams might include telemarketers or a social media manager to help generate leads and a call center for follow-up customer service and processing transactions. In many high-ticket sales situations such as cars or furniture, the sales manager may act as a "closer" to help the floor salesperson with negotiations.

In B2B markets, team selling is common. Many industrial products are too complex for one person to have all of the expertise to complete a deal. Specialists help out at various stages of the process. Sales cycles in B2B markets can be very long, sometimes, a year or even longer. A **sales cycle** is the time it takes to complete the sale, starting with the first contact with the customer and ending with the purchase agreement. A sales team can provide continuity if there are personnel changes during the sales process.

18.3 THE SALES PROCESS

A typical **sales process** involves six stages: prospecting, pre-approach, approach, presentation, close, and follow-up. The amount of effort put into each stage depends on the selling situation. For example, a salesperson working in a furniture store may have a few moments from the time a customer walks into the store until the approach while a field salesperson will spend significant amounts of time on prospecting and the pre-approach stage.

Prospecting

Prospecting is the process of identifying and qualifying potential customers. This involves identifying potential customers, or "leads," and then qualifying them, or determining if the prospect has the willingness, financial capability, and authority to make the purchase.

In a traditional corporate setting, marketing's responsibility is to generate qualified leads for the sales team to pursue. For example, the marketing team may set up a booth at a trade show to collect names and company information of those who stop by the booth. Or the company might publish a white paper, or report, about a product and ask for an email address from anyone downloading the report Chapter 19.6). These would be leads, or people who have expressed an interest in the product. Then these leads would be qualified, or screened, to make sure they have the ability to make a purchase before asking a salesperson to meet with the prospect.

Having identified a qualified prospect, the next step is to create an opportunity to make a sales presentation. Usually this involves making an appointment for the sales rep to meet with the customer.

Pre-Approach

The pre-approach phase involves collecting information and planning the strategy to take when making the presentation. The effort put into this stage is a function of time available and the size of the potential sale. In a B2B situation, you should be aware of all publicly available information about the company and the person you will be meeting with. If this is a repeat customer, you should be aware of the company's purchasing history and any problems the customer may have had with your product in the past. Finally, it is helpful if you know some personal information about the prospect. Knowing the client's marital status, whether there are children in the household, college affiliation, interest in sports, or other hobbies will help make a personal connection with the prospect.

Approach

The goal of the approach, or initial contact, with the prospect is to create rapport and to clarify the roles for the meeting. The evaluation of your product also involves an evaluation of the source (Chapter 2.2), so it is important to establish that you are someone who can be trusted. Prospects won't be comfortable with your product if they aren't comfortable with you as a person. Some salespeople use humor as a way of "breaking the ice" while others find spending a little time talking about what is happening in the person's life is a way to establish rapport. It is a mistake to start "selling" before the prospect is comfortable with you and your role as a salesperson.

Over time, as the business relationship develops, it is not uncommon for buyers and sellers to become friends who actually look forward to the occasional sales call.

Presentation

The presentation is your opportunity to demonstrate how your product will solve the customer's problem. There are three formats for a sales presentation: stimulus-response, formula, and need satisfaction. Stimulus response is used in retail selling and for "up selling," or encouraging customers to increase the size of the purchase or to make additional related purchases. With stimulus-response, salespeople are trained to recognize specific cues or stimuli and to offer the customer a product in response. The classic example of stimulus-response selling is: "Do you want fries with that?" Formula selling, or a "canned presentation," is where the salesperson works from a script. This approach is common in telemarketing and as a training tool for new salespeople.

Rather than offering a specific solution, as in stimulus-response or formula presentation, consultative selling requires a need-satisfaction approach. This involves asking questions to uncover needs and then working with the customer to develop a solution. A combination of open-ended questions to identify areas of opportunity and closed-end questions, or "probes," to clarify specific issues will help develop a good understanding of the prospect's situation. The better your understanding of the prospects' needs, the better your chances of satisfying them.

When it is clear you have uncovered all of the needs, it is time to develop solutions. Hopefully, your product will be part of the solution. Remember, 80% of sales are made after at least five sales calls, so not all solutions will involve a sale. As you present the advantages of using your product, the prospect will ask questions. These are objections or concerns the prospect may have about the proposed solution. You handle the objection by restating the question to make sure you understand what the concern is. If the concern is about a fact, it is a misunderstanding that can be cleared up with information.

248 Close

Closing is the process of converting prospects into customers. This is where you ask the prospect to do what you want them to do. ChangingMinds.org offers 71 different closing techniques (http://changingminds.org/disciplines/sales/closing/closing_techniques.htm). Always ask for the order. Don't hint. If you don't ask the prospect for the order, you have made the decision for them. Think about it. The worst that could happen is that the prospect would say no. If you don't ask for the order, there is a 100% chance that the answer is no.

Follow-Up

After the sale has been made, the relationship with the customer continues to develop. The salesperson will follow up with the customer to make sure that the product was delivered on time and is performing as expected. This post-purchase service builds trust and makes it easier for the customer to make a repeat purchase. Also, staying in touch with the customer after the sale is a good source of market information. In addition to knowing the timing of repeat purchases, the salesperson might identify opportunities to sell additional products to the customer.

> "They want to be able to measure every single impression, measure every single action that drives the user to actually convert"
>
> **Kevin Heung**

18.4 SALES MANAGEMENT

There are two aspects to sales management: sales force strategy and sales force management. Sales force strategy looks at the role of personal selling in the overall promotional mix and customer coverage. For a consumer packaged goods company, the primary emphasis may be on mass-market communications to develop brand awareness with the end user while personal selling deals with relationships with other members of the distribution channel. On the other hand, for a manufacturer of shipping containers selling to other businesses, personal selling may be the primary element of the promotional mix.

Customer Coverage

Customer coverage deals with how often salespeople should be calling on customers. Here the 80–20 rule comes into play (80% of your business comes from 20% of your customers). You want to be sure that the 20% of you customers who do most of your business are well taken care of. On the other end of the spectrum, you have the 80% of your customers who do 20% of your business. You want to make sure you don't lose money serving these smaller customers.

To deal with this issue, many businesses classify customers in terms of "A," "B," and "C" accounts. "A" accounts are the 20% who do most of the business with you. You might want salespeople to call on these accounts quarterly or even monthly. "B" accounts are customers and prospects with the potential to become high-volume customers. These are the accounts you would want your sales force to pursue in order to generate new business. "C" accounts are smaller customers who do not have the potential to become high-volume customers. You might service these accounts online or through a call center to minimize the cost. A salesperson would only call on one of these accounts if a situation comes up that can't be handled otherwise.

In order to meet these varying requirements, salespeople are assigned a number of accounts as their sales territory. From a salesperson's perspective, "A" accounts are the primary source of income, and "C" accounts cost more to call on than they are worth. "B" accounts represent an opportunity for the salesperson to increase sales in the territory.

The sales manager's job is to create territories where the number of "A" accounts is small enough that the salesperson can call on them regularly yet large enough that the salesperson has a big enough book of business to earn a living—but not a great living. You want your salespeople to be "hungry," or willing to work hard to boost their income. There should be enough "B" accounts in a territory, so a salesperson who develops new business will make a good living. "C" accounts should be distributed fairly so no one person bears the burden of calling on these accounts.

Sales Force Management

Sales force management covers a wide range of issues including recruitment and selection, assimilation, training, motivation, compensation, supervision, and performance evaluation.

Recruitment and selection involves the hiring of new salespeople. Turnover in many sales jobs is high, so sales managers are always on the lookout for good people. The goal is to have a large pool of potential applicants so that when an opening occurs, there are people ready to step in.

Not all applicants will make good salespeople. Some don't have the aptitude, and others don't have the temperament to make successful salespeople. The selection process is intended to screen out applicants unlikely to be successful. This might include a combination of aptitude testing, shadowing existing salespeople, and pre-employment tasks.

Assimilation is the process of getting the new hire familiar with the procedures and the culture of the sales organization. The recruit will need to understand the dress code, how to interact with colleagues, support staff, and managers, and the other "unwritten rules" in order to be effective.

Training is a significant cost center in sales management. There is the cost of the initial sales training for the new hire as well as ongoing training to improve technique and to expand the number of products the salesperson can deal with. Some companies see the initial sales training as critical to success in the organization and hire inexperienced sales people, or "green peas," so they can be trained to the company's standards. Other companies prefer to hire experienced salespeople from other companies. This saves the cost of initial training for the experienced rep, but the experienced rep might move again if another firm makes an even better offer. When these experienced salespeople are hired away from a competitor, or "poached," it can create ill will between the competing firms.

Motivation is an important part of the sales manager's job. Salespeople should be happy and hungry. Even highly successful salespeople deal with rejection every day and can use some emotional support. Under-performing salespeople need to understand how their efforts can improve their financial situation.

Most sales compensation packages are performance based, and salespeople will do whatever earns them the most money. This doesn't necessarily mean that salespeople are greedy; money is how you keep score in sales. There is a trade-off between guaranteed income (salary) and performance-based compensation (commission). Most compensation packages have some of both. The higher the proportion of salary, the more control you have over the salesperson's activity, but they are not as "hungry," or having to work hard, to make sales in order to earn the income they desire. The higher the proportion of commission, the more effort salespeople will put into generating transactions; however, they may be reluctant to perform some of the other roles expected of the salesperson such as market research, calling on "C" accounts, or reporting.

Sales supervision involves working with the salesperson to set goals and to develop skills. Many sales managers will accompany salespeople on sales calls to monitor progress and to show, by example, how to work with accounts.

Performance evaluation looks at sales results as well as other things such as activities that generate new sales, opening new accounts, non-sales-related activity, such as training or attending sales meetings, and reporting on what is happening in the field. The performance metrics should be tied to the compensation package so that it is in the salesperson's interest to perform appropriately on all activities.

(ENDNOTES)

1. Agnihotri, Raj, Leff Bonney, Andrea Leigh Dixon, Robert Erffmeyer, Ellen Bolman Pullins, Jane Z. Sojka, and Vicki West, 2014, "Developing a Stakeholder Approach for Recruiting Top-Level Sales Students," *Journal of Marketing Education* 36 (1) 75–86.
2. http://www.smartcompany.com.au/marketing/sales/15046-20100611-how-many-calls-should-it-take-to-make-a-sale.html. Accessed September 21, 2015.
3. http://money.usnews.com/careers/best-jobs/retail-salesperson. Accessed May 29, 2018.
4. http://ultimatelead.com/2013/11/04/cost-b2b-sales-call/. Accessed September 21, 2015.
5. https://money.usnews.com/careers/best-jobs/sales-representative. Accessed May 29, 2018.

DIGITAL MARKETING

CH 19

The world has gone digital. This is especially true for the Marketing profession where technology has affected marketing at all levels of the organization. In addition to being a platform for e-commerce, marketers see digital, social media, and mobile marketing as a means of facilitating individual expression, as a decision support tool, and a source of market intelligence[1]. And the explosion in marketing technology products has supported this prediction. In 2011, MARTECH Today® identified 150 marketing technology products. By early 2016, there were nearly 4,000 products on the market[2]. It is estimated that the CMO of an enterprise-level organization deals with 28 different marketing technology solutions[3].

It's not just CMO's who deal with marketing technology. Digital marketing is essential for entry-level marketers as well. A Walker Sands study found that more than half (53%) of entry-level marketers had led a martech purchasing decision in the last three years[4].

The point is, if you are a young person embarking on a marketing career, it is expected that you will have some familiarity with digital marketing. This is one area where youth can be an advantage.

19.1 WHAT IS DIGITAL MARKETING?

We define **digital marketing** as any technology-mediated marketing activity. This includes marketing using digital channels of communication such as social media, internet, and mobile devices; e-commerce; and computer-assisted marketing activity such as automated marketing, programmatic advertising, and marketing analytics (Chapter 4.3).

More importantly, digital marketing is marketing. While new media and new technologies offer new and improved ways to connect with customers, they are not an end in and of themselves. There needs to be a solid strategy driving the overall marketing program. Digital marketing is an increasingly important element of a comprehensive marketing strategy, but without focus and direction, it can be a waste of money. This is part of the lesson we learned from the dot com bust in the early 2000's when anything internet was funded because it was cool. Around that time, I remember meeting with a 19-year-old young man who was entering college as a marketing major. He had been CEO of an internet startup, had burned through $5 million in venture capital and all he had left to show for it was his Jaguar (a luxury car). After all that, he felt it would be a good idea to learn about marketing.

Omni-Channel Marketing

As the number of options for reaching consumers increases, the marketing discipline has moved from the idea of "channel silos," where a distinct strategy was developed for each marketing channel, i.e., an in-store strategy, a television advertising strategy, and internet marketing strategy; to an integrated marketing strategy. The idea behind **omni-channel marketing** is to create a seamless customer experience regardless of which channel or device a customer uses to interact with the brand. This approach includes traditional marketing activity in addition to digital marketing.

In their marketing blog, HubSpot describes Disney's omni-channel approach for visitors to its theme parks. A family thinking of visiting the happiest place on earth starts the journey by visiting Disney's mobile-friendly trip planning site. Once the trip is booked, they use the My Disney Experience tool to plan the trip from where to dine to securing the FastPass+ (a virtual queuing system). In the park, the mobile app helps navigate through the park and estimates wait times for the various attractions. Finally, the Magic Band is a hotel room key, stores pictures taken in the park with characters, can be used order food, and integrates the FastPass+. All one seamless customer experience[5].

"A lot of places are moving toward connecting real life with digital life"

Marketing Professional

Advantages of Digital Marketing

Why is digital marketing such a big deal? The answer is digital has some significant advantages over traditional marketing. The cost of reaching an audience through digital media is a lot lower than with traditional media. Unlike television advertising, where the major expense is air time—or access to the distribution network; it costs very little to gain access to the internet. This allows you to put more resources in the content of the message rather than in buying access. This also reduces the overhead needed for a small startup find its market.

Another advantage of digital marketing is its immediacy. Customers have access to your brand 24/7 and you get instant feedback on your marketing activity. I was creating a YouTube channel for this book and was getting feedback before I had finished posting the second video. This immediacy allows for **optimization** of digital marketing activities. Optimization is a process that involves using customer feedback to make continuous incremental improvements to improve the effectiveness of your marketing activity.

A/b testing is a common approach used for optimization. With a/b testing, you post at least two versions of your marketing message and let the audience response tell you which is best. Dozens, or even hundreds of a/b tests can help optimize every aspect of the message: copy, content, color, graphics … you name it.

Unlike traditional media, which are based on one-way communication; digital media allow for interactivity. Rather than trying to plan the entire marketing campaign in advance, it is important to allow for customer feedback. They will help you decide which approach works best for them.

Finally, digital media support behavioral segmentation. In traditional market segmentation schemes, demographic information is the most common approach because we know who our customers are, but we can't see what they are doing. In the digital arena, it is just the opposite. Much online tracking is anonymous and based on cookie (small tracking programs embedded in websites) data. So we don't know who our customers are, but we do know what they've been doing.

In the remainder of this chapter, we'll look at some of the major elements of a digital marketing program: the website, content marketing, search engine marketing, social media marketing, email marketing, mobile marketing, and automated marketing.

19.2 THE WEBSITE

A website is a critical element of any digital marketing program. There many roles the website can play depending on your overall strategy, but a permanent online presence is the hub for digital activity. The home page should express your strategy and is a starting point for the user experience. The quality of the site, in terms of content and relevant key words, is important in improving organic search rankings (19.4).

In e-commerce, the home page is the storefront, signaling the shopping experience to be had.

In addition to the home page, the website may contain several sister, or subordinate sites linked to the home page. This is where the user experience comes to life. Both the ease of navigation and the ability to direct customers to relevant content all play role in user interaction and user experience (UI and UX). A customer should be able to find relevant content in a subordinate site quickly by navigating from the home page.

A good website gives you a place to send customers who respond to other marketing activities. There should be a page directly related to every call-to-action (CTA) in your campaign. If an email campaign includes a link to participate in a webinar, there should be a page explaining what the webinar is about and providing an opportunity to sign up. Rather than taking you to the home page, the link should take you directly to the subordinate page explaining the webinar. This "deep landing" makes it easier for the customer to comply with your request. If the link took you to the home page, there would be several extra clicks before you got to the webinar site. Each extra click is an opportunity for the customer to lose interest. For an e-commerce site, a banner ad featuring red tennis shoes should take the customer directly to the page featuring red tennis shoes.

Conversion, or the point at which the subject of a marketing message performs the desired action, is an important metric in evaluating the effectiveness of digital marketing activities. In an email campaign, a conversion might mean the customer opened the email. Another conversion might be that the customer clicked on a link to your website. Another conversion might be that the customer actually participated in the webinar. The idea is to measure each step of the buyer's journey to identify strengths and weaknesses of the campaign. Conversion is a common KPI (key performance indicator) in digital marketing.

19.3 CONTENT MARKETING

Relevant content is the fuel that makes digital marketing work. Regardless of the platform or medium, people online are looking for something to engage with. That something may be a video, it may be a product, it may be the answer to a question, it may be something to share with friends; whatever it is, the solution to their problem lies in the content they find. The two most common goals for content are education and entertainment. In a B2B setting, education might be the primary goal; while entertainment might be the goal for a consumer oriented site. Actually, a little of both never hurts.

Context is an important consideration in whether or not content is relevant. A person leaving a party at 3:00 in the morning might find a mobile ad for a nearby all-night pizza parlor to be relevant. A recruiter doing a background check on a potential job applicant might find the pizza ad to be irrelevant.

Common vehicles for online content include video, blogs, white papers, and product information. Content can be owned or earned. Owned content is content you create. It is important to keep developing fresh content to keep people engaged with your program. Earned content, or user-generated content, is provided by users. When users post content to the web, it has more credibility than when the marketer creates the content. In e-commerce, customer ratings are an important form of earned content.

One way to reduce the cost of developing fresh content is to re-purpose it for different channels and for different audiences. For example, a research project might lead to the publication of a white paper (a research paper that is not subject to peer review) in a trade journal. Then the paper could be posted online to reach those who don't subscribe to the journal. In addition, an infographic could be created from the white paper as another form of content. Then perhaps, a webinar allowing prospective customers to interact around the white paper. Finally, a series of blog postings could highlight different elements of the paper.

19.4 SEARCH ENGINE MARKETING

Search engine marketing (SEM) is a powerful way to reach customers. The reason is simple. When people use a search engine such as Google or Bing, they are searching with intent, i.e., they are looking for something specific. They are telling you what is relevant to them in that moment. There are two approaches to search engine marketing: paid search and organic search. Paid search and organic search complement each other. Paid search can drive traffic to your site, improving organic results; while having both sponsored and organic results showing on the same page increases the impact of the listing.

Paid Search

Paid search, or "pay-per-click" involves creating clickable ads and paying to have them displayed in the sponsored listings. These listings are created dynamically when a person searches for a specific term. The advantage of paid search is that you have control over when your ad is displayed. This is especially important for new products where the goal is to create awareness of the new product because customers can't search for something they don't know exists (Chapter 2.2). With paid search, you can introduce your product to people who might find it relevant based on the context of their search.

There are two major components to a paid search campaign: selecting the appropriate search terms (known as key words) and designing clickable ads appropriate for the terms you have selected.

Key Word Selection

Key word selection is an art as well as a science. The goal is to identify search terms likely to be used by people who might be interested in what you have to offer. If the key words are too broad, you will attract clicks from people who aren't interested in your offering, wasting money. If your key words are too specific, you might not get enough clicks. A typical AdWords (Google's paid search application) campaign may involve selecting dozens, hundreds, thousands, even millions of search terms to support your overall strategy. Google has a "keyword planner" tool to guide you through the process of selecting search terms for your campaign: https://adwords.google.com/KeywordPlanner.

After selecting the appropriate search terms, you need to buy the right to have your ad served when a person searches for the term you have selected. This is done through an auction process. You establish how much you would be willing to pay for a particular term and establish a daily maximum you are willing to pay. Depending on how many other people are trying to use the term it may cost from a few cents to several dollars for each click. The average cost per click in AdWords is around one or two dollars[6].

This is not the end of the process. Because you get real-time feedback on the effectiveness of your search terms, there is a continuous process of tweaking the list to improve, or optimize, the performance of your list. This is an area where a/b testing can really pay off.

> "I really appreciate the startup community and the opportunity that you get—being able to move up quickly based on how hard you work—versus the old-style corporations where you had to climb the corporate ladder."
>
> **Felicia Terwilliger**

Creating the Ads

Having successfully purchased a great search term, you need to design a clickable ad related to that particular term. Again, relevance is the magic ingredient. You know what term the person is searching for and you know what your offering is. You want to design an ad that will be attractive to a potential customer. The goal is conversion—to entice the customer to click on the ad. It is important to be as specific as possible with the ad because you don't want to attract (and pay for) clicks from people who have no interest in your offering. It is also important for the ad to lead to a deep landing—to take the customer directly to the part of the website related to the offer.

Just as there may be thousands of key words in your list, there may be tens of thousands of ads to support the campaign. It is not uncommon to develop multiple ads for each key word selected. This is an opportunity to leverage content you have developed to support the brand. Different features or different graphics can be used to develop alternative versions of the same ad. This is another area where a/b testing is helpful. By continuously tweaking the content of the ads, you are optimizing their effectiveness.

Fraud is becoming a significant issue in search engine marketing. Unscrupulous website operators will generate "click bait" style copy that encourages people to click on ads through misleading or sensational "come-ons". Stacking, or serving multiple ads at the same place, means that a person may click on several ads that are not even visible to the person. The Media Ratings Council (http://mediaratingcouncil.org/) is an industry group that develops standards for what it means for an ad to have been seen.

Retargeting

Retargeting is a follow-up approach to search advertising. Rather than serving ads based on a person's search terms, ads are served based on the person's prior online activity. When a person visits your website (either by clicking on an ad, or through an online search) a tracking cookie, called a pixel, embedded in the website tracks the person's online activity. The fact that they visited your site indicates a certain level of interest. As a consequence, ads that retarget a person who has already visited your site have a higher conversion rate than search ads.

Organic Search

Organic search refers to the websites that appear as unpaid responses to a search term. The purpose of a search engine is to deliver relevant content to users and it is important that the organic results are useful to the user. Getting good placement in organic search results is important because 90% of clicks go to the organic rather than to the sponsored links, and 90% of Google searchers don't go past the first page of results[7].

Search engine optimization (SEO) refers to activity designed to improve your website's rankings in the unpaid search results. Search engine operators are continually revising the criteria they use to rank search listings to improve their relevance to their users. The actual criteria are a tightly guarded secret. Marketers, keep trying to figure out what the criteria are in order to improve their organic results. Figure 19.1 shows one such estimate developed by Open Umbrella (openumbrella.org). Based on analysis of 182 websites, they estimate that the two most important criteria for determining search rankings are the number and quality of the links to the site (30%) and fresh content (23%).

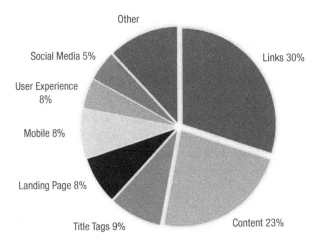

FIGURE 19.1   Factors that Improve Organic Search Rankings

By paying attention to these criteria, marketers can improve their organic results. Moz, an online search agency, offers an excellent "Beginner's Guide to SEO," https://moz.com/beginners-guide-to-seo.

19.5 SOCIAL MEDIA, EMAIL, AND MOBILE MARKETING

Social media, email, and mobile are three important channels of communication in the digital environment. Each channel has unique characteristics that impact the content used to reach customers.

Social Media Marketing

With mistrust of business increasing following the financial crisis of 2007–2009, consumers are increasingly turning to word of mouth as a form of advertising they can trust. 90% of consumers trust recommendations from people they know and 70% of consumers believe in customer opinions posted online[8]. This is why social media has become such an important element in digital marketing. It is the online analog of word of mouth communication.

Merriam-Webster defines **social media** as "forms of electronic communication (such as Web sites) through which people create online communities to share information, ideas, personal messages, etc.[9]" The key distinction between social media and other forms of communication is people sharing information with other people. When a friend likes something on Facebook, it is much more believable than a claim made by an advertiser.

From a marketing perspective, the goal in social media marketing is to get people to share content rather than to consume content. When a person re-tweets something to their network, the tweet takes on a whole new level of credibility. So what makes content shareable? Andy Wiedlin suggests four approaches to developing shareable content: Identity, heart, nostalgia, and humor[10].

Identity content highlights a person's sense of self. For example, a cartoon that expresses the frustration of introverted people living in a land of extroverts is likely to be appreciated and shared by people who are introverted. Heart isn't about the organ that pumps blood through your body, it's about content that is uplifting or inspirational. Nostalgia content helps people remember some of the good times in their past. Humor … well humor is supposed to be funny.

Sometimes social media content is so shareable that it goes viral. That means it is spread rapidly through the web through social media platforms. Good viral content can reach an audience of millions in days, or even hours. For example, on May 19, 2016, Candace Payne posted a video of herself laughing while wearing a Chewbacca (a character from the Star Wars movie franchise) mask. Within five days, it had garnered 140 million views, making it the most viewed Facebook Live video in Facebook's history[11].

While the goal of every marketer is to create content that goes viral, it isn't that easy. You can't predict which combination of content and circumstances will make a particular work take off. You can, however, improve your chances by making sure your content is shareable and relevant to your target audience.

Email Marketing

Email is a medium that allows you to develop relationships with customers. Unlike search advertising, you are directly communicating with a person known to you. This is especially important in B2B marketing where sales cycles can take months or even years. The two key issues in email marketing are developing and maintaining the list of email addresses, and developing effective emails.

A successful email campaign depends on having the email addresses from prospective customers and having permission to use the email address for business communication. Email addresses can be gathered through a number of means. For example, customers visiting a trade show may leave their information when they visit your booth, or a person may provide an email address in exchange for some relevant content on your website. In these situations, permission to communicate is implied and the initial email to these people should provide an opportunity to unsubscribe or to manage the types of emails they are willing to receive.

Email is also a vehicle used to install malware (hostile or intrusive software) and for phishing (attempting to obtain sensitive information such as passwords by pretending to be from a trusted source). This is why people avoid "cold call" emails, such as those generated from a purchased list. This is why it is important to use email for people who opt in to receiving materials from you.

There are three levels of conversion to keep in mind when designing the email: did they receive it, did they open it, and did they respond to the message. The first level is whether or not the person receives the email. MailChimp® estimates only 79% of permission-based emails reach their target[12]. Spam filters and internet service providers (ISP's) block the rest because they appear to be spam—junk email.

The first thing a person sees when they receive your email is the subject line. This is probably the most important element of the email. The subject line determines whether the person opens the email or simply deletes it. The subject line needs show the recipient that the content is relevant, and is interesting enough to make the person want to open the email. Personalization in the subject line can improve conversion (opening the email). People always notice their names.

If a person opens the email, there needs to be a payoff. There should be content of interest to the recipient. The payoff might be information, it might be entertainment, or maybe a little of both. This is another place where brand-related content can be re-purposed.

Finally, you want to provide a way for the recipient to respond to the email. You can ask them to reply to the email, but it is more common to provide links to your website in the body of the email. Some email communications might have more than one area of content. For example, click here for a white paper, and click there for a product demonstration. The option selected is an indicator of the level of the person's interest in your offering.

Mobile Marketing

With the near universal adoption of smartphones (comScore reports 79.1% penetration in January 2016[13]), mobile marketing is an increasingly important channel of communication. We live with our smartphones. We check them when we get up in the morning and check them before going to bed at night. We use them to read emails, to watch television, to surf the web, even to pay our bills. Oh yes, we also use them to make phone calls. A recent study found people use their smartphones five hours each day checking them 85 times.[14]

Because of the intimate relationship we have with our mobile devices, mobile marketing creates opportunities to connect with customers in ways that are impossible with other communication media. In addition to all of the data associated with the functions of the device (contact list, appointments, photos, email, etc.) a smartphone captures context information. It knows the time of day, it knows where you are, it knows whether or not you are moving, it even knows what angle you are holding it at.

Beacon technology uses low-power Bluetooth transmitters to communicate with to nearby mobile devices[15]. This allows retailers, for example to monitor a customer's activity while in a physical store as well as to send targeted ads to the device.

19.6 AUTOMATED MARKETING

Although we have not yet achieved the technological singularity—when computers take over the world—advances in information technology have enabled marketers to automate some of the marketing process. Marketing automation has roots going back to the 1980s with automated contact management systems.[16] The goal was, and continues to be, to automate tasks that don't require face-to-face interaction, so salespeople can spend more time working with their best prospects. Although the term "automated marketing" usually refers to advances in customer relationship management in the B2B arena, programmatic advertising is bringing automation to the consumer sector.

Customer Relationship Marketing

CRM, or customer relationship management, is a blanket term that covers software to support a variety of automated marketing activities. It usually involves integration of internal databases such as sales, marketing, customer service, and technical support, as well as managing communication with current and prospective customers. Salesforce®, Microsoft®, Oracle®, and SAP® are the leading providers of CRM software at the enterprise (large organization) level. CRM may or may not include sales force automation or marketing automation. **Sales force automation (SFA)** software automates activities such as inventory control, sales processing, tracking of customer interactions, sales forecasts, and performance monitoring.[17] **Marketing automation** software emphasizes marketing-related activities such as lead generation, segmentation, lead nurturing, lead scoring, relationship marketing, customer retention, and marketing ROI (return on investment).[18] The leading companies in automated marketing are HubSpot, Infusionsoft, and Marketo.[19]

The Sales Funnel

Automated marketing is frequently performed in conjunction with a sales funnel (Figure 19.2). The funnel represents the buyer's journey and different tactics are appropriate at different stages of the process: top of funnel, middle of funnel, bottom of funnel. The software develops a lead score for each prospective customer. The lead score takes into account all of the interactions with the customer, estimating their readiness to buy. When it appears the customer has reached the bottom of the funnel and is close to being ready to purchase, the software turns the lead over to the company's sales force to close the deal.

The goal with top of the funnel tactics is lead acquisition. At this point you don't know who your prospective customers are, so outreach tactics (such as search engine marketing) help create awareness of the product. At some point the person will provide some identifying information—say providing an email address in exchange for access to a report. Once the person has entered the top of the funnel, the automated

marketing program can begin a pro-
grammed series of communications
with the person designed to get more
personal information and to start
developing a lead score. For example,
after providing an email address for
a report, the prospect may receive an
email invitation to a webinar. In order
to attend the webinar, the person has
to complete a short form giving their
job title and the company they work
for.

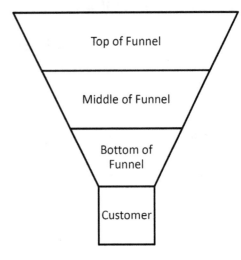

FIGURE 19.2   Sales Funnel

When there is enough information
on the prospective customer, they are
moved to the middle of the funnel.
The goal with middle of the funnel
tactics is to nurture the customer.
Content at this stage of the process is to educate the customer about the company's
offering and to determine which specific products the prospect might be interested
in. For example, the customer might receive an email summarizing a blog posting about data security. The next week they might receive another email talking
about data storage. The prospect's responses to these communications indicate
the level of interest and the areas the person is interested in. The software monitors the person's activity and demographic profile, continually updating the lead
score.

Once the lead score has reached the point where the prospect seems to be close
to making a purchase, the prospect is turned over to the sales staff who attempt to
convert the prospect into a customer. If the prospect does not make a purchase, they
are recycled to the middle of the funnel for additional nurturing.

Programmatic Advertising

Programmatic advertising uses artificial intelligence and real-time bidding to
automate the placement of online ads. While still a young technology, it is gaining ground quickly. According to eMarketer®, by 2016 programmatic accounted
for more than two thirds of digital advertising and continues to grow as a
proportion of overall digital advertising.[20] In addition, programmatic advertising is starting to be used with traditional ad media such as television and direct
marketing.

(ENDNOTES)

1. Lamberton, Cait and Andrew T. Stephen, 2016, "A thematic Exploration of Digital, Social Media, and Mobile Marketing: Research Evolution from 2000 to 2015 and an Agenda for Future Inquiry, *Journal of Marketing,* 80 (November) pp. 146–172.

2. https://martechtoday.com/infographic-marketing-technology-landscape-113956, accessed October 26, 2016.

3. "Tomorrow's Marketer," Marketo and Forbes Luncheon, June 22, 2016, San Francisco, California.

4. Perro, Dave and Sarah Dietze, 2016, "Walker Sands State of Marketing Technology 2016: Understanding the New Martech Buyer's Journey," http://www.walkersands.com/New-Martech-Buyer-Journey accessed October 26, 2016.

5. http://blog.hubspot.com/marketing/omni-channel-user-experience-examples#sm.000t5gnsz 109idleqfm2idex8sfeq, accessed October 26, 2016.

6. http://www.wordstream.com/blog/ws/2015/05/21/how-much-does-adwords-cost, accessed September 14, 2015.

7. http://www.protofuse.com/blog/first-page-of-google-by-the-numbers/, accessed September 14, 2015.

8. Kotler, Philip, Hermawan Kartajaya, and Iwan Setiawan, 2010, *Marketing 3.0: From Products to Customers to the Human Spirit, Hoboken, N.J.:Wiley p. 30.*

9. http://www.merriam-webster.com/dictionary/social%20media, accessed October 28, 2016.

10. Wiedlin, Andy, "Media Trends & the Emergence of Shareable Content," in-class presentation, San Francisco State University, September 19, 2016.

11. https://en.wikipedia.org/wiki/Chewbacca_Mask_Lady, accessed October 28, 2016.

12. https://mailchimp.com/resources/guides/how-to-avoid-spam-filters/html/, accessed October 28, 2016.

13. https://www.comscore.com/Insights/Rankings/comScore-Reports-January-2016-US-Smartphone-Subscriber-Market-Share, accessed October 28, 2016.

14. Andrews S, Ellis DA, Shaw H, Piwek L (2015) Beyond Self-Report: Tools to Compare Estimated and Real-World Smartphone Use. PLoS ONE 10(10): e0139004. doi:10.1371/journal.pone.0139004, accessed October 28, 2016.

15. http://www.cio.com/article/3037354/marketing/6-things-marketers-need-to-know-about-beacons.html, accessed October 28, 2016.

16. http://www.destinationcrm.com/Articles/PrintArticle.aspx?ArticleID=42412. Accessed September 23 2015.

17. http://whatis.techtarget.com/definition/sales-force-automation-SFA. Accessed september 23, 2015.

18. Marketo, 2013, *The Definitive Guide to Marketing Automation,* http://www.marketo.com/definitive-guides/marketing-automation/, downloaded September 23, 2015.

19. http://www.enterpriseappstoday.com/crm/slideshows/7-marketing-automation-leaders.html, accessed October 28, 2016.

20. https://www.emarketer.com/Article/More-Than-Two-Thirds-of-US-Digital-Display-Ad-Spending-Programmatic/1013789. Accessed May 30, 2018.

ENVIRONMENTAL SCANNING

CH20

f you remember from Chapter 4, there is no such thing as a good decision or a bad decision at the time you make it. The best we can do is to make "defensible" decisions. Based on the information available to us at the time, we do what we think is right. The more information we consider, the more defensible the decision will be.

Environmental scanning is a systematic approach to identifying information that might be relevant to the situation at hand. By carefully considering as many different areas as possible, you are more likely to identify important information that might have been overlooked otherwise. This makes your decisions more defensible, which increases the probability that they will turn out to have been good decisions.

20.1 MARKETING MYOPIA

In 1960, Theodore Levitt (an American economist, professor at Harvard Business School and an editor of the *Harvard Business Review*) published the now classic *Harvard Business Review* article, "Marketing Myopia."[1] In this article, he claimed that every industry was once a growth industry. When industries go into decline, it is not because of changing market circumstances but because of short-sighted managers in the industry focusing on their specific product rather than on the benefit customers received from the product. Thus, the passenger railroad industry is a shadow of its former self because managers believed they were in the railroad business rather than providing transportation services. Instead of embracing air travel as an opportunity to provide transportation services, the railroads lost passenger traffic to the airline industry.

The automobile industry is going through dramatic changes as ride-sharing companies such as Lyft™ and Uber, and car-sharing companies such as Zipcar®, are changing the way people think about cars. To avoid marketing myopia, Mark Fields, CEO of Ford Motor Company recently announced that, rather than being a "car company," Ford is now in the "mobility industry[2]." This shifts the company's focus from the product, to the benefit customers receive from the product. (Ironically, Fields was fired for not moving quickly enough towards ride sharing and autonomous vehicles—as well as for a slump in car sales[3])

According to Levitt, there are four conditions likely to spawn marketing myopia:

1. The belief that growth comes from an increasing and more affluent population.
2. The belief that there is no competitive substitute for the product.
3. Too much faith in mass production and an emphasis on selling rather than on marketing.
4. Preoccupation with technical aspects of the product.

Environmental scanning is the process of systematically monitoring external and internal data that may impact future plans. Understanding trends in the sociocultural, economic, competitive, and political environments will give early warning of opportunities and threats to be aware of as you develop your marketing plans.

20.2 WHAT IS ENVIRONMENTAL SCANNING?

There are two dimensions to consider when determining which factors or environments to include in your environmental scan: macro vs. micro and internal vs. external. Macro issues are things that affect every business while micro issues are unique to your specific situation. External issues are things over which you have no control while internal issues are things you have the ability to change. Figure 20.1 locates the common environments considered along these two dimensions.

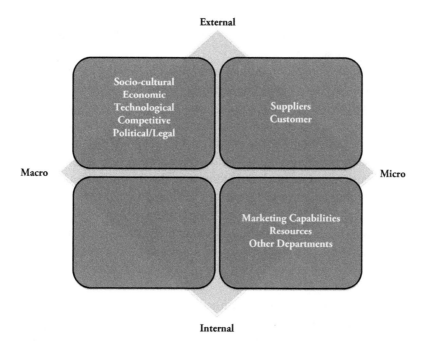

External

| Socio-cultural
Economic
Technological
Competitive
Political/Legal | Suppliers
Customer |

Macro ⟷ Micro

| | Marketing Capabilities
Resources
Other Departments |

Internal

FIGURE 20.1   Environmental Scanning Framework

269

In the upper left quadrant, we have external macroenvironment issues such as the social, economic, technological, competitive, and political/legal environments. The upper right quadrant contains external microenvironments. The lower right quadrant contains internal microenvironments. The lower left quadrant is empty. Unless you are a magician or have super powers, there aren't many issues that affect the entire economy over which you have control.

External Macroenvironments

External macroenvironments are areas outside of your control that affect all businesses. Although there is little you can do to influence trends in these areas, it is important to be aware of them as you develop your marketing plans. It is easier to swim with the current than to struggle against it.

Sociocultural Environment

The sociocultural environment looks at demographic and cultural trends such as population growth, living patterns, attitudes, and values. These are many of the same variables used for market segmentation (Chapter 5.2). Monitoring developments in this area will help keep your segmentation in step with market conditions. You are always looking for growing segments, and the earlier you identify opportunities, the stronger your market position will be. Similarly, if the segments you have targeted are becoming less attractive, you have time to redeploy your resources to more promising areas.

For example, the population in the United States is growing but not as fast as the rest of the world. Population is estimated to reach 417 million by the year 2060. The demographic profile will be older and more diverse. By 2030, one in five Americans will be older than 65, and by 2044, more than half of the population will belong to a minority group, and immigration will play a significant role in population growth. By 2060, 20% of the population will be foreign-born.[4]

Multigenerational households are increasing. The number of multigenerational households has doubled since 1980, with 18% of the population living in multigenerational households in 2012. Much of the growth has been with younger people aged 25–35, with nearly one out of four living in multigenerational households. The reason for this increase is a combination of lost job opportunities during the Great Recession as well as young people marrying later and staying in school longer than previous generations.[5]

From a religious perspective, the United States is still predominately Christian although the country is becoming less religious. The percentage of the population identifying as Christian decreased from 78% in 2007 to 70% in 2014 while those reporting no religious affiliation increased from 16% to 22% of the population. Most of the decline came from mainline Christians while evangelical Protestants and non-Christian religions saw some growth during this period.

> "Some really good advice when I first started was, 'It's OK to ask for help, but don't ask for help until you've tried to Google the answer.' That doesn't necessarily mean actually looking it up on Google, but try to find the answer yourself before you just say, 'Hey, I can't do this, somebody help me.'"
>
> **Ariana Raftopoulos**

Economic Environment

You can make money in an "up" economy and you can make money in a "down" economy as long as you know whether you are in an up or a down economy. The Conference Board (www.conference-board.org) tracks a number of economic trends. The Leading Economic Index® is a composite of ten leading economic indicators which can give a clue to the direction the economy is headed. The Consumer Confidence Index® tracks consumer perceptions of market conditions.

Ultimately, we are interested in how much money people have to spend on our products. The median gross income per household was $53,000 in 2013.[6] As marketers, we are more interested in disposable and discretionary income. **Disposable income** is the money left over after taxes have been paid and is available for necessities such as rent, utilities, medicine, and food. **Discretionary income** is the money left over after taxes and living expenses have been paid. This money is available for luxuries or for savings. Many consumer-oriented products are discretionary purchases.

Technological Environment

One of the major causes of marketing myopia is not paying attention to technological advances in other industries. Look at the impact streaming services such as Pandora® or Spotify® have had on both recorded and broadcast music.

Going forward, the digital revolution continues. Among the top ten technological trends identified by Gartner®, a technology research and consulting firm; nine are primarily digital: computing everywhere, the internet of things, data analytics, context rich systems, cloud computing, smart machines, web-scale IT, software-defined applications, and digital security.[7]

3-D printing, or additive manufacturing, is another emerging technology with the potential to disrupt existing businesses and create new ways of developing and producing physical goods.

Competitive Environment

Scanning the competitive environment includes looking at the levels of competition, industry structure, and factors that drive competition. There are three levels of competition to consider. The most specific is **brand competition** or head-to-head competition. This is direct competition in the same product category. For example, Coke® is competing against Pepsi® and all of the other cola products out there. Brand competition is what we usually think of when we talk about competition. While it is important to keep tabs on your direct competitors, it is also helpful to step back and look at the larger picture.

Product competition, or industry-level competition, recognizes that in addition to your direct competitors, you face indirect competition from alternative products. Thus, in addition to competing against Pepsi in the cola market, Coke is competing with ice tea, milk, lemonade, water, and other nonalcoholic beverages. And, ultimately, we are all competing for the consumer's discretionary income. A customer may choose to buy a Coke or decide to go to the movies or to make a down payment on a yacht or even to put the money into savings.

Industry structure has a major influence on competitive behavior. A company that enjoys a monopoly has no brand-level competition, and the major emphasis is to prevent customers from switching to substitute products. In an oligopoly, where a small number of players dominate the market, or in monopolistic competition, where brand-based barriers to entry create the same effect, game theory comes into play. It is important to anticipate competitor response to any market action. Most consumer products are in mature industries (Chapter 8.1) and are dominated by a small number of companies. For example, Kellogg's® and General Mills® dominate the breakfast cereal market.

Michael Porter's five forces model provides a good framework for assessing industry attractiveness. In this model, he identifies five forces that impact the attractiveness of an industry: threat of new entrants, bargaining power of suppliers, bargaining power of buyers, the threat of substitute products, and industry rivalry.[8] A new entrant to the industry will put downward pressure on profitability as the new player aggressively builds market share. When buyers or suppliers have high bargaining power, they are more likely to capture a larger share of channel profits. The availability of substitutes puts a limit on prices, while intense rivalry within an industry can lead to price competition, lowering the overall profitability of the industry.

Political/Legal Environment

The political/legal environment deals with restrictions placed on business by government. In the United States, commerce between the states is regulated at the federal level while commerce within the state is regulated at the state level. In addition, local governments may have additional regulations within their jurisdictions. Overall, the intent of business regulation is to increase competition and to protect consumers.

Because commerce is regulated at the state level, the rules will vary from state to state. The **Uniform Commercial Code (UCC)** is an attempt to bring consistency to business law among the states. The UCC is not law but rather a series of recommendations for states to consider as they develop their own set of regulations.

Most industries are subject to government regulation at some level. In most cases, the legislature will pass a law stating the objectives of the regulation and then create a regulatory body to interpret the law and to issue specific rules as the case may be. Thus, the Environmental Protection Agency was created by the Federal Clean Air Act of 1970 and the Clean Water Act of 1972. These regulatory agencies issue proposed rules in the Federal Register and invite comment from affected parties before the regulations go into effect. Other federal regulatory agencies include the Food and Drug Administration (FDA), which regulates food products, and the Consumer Product Safety Commission (CPSC), which sets safety standards for consumer products.

Many trade associations as well as businesses engage in lobbying activity. A lobbyist is a person who meets with legislators and regulatory agencies to influence proposed regulations of business. Because regulations can have a significant impact on business operations, it is important to make sure the business's perspective is represented in the process.

Some industries are self-regulated. This means that the industry sets up its own regulatory body to issue rules related to the industry. Some of these self-regulating organizations such as the Financial Industry Regulatory Authority (FINRA) are created to interpret laws related to the industry. Other self-regulating organizations such as the National Association of Realtors (NAR) or the American Medical Association (AMA) regulate the industry in the absence of government regulation.

External Microenvironment

The external microenvironment deals with things you do not control but are unique to your business. Namely, customers, intermediaries (Chapter 13.3), and suppliers. You can't force someone to be your customer, but you do have the ability to choose the market segments you want to target. Part of the environmental scan is to review the customers you are currently serving and to identify new potential markets. This way, as current markets mature, there will be opportunities for continued growth.

In the same vein, while you don't have control over the intermediaries you work with, you do have control over the intermediaries you choose to work with. Channel partners should be aligned with your overall marketing strategy.

It is always good to have more than one supplier for each resource in your supply chain. There are two reasons for this. First, if you only have one supplier, you are at that supplier's mercy. If the supplier decides to raise prices, your only choice is to accept the increase. If you have more than one supplier, you can always shift your business to an alternate supplier should circumstances require it. The other reason is that the more suppliers you work with, the better market intelligence you will have as each supplier's salespeople will have information about market conditions.

Internal Microenvironment

The internal microenvironment looks at the internal capabilities and culture of your organization. In order to create need-satisfying offerings for your customers, you need to understand your customers and the external business environment, as well as the internal capabilities of your organization. In order to do this, marketers need to become "boundary spanners," meaning we need to create relationships with others inside and outside of the company in order to do our job. Many people find this to be one of the benefits of a marketing career.

Both internal resources and corporate culture will have an impact on your marketing strategy. Corporate culture looks at the values, norms, and beliefs within an organization. Some organizations reward risk taking and some are focused on profit while others may be more people centered. The point is that successful strategies will be aligned with the corporate culture rather than at odds with it.

Internal resources looks at the relative strength of the various functional areas within the business. Operating procedures, research and development, financial condition, employee skills, physical facilities, and leadership need to be taken into account. Most business schools provide exposure to the various business functions as part of the basic preparation for a business career.

Ideally, you will be able to articulate your distinctive competencies by asking: "What is it that we do better than everybody else that people are willing to pay us money for?" Better yet, this should be your "elevator pitch," meaning you can clearly state it in 30 seconds or less.

(ENDNOTES)

1. Levitt, Theodore, 1960, "Marketing Myopia," *Harvard Business Review* (July/August), 45–56.
2. "The Future of Personal Transport," The Economist January 9, 2016.
3. https://jalopnik.com/why-mark-fields-was-fired-1795431562, Accessed May 30, 2018.
4. Colby, Sandra L., and Jennifer M. Ortman, 2015, "Projections of the Size and Composition of the US Population: 2014-1060," US Census Bureau.
5. http://www.pewsocialtrends.org/2014/07/17/in-post-recession-era-young-adults-drive-continuing-rise-in-multi-generational-living/. Accessed September 27, 2015.
6. http://quickfacts.census.gov/qfd/states/00000.html. Accessed September 27, 2015.
7. http://www.gartner.com/newsroom/id/2867917. Accessed October 15, 2015.
8. Porter, Michael, E, 2008, "The Five Competitive Forces that Shape Strategy," *Harvard Business Review,* (January), 78–93.

274

STRATEGIC MARKETING

CH21

An old joke has the pilot of an airliner coming over the speaker with the following announcement: "I've got good news and bad news. The bad news is we have no idea where we're going. The good news is that we're making excellent time." Up until now, we've focused on understanding customers and the processes we use to create need-satisfying offerings. Strategic marketing asks these questions: "Where are we going with all this?" What is the vision of the future, and what things do we need to do to achieve that vision?"

21.1 WHAT IS STRATEGIC PLANNING?

Strategic planning is the process of determining what an organization is, who it serves, what it does, and why it does what it does, with a focus on the future.[1] *Strategic marketing* is the process of identifying long-term market opportunities and developing the organization's resources and capabilities to match those opportunities. This involves establishing objectives that will take more than a year to achieve. Frequently, a three- to five-year planning horizon is used. The process involves working with employees and other stakeholders who are working toward common goals and getting agreement as to the intended outcome and the organization's direction in a rapidly changing environment.

The output is a strategic plan, or a document used to communicate the organizations goals, the actions needed to achieve those goals, and all of the other critical elements developed during the planning exercise.

There are four elements to the strategic planning process: analysis of the current internal and external environments, strategy formulation, strategy execution, and evaluation and refinement of the process based on the result. In Chapter 20, we discussed the environmental analysis. In this chapter, we'll focus on matching long-term strategies with market opportunities. In Chapter 22, we'll look at implementing and evaluating the strategy.

21.2 HIERARCHY OF GOALS

There is a hierarchy of goals in the planning process, starting with vision and mission, then long-term objectives or goals, followed by strategies to achieve those goals, and ultimately, specific tactics or short-term activities to achieve the goal. Because strategic planning happens at multiple levels of the organization, there is a top-down flow to the goal-setting process. Decisions made at lower levels of the hierarchy need to support the overall direction established at the top.

Vision and Mission

An organization's vision describes the scope and direction of the business and is the responsibility of the founder or top management. The vision sets the broad parameters for the organization. What would be the impact of the organization's long-term success? What is the business we are in, and how will we operate as an organization? The vision may or may not be articulated in a formal vision statement.

An organizations **mission** is a formal statement that describes the overall purpose of the organization and identifies its customers, products, processes, and values. The mission is frequently intended to be inspirational as well as functional. The mission statement needs to be specific enough to provide guidance but vague enough to allow managers to adapt to changing market conditions. Adhering to a mission statement that defines the business too narrowly is a cause of marketing myopia (Chapter 19.1).

The test of a good mission statement is that when a person in the organization comes up with a bright idea, the mission should tell the person whether or not the idea is something the company is likely to support.

Mission statements can happen at any level of a business. There can be a corporate-level mission, a business-level mission, a department-level mission, or even a personal mission statement.

Objectives, Strategies, and Tactics

Objectives, or goals, are the long-term accomplishments that the organization wants to achieve. The result would be a sustainable competitive advantage. If, by the end of the planning horizon, these things have happened, the plan will have been a success.

In order to be useable, an objective needs to be specific, time constrained, measurable, and relevant. This means it needs to be quantifiable. You may have heard the business term, "making the numbers." This refers to the achievement of quantifiable goals. If the goal can't be expressed in numbers, it can't be measured.

For example, a good marketing objective may look something like this: In five years, we will have diversified our revenue base so that at least 25% of annual revenue comes from new products. Here is a bad way to state that same objective: For the next five years, we will diversify our revenue base by focusing on new products. The first version is specific and measurable. The second version is not. What does it mean to "focus" on new products?

A **strategy** is a broad initiative or action you will undertake to help achieve the objective. A strategy usually takes more than a year to execute, and the result will be significant progress toward meeting the long-term objectives. For example, if the objective is to generate 25% of sales from new products, a strategy might be to create a new product development team.

Tactics are short-term activities to achieve the strategic goals. The timeframe for a tactic is usually less than a year, frequently monthly or weekly. For example, if the strategy is to create a new product development team, a tactic might be to hire a new product manager in the next three months.

Corporate-Level Issues

Sitting at the top hierarchy of goals is the corporate level, or "C Suite" (Chief Executive Officer, Chief Operating Officer, Chief Financial Officer, Chief Marketing Officer, etc.). This is the level where the vision, mission, and corporate-level objectives are established. Corporate-level objectives become constraints on the planning process at other levels in the hierarchy. All of the activity at subsidiary levels should be in support of these corporate objectives.

In large conglomerate organizations, corporate determines the business portfolio, or the mix of business units in the corporation. The Boston Consulting Group matrix introduced in Chapter 8.4 was originally developed as a tool for managing corporate business portfolios.

Business Unit Level Issues

A business unit (or strategic business unit) is an independent profit center. A large corporation may have several business units, each responsible for developing and executing strategic plans for the unit. A smaller business may consist of a single business unit. At the business unit level, the primary concern is efficient use of resources in order to maximize return on investment (ROI).

Functional Area Issues

Each business unit may contain several specialized functional areas such as marketing, operations, accounting, finance, administrative, information technology, research and development, etc. Each of these functional areas is responsible for helping the business achieve its strategic objectives. Each functional area needs to develop plans to support its mission. The marketing plan is one of several functional-level plans.

Business Plan vs. Marketing Plan

Strategic planning is done at the business unit level as well as at other levels within the organization. Because of this, there can be confusion between the business plan and the marketing plan. All business plans require key marketing input such as customer analyses and sales forecasts. The major difference is at the strategy level. For a business plan, strategies developed to achieve corporate objectives would be based on the various functional areas within the company. There might be a financial strategy and an operations strategy, as well as a marketing strategy involved. For a marketing plan, strategies would involve the marketing mix. There might be a product strategy, a pricing strategy, a promotional strategy, etc.

21.3 DEVELOPING THE MARKETING PLAN

Figure 21.1 illustrates the strategic planning process from the perspective of the marketing team. The vision and mission and corporate-level objectives are determined at the "C Suite" level, and unless you are one of the "C's," i.e., CEO or CMO, these are probably given to you. You will be responsible for the activities to achieve the objectives, including the environmental scan, situation analysis, developing strategies, tactics, and evaluation.

Environmental Scan

In Chapter 20, we described a general approach to scanning the business environment. And it is always a good idea to keep abreast of developments in the broader environment. However, when it comes to developing a marketing plan, the environmental scan needs to be put in context. Given the objectives you are trying to achieve, what are the key issues you've identified in the environment that could have an impact, either positive or negative, on your ability to

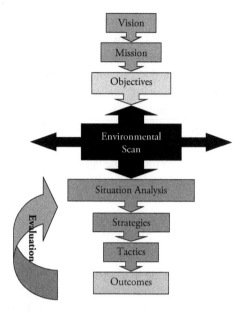

FIGURE 21.1 Strategic Planning Process

achieve the objectives? It is these—and only these—strategic issues that you will bring into the situation analysis and the rest of the planning process.

Situation Analysis

The next stage of the planning process is the **situation analysis**, or the study of past and present data to identify trends, forces, and conditions with the potential to influence the performance of the business and the choice of appropriate strategies. The goal is to evaluate the issues identified in the environmental scan in terms of whether they are positive or negative and in terms of your ability to influence them.

One of the most basic approaches to evaluating these key issues is a **SWOT** analysis (Figure 21.2). A SWOT analysis evaluates internal and external factors in terms of whether they are positive or negative. Internal factors are considered strengths if they are positive and weaknesses if they are negative. External factors are considered opportunities if they are positive or threats if they are negative.

Strengths are favorable issues within your control. These are the source of your distinctive competencies that can be used to position your business relative to the competition (Chapter 6.2). You are looking for

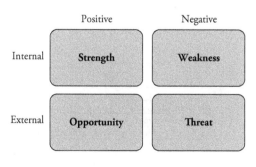

FIGURE 21.2 SWOT Analysis

areas where you are providing something of value to customers that none of your competitors is providing. Remember, you will need to meet key aspects of your competitors' offerings just to be taken seriously in the category. What is it you are better at than anyone else that customers are willing to pay you money for? Weaknesses are internal negatives.

Opportunities are trends in the external environment that are considered positive, given your internal situation and the objectives you are trying to achieve. Strategies that take advantage of these favorable conditions are likely to be successful. Similarly, threats are trends in the external environment that could make it difficult to achieve your objectives.

Developing Strategies

A **strategy** is a plan of action or policy that will lead to achieving the long-term objectives. The key to developing strategies is to use the environmental scan and SWOT analysis to focus your efforts on areas that will be most productive. You do this by proposing actions that will take advantage of the positives in your analysis and/or minimize the negatives. For example, if our objective was to have 25% of our revenue come from new product sales, and our SWOT analysis showed we had no internal capability to develop new products (a weakness) but were in a strong financial position (a strength), one strategy might be to create an internal new products development department. An alternative strategy might be to contract with an outside design firm to create new products for us. Both of those strategies take advantage of our financial position and minimize our weakness in new product capability.

Just as we did with the new product development process (Chapter 7.3), the first stage in strategy development is to generate as many alternatives as possible that take advantage of the positives and/or minimize the negatives. After generating the list of alternatives, it should be subjected to a cost-benefit analysis. What resources will be required to implement each strategy, and what is the impact we expect if the implementation is successful? Figure 21.3 is an example of an evaluation matrix.

In this example, our objective is to achieve 25% of sales from new products within five years. Using the process described above, we've identified six possible strategies that will result in an increase in sales of new products. For each strategy, the benefit is the increase we would see in sales from new products if the strategy is successful, expressed as a percentage of sales from new products. This is reduced

	Strategy					
	A	B	C	D	E	F
Expected Benefit	5%	20%	15%	30%	10%	10%
Probability of Success	.8	.4	.333	.5	.8	.5
Expected Outcome	3.75%	8%	5%	15%	8%	5%
Resources Required	$10,000	$100,000	$100,000	$150,000	$50,000	$75,000
Cost/% Increase	$2,666	$12,500	$20,000	$10,000	$6,250	$15,000

FIGURE 21.3   Strategy Evaluation Matrix

by the estimated probability that the strategy will be successful if implemented to give us the expected benefit. The cost of implementing the strategy is divided by expected benefit, giving us an estimate of the cost of achieving a 1% increase in sales from new products.

For example, Strategy A will give us 5% of sales from new products, and there is an 80% probability that the strategy will be successful. The cost of implementing strategy A is $10,000, which gives us a cost/benefit of $2,666 for each 1% increase in sales from new products.

If the objective is to get 25% of sales from new products, we would need to implement enough strategies to achieve our objective. We would start with the most cost-effective strategy, "Strategy A," and then add additional strategies going from least expensive to most expensive until we have a reasonable chance of achieving our objective. In this case, we would recommend implementing strategies A, E, and D. This would give us an expected increase of 26.5% and require an investment of $210,000 to achieve the objective.

With this approach to developing strategies, you are connecting the internal capabilities of the organization with the realities of the business environment. It is important to move quickly in implementing strategic plans. There may be a limited timeframe, or strategic window, when the opportunity matches the organization's resources.

Product/Market Growth Matrix

In a 1957 *Harvard Business Review* article, Igor Ansoff, known as the father of strategic management, outlined four basic strategies for increasing sales.[2] These four strategies, penetration, market development, product development, and diversification, are expressed as a 2 × 2 matrix with markets on one axis and customers on the other (Figure 21.4). The least risky strategy for increasing sales is a **penetration strategy**, or selling existing products to existing customers. However, there is a limit to how much of an increase you can achieve with this approach. As more and more customers adopt the product, you reach a level of market saturation where the majority of your existing target market is using the product.

If the market is saturated, you will need to look to new markets or to new products to grow your business. A **product development** strategy involves introducing new products to your existing customers while a **market development** strategy involves identifying additional market segments that might see the benefit in your existing product offerings. Both of these strategies are riskier than a penetration strategy. With product development, you know the market but are dealing with unfamiliar products.

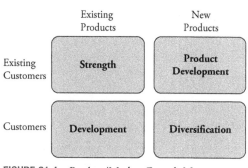

FIGURE 21.4   Product/Market Growth Matrix

With market development, you are dealing with familiar products but don't know the new customers.

A **diversification** strategy involves marketing new products to new market segments. This is the riskiest growth strategy because you don't have experience with either the products or the markets you are working with. Diversification is appropriate when market conditions have shifted to the point where the product is in the decline stage, and the market segment is shrinking. One reason diversification can be so risky is that the company may have been losing money for a long time before recognizing the need to diversify away from unfavorable market conditions. In that situation, the business may no longer have the resources needed to effect the change.

Tactics

Tactical issues are the intermediate steps needed to implement the plan. There needs to be a plan deploying the marketing mix for each target segment. In addition, an annual budget and timetable need to outline what activities are to happen, how much they will cost, and who is accountable for the results. Finally, there should be contingencies, or changes to the plan, to be implemented if the actual results are different than what was anticipated. These contingencies and the factors that would invoke them should be in place before the plan is implemented.

21.4 THE MARKETING PLAN

A marketing plan is a document outlining the organization's objectives, strategies, and marketing activities, resources needed to support the plan, and timetable for implementation. The format of the marketing plan depends on the audience for the plan and on the unique characteristics of the business. If the marketing plan is intended for external audiences such as investors, or for public relations purposes it will have less detail and will be written in a way that puts the business in a positive light. If the plan is intended for an internal audience, it will have more detail and a stronger emphasis on the tactical activities required of the people responsible for implementing the plan.

Having said that, here is a basic outline for a generic marketing plan:

I. Executive Summary

- Briefly review the highlights of the plan and its role in achieving higher-level strategies and objectives

II. Situation Analysis

- Internal Analysis: company background, products, markets, past results, distribution, positioning

- External Analysis: environmental scan, competitor analysis, key trends
- SWOT Analysis: critical success factors

III. Marketing Objectives
IV. Marketing Strategies
 V. Marketing programs

- Sales forecast, target markets, product, price, promotion, distribution

VI. Execution

- Budgets, timetable, evaluation metrics, contingencies

Planning in Uncertainty

The strategic planning process described above works best with established businesses; however, for businesses where there is a high degree of uncertainty, such as with a startup or in a highly volatile industry, Stuart Read, professor of strategic management, Williamette University, Salem, Oregon, and colleagues suggest an alternative approach similar to that used by experienced entrepreneurs.[3] Traditional market planning starts with a stated objective and develops a plan to achieve the objective. The entrepreneurial approach starts by assessing the resources available to you and then interacting with people you know or meet to generate possible business ideas. Figure 21.5 illustrates this entrepreneurial approach. This process leads to new business ideas that are supported by the commitments you generated. As you

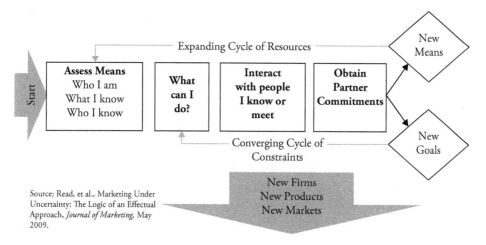

Source: Read, et al., Marketing Under Uncertainty: The Logic of an Effectual Approach, *Journal of Marketing*, May 2009.

FIGURE 21.5 Planning in Uncertainty (Stuart Read, Nicholas Dew, Saras D. Sarasvathy, Michael Song, and Robert Wiltbank, "Marketing Under Uncertainty: The Logic of an Effectual Approach," *Journal of Marketing*, vol. 73, no. 3, pp. 4. Copyright © 2009 by American Marketing Association. Reprinted with permission.)

work with more partners, you expand your capabilities and the options available to you for creating additional business opportunities.

There are two recommendations for people starting businesses in an uncertain environment. First, traditional market research may be less effective than a networking approach. In the process of sharing your ideas with others, you will uncover business opportunities at the same time that you are identifying potential stakeholders in the business. Second, avoid the "more for less" pricing strategy common with new businesses. Instead, pricing decisions should be negotiated at the same time that the business idea is being developed.

21.5 SALES FORECASTING

There is a saying among salespeople that "nothing happens in business until somebody sells something." This isn't completely accurate. The saying should be that "nothing happens in business unless there is a sales forecast." A sales forecast is a prediction of what a business's sales will be in the future. This prediction is a critical piece of information for all marketing plans and for all business plans. Without an estimate of future sales, you can't plan for inventory, for cash flow, or for growth.

Terminology

Before we look at some of the methods used to develop sales forecasts, it might be helpful to go over some of the terminology we'll be using: market size, market potential, sales potential, market share, and market factor. Market size can be expressed either in terms of dollars or in terms of units. Dollar sales are important for financial planning while unit sales are important for inventory and production planning. However, you need to look at both dollars and units together to get a clear picture of the market situation. For example, in 2013, domestic box office receipts (dollar sales) were up while ticket sales (unit sales) were down.[4] Was it a good year or a bad year for the movie industry? Dollar sales were up, so you might say, "Yes," but unit sales were down, so you might say, "No." When you put them together, you get a clearer picture: fewer people attended the movies, which isn't healthy, and revenue increased because of an increase in ticket prices.

Market potential is the upper limit of demand. It speaks to that magical world where every person who was a potential customer bought your product. Of course, that never happens. Sales potential is the upper limit of demand for your company. It is market potential limited to the geographic areas you serve and the distribution channels you use.

Market share is the portion of a market captured by a single entity, usually expressed as a percentage. A market share of 30% means that your business accounts for 30% of sales in that particular market. **Relative market share** is the ratio of your market share compared to that of your largest competitor. It is a measure of relative strength in the market, or market power. A relative market share of 2 means that your market share is twice as big as that of your closest competitor. A relative market share of ½ means your competitor's market share is twice as big as yours.

A market factor is something that is measureable in a market and is related to demand.

Forecasting Methods

The goal of sales forecasting is to develop an actionable estimate of future sales based on sales potential, your marketing plans, known mitigating factors (such as the opportunities or threats identified in the environmental scan), and unknown mitigating factors. One unknown mitigating factor, especially common with new product introductions, is over optimism. Some suggest cutting any sales estimate for a new product in half to take over-optimism into account.

There are several methods used to develop sales forecasts, and the proper approach to use depends on the structure of the industry. Common approaches include market factor analysis, surveying knowledgeable people, statistical methods, market testing, and the chain ratio method.

Market Factor Analysis

Market factor analysis takes advantage of the relationship between your product and a known market factor to develop a sales forecast derived from the forecast of the market factor. For example, in industrial markets where demand is derived, the forecast for component parts can be determined based on the predicted sales of the end product. Thus, a sales forecast for the tire industry would be derived from the sales forecast for automobile sales. Every car built in the current year will require at least four tires, so we have a solid forecast for OEM (original equipment market) sales for tires. In addition, we know how many cars have been produced in the past, so we can develop a forecast for aftermarket, or replacement, tire sales. A tire lasts three to four years, so the replacement market forecast would be a percentage of the number of cars built three and four years ago that are still being driven.

The advantage of market factor analysis as a forecasting tool is that it is relatively easy to implement and can be very reliable. The disadvantage is that it only works well in markets where there is a known market factor and where demand is relatively stable. This approach would not be very helpful in markets with volatile demand such as the market for fashion-oriented products.

"Ten years ago, you'd figure out a whole bunch of things about what to say and do for your brand and then you'd just go and do them. Now that's part of the process, but there's a lot of slack you leave in the plan for social response, for pop culture response, for how the data shows things are performing. So you plan in evolution and optimization rather than just building a campaign, launching it, and waiting eight weeks to see how you did."

Justin Garrett

Survey Knowledgeable People

People working in an industry tend to have a pretty good idea of what is happening within their companies as well as a sense of what is happening with their competitors. Surveys of customers, the sales force, and senior management can be used to develop sales forecasts. A **buyers' intentions survey** involves asking customers what they anticipate purchasing or consuming in the upcoming period. This could be either a formal survey or an informal approach such as chatting with customers at a trade convention or a networking event. The survey of buyers' intentions works best in B2B markets where there are a relatively small number of buyers and where the buyers are likely to be planning their purchases in advance. The advantage to this approach is that the customer is telling you what demand will be. The disadvantage is that a customer might overstate purchase quantities as a tactic to negotiate better terms for deal. Also, this approach assumes customers will be loyal. It doesn't help if your best customer is planning in increasing purchase quantities but will be doing business with someone else in the future.

A **sales force survey forecast** asks salespeople to estimate what they believe their customers will be purchasing in the coming period. Again, this approach works best in B2B markets where salespeople tend to have longer-term relationships with their customers. The advantage is that it is easier to get cooperation because the salespeople work for you. The disadvantage is that in the mind of the salesperson, asking for a sales forecast may be perceived as setting a sales quota. In that case, the salesperson is likely to give a lowball estimate in order to increase the likelihood of exceeding the quota.

Senior executives in a business tend to hold the position because they have a very good sense of what is happening in the industry. Some forecasting methods ask senior managers for an informed opinion about potential demand. This approach works best in the early stages of strategic projects where detailed plans are not yet available. The **Delphi method** is an approach developed in the 1950s to generate consensus among experts. With the Delphi method, top managers are surveyed and the results tabulated anonymously. After seeing the results, managers make another forecast, which is tabulated and shared. Eventually, they forecasts will begin to converge.

Statistical Methods

Statistical methods such as trend analysis are based on the assumption that past performance is an indicator of future results. The basic approach is to use regression analysis to identify trends in past sales data and then to project these trends into the future to develop the sales forecast. In practice, the statistical models used to project trends are more sophisticated, allowing for cyclical adjustments, and include multiple variables that may have an impact on sales. This approach works best in industries with relatively stable demand. Once the model has been developed it can be updated continuously, making it relatively easy to develop statistical forecasts. The disadvantage is that it ignores environmental factors not included in the model. As a consequence, trend analysis is more effective for shorter-term forecasts, say a year or less.

Market Testing

Sometimes, the only way to estimate future demand for a product is to put it on the market and see how people react. Market testing involves a limited product introduction on a small scale, as an experiment, in order to estimate potential sales for the product. The results of the market test can be extrapolated to your business's sales potential in order to develop the sales forecast. This approach is used in new product development (Chapter 7.3) and where demand is difficult to forecast using other methods. The advantage to market testing is that it can give reliable information relevant to the specific product. It also gives you the ability to fix any problems identified in the marketing program before the full-scale product launch. The disadvantage is that market testing is expensive and time consuming. The longer the product is in test market, the better chance competitors have of imitating the product.

Chain Ratio Method

In Chapter 5.2, we learned that business opportunities can be identified using multiple segmentation criteria to define a market segment. The chain ratio method of forecasting takes a comparable approach to developing a sales forecast. The basic idea is to start with the market potential for your product and then reduce the forecast with a series of assumptions based on the marketing plan. Different forecasting methods might be used at different stages of the forecast.

Let's say, for example, we have been selling a product in a five-state region, and we are planning on expanding our coverage to all 50 states. Here's how the chain ratio method might work to develop a sales forecast for the new territory. Last year, we sold 1,000,000 units. We know we have a 40% market share in our current market area and that our market area contains 20% of the nation's population. The average customer purchases our product five times a year, and the average price is $10.

We start with market potential. Our 200,000 customers are 40% of the regional market, so the regional market potential is 500,000. Our region is 20% of the nation, so the market potential is 2,500,000 customers. This means there are 2,000,000 potential new customers in the new territory.

From trend analysis, we predict the market will increase 5% next year, which gives us a potential of 2,100,000 customers.

Market research tells us that the product is not as popular nationally as it is in our region, so we would expect 10% fewer customers with the national rollout. This gives us an estimate of 1,890,000 customers.

Using the Delphi method, senior management estimates we will have a 10% market share nationally in the first year of introduction (this includes our current region). This gives us a sales estimate of 189,000 customers.

Market research indicates that customers in the new territory will buy the same quantity as our current customers, which gives us a unit forecast of 945,000 in the first year.

A/B testing suggests that prices are very inelastic for this product, so we will increase the price by 20% to $12 and anticipate only a 5% decrease in demand. This gives us a final sales forecast of 897,750 units or $10,773,000.

The value of the chain ratio method is that each step of the process gives us a metric we can use to help evaluate the plan after it has been implemented (Chapter 22.3). If sales are coming in below forecast, we have several places we could look to find the problem: Did the overall market increase 5% as expected? Was the market research suggesting 10% fewer customers accurate? Did we achieve the 10% market share as predicted? Did customers in the new territory buy in the quantities expected? Were customers more sensitive to the price increase than we thought?

Using a Sales Forecast

The first thing to understand when working with a sales forecast is that it is an estimate. There will always be an element of uncertainty. In his book, *Men and Rubber: The Story of Business,* Harvey Firestone, no believer in sales forecasts, said he could predict sales up to the amount of back orders he had at the factory.[5] How much money to invest in developing the forecast is a function of cost and benefit just as it is with any market research project (Chapter 4.1).

With that in mind, it is a good idea to develop at least three sales forecasts: the best-case scenario, the worst-case scenario, and the most-likely scenario. The best-case scenario is what would happen if everything goes right, and the worst-case scenario is what would happen if everything went wrong. The most-likely scenario is the actual sales forecast.

If you can't live with the consequences of the worst-case scenario, don't implement the plan. If you can live with the worst-case scenario, then implement the plan using the most-likely scenario as the sales forecast. At the same time, develop contingency plans anticipating what you would change if the best or worst cases were to develop. That way you can move quickly to adapt if the results are different than anticipated.

(ENDNOTES)

1. http://balancedscorecard.org/Resources/Strategic-Planning-Basics. Accessed September 30, 2015.

2. Ansoff, Igor, 1957, "Strategies for Diversification," *Harvard Business Review* 35 (5) Sep–Oct, 113–124.

3. Read, Stuart, Nicholad Dew, Saras D. Sarasvathy, Michael Song, and Robert Wiltbank, 2009, "Marketing Under Uncertainty: The Logic of an Effectual Approach," *Journal of Marketing* 73 (May), 1–18.

4. http://www.boxofficemojo.com/yearly/?view2=domestic&view=releasedate&p=.htm. Accessed October 2, 2015.

5. Firestone, Harvey, and Samuel Crowther, 1926, *Men and Rubber: The Story of Business*, New York: Doubleday, Page, and Co.

EXECUTION

CH22

W hen your plan meets the real world, the real world wins. As we move forward with the implementation of a marketing plan, there are two questions to consider: "Are we doing the right things?" and "Are we doing things right?" Understanding customers and the marketing mix are all intended to ensure we are doing the right things. In this chapter, we'll look at how plans are implemented to ensure we're doing things right.

22.1 IMPLEMENTING THE PLAN

In their 2003 *Harvard Business Review* article, Nitin Nohria, the current dean of Harvard Business School, and colleagues identified four basic management practices that separate winning companies from losing companies: strategy, execution, culture, and structure.[1] In Chapter 21.4, we discussed a process for developing strategies linked to the company's internal capability and the realities of the external business environment. Having a clear and focused strategy is the first step in implementing the plan.

Execution is the emphasis on internal operations. The people closest to the customer need have a clear understanding of what is expected. The emphasis is on delivering a customer experience that consistently meets customer expectations. Customers won't reward you for exceeding their expectations, but they will punish you if you fail to meet their expectations.

A performance-oriented culture has clear communication around values and expectations, good communication, and rewards performance. Everyone in the organization, not just managers, needs to understand what is expected of him or her and how he or she is going to achieve his or her goals. Exceeding the performance goal is not a time to rest, it is an accomplishment to be rewarded and an opportunity to find additional ways to contribute. Obviously, financial rewards should be tied to performance. Top-performing organizations go beyond financial rewards and provide recognition for people's achievements.

Organization Structure

There is no one type of organization structure that works best for all companies. A business can be successful with any organizational structure as long as the structure is aligned with the organization's objectives and with the needs of its customers. Furthermore, in today's fast-moving business environment, the structure should be flat and flexible.

A flat structure eliminates unnecessary layers of bureaucracy and pushes decision-making authority as close to the customer as possible. With a strong marketing information system (Chapter 4.2), there is less need for managers to monitor progress and to share information. Computers do that. Managing involves communicating goals, scheduling tasks, listening, and recognizing success. A flexible organization is continually rethinking the organization structure to be sure it is aligned with the current strategy and market conditions. At a minimum, a review of the current structure should be part of the strategic planning process.

Types of Structures

There are four organizational structures frequently used in marketing organizations: functional structure, geographic structure, product structure, and market structure. A functional structure is the traditional corporate structure, with the various marketing

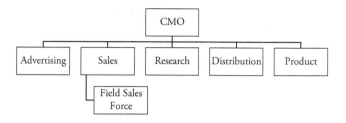

FIGURE 22.1   Functional Organization

functions reporting to the Chief Marketing Officer (CMO) or V.P., Marketing. Figure 22.1 is an organization chart illustrating the functional organization. Each box represents a marketing function, and the lines connecting the boxes represent the lines of communication and authority. The advantage to this structure is in its simplicity. The disadvantage is that it may not provide adequate product-level support in large companies with a wide variety of products and market segments. Also, this structure can lead to competition among the various functional areas for budget and status.

Businesses competing on a national or global scale frequently organize their sales force along geographic lines. General marketing functions are conducted at the corporate level, and the sales force is deployed geographically. This structure allows for field salespeople to maintain close contact with customers in their district.

Companies with a wide variety of products or brands often use a product or brand management structure. With this structure, the marketing function is organized around product groups, with a product manager or a brand manager responsible for managing a product or a group of products. The advantage of this type of organization is that by making a manager, or "champion," responsible for each product, the marketing program can be fine tuned for that product, and there is less chance for minor brands to be ignored.

Companies with different customer groups may use a market or customer organization. This is effective when different types of customers deal with the product differently. For example, with component products such as tires, the original equipment market involves selling thousands of tires to a handful of automobile manufacturers. The replacement parts market, or aftermarket, involves packaging the product for consumer purchases and distributing through a large number of repair shops and auto parts stores. It would make sense to develop separate marketing programs for these two customer types. Similarly, in consumer markets, there may be national accounts, such as Macy's® or Walmart®, where you deal directly with the customer and smaller regional accounts you serve through intermediaries.

Tactical Plans

One of the biggest disconnects in the strategic planning process is making the leap from "we will achieve 25% of sales from new products within five years" to "what am I supposed to do Monday morning?" Tactical plans are the short-term activities that need to happen to keep the organization on track to achieve the long-term objectives. Each management unit should know what is expected in the current period, how it is to be achieved, the relevant time frame, and a sense of which activities have priority over others. In a performance-oriented culture, these expectations are clearly expressed at every level of the organization, and the reward structure encourages completion of the activities.

> "One thing that tends to get underplayed is that you have to live successfully within the organization … there are people who are calling the shots and you need to make sure you have access to them."
>
> Steve Pollyea

Budgeting

Budgeting is how tactical plans are made real. For most businesses, resources are limited, and money has to be allocated where it will benefit the business most. The budget process involves developing a top-down budget, a bottom-up budget, and negotiations to reconcile the two. The top-down budget is determined at the corporate level and is the organization's investment in marketing. There is an expectation of a certain return on this investment.

The bottom-up budget is developed by the marketing manager. Looking at the objectives in the marketing plan and the strategies deployed to achieve them, what are the activities that have to happen in order to be successful? For example, in Chapter 21.2, we suggested hiring a new products development manager as a tactic. This is an example of an activity used to develop the budget. You need to estimate how much it will cost to hire the new person, and what it will cost in compensation after the person is hired. The bottom-up budget is determined by specifying all of the activities, or tactical plans, and what it will cost for each activity. The sum of these activity costs is the bottom-up budget.

Usually, the bottom-up budget is higher than the top-down budget, meaning that the marketing manager estimates it will cost more to achieve the objectives than the corporate budget allows. This requires negotiation to develop a realistic budget. As a marketing manager, you need to be able to defend each budget item and to explain the consequences of cutting something from the budget. The end result may involve adjusting both budgets until they agree and, perhaps, rethinking the expected outcomes in light of the changes to the budget.

There is more to budget negotiations than simply allocating resources. In a large organization, budget represents power, and the bigger a person's budget, the more responsibility and status that person has. This means that there is often a political dimension to budget negotiations.

22.2 CONTROLLING THE PLAN

Controlling the plan involves measuring actual performance, comparing it to planned performance, and making necessary changes as required. As the goals were established when the marketing plan was developed, the issue in controlling is measurement.

Metrics

A **metric** is a quantifiable measure used to track, monitor, and to assess the success or failure of a business practice. These are the "numbers" people talk about making.

In order to be useful, a metric needs to be objective, quantifiable (it has to be a number), timely, and relevant. It is important to measure things critical to the success of the plan rather than measuring things because they are easy to measure. There is an old saying in management: "That which is measured, improves." This is because we tend to focus on things we know other people will be paying attention to. For example, if the marketing department is trying to develop new product capability, and people are required to turn in a monthly expense report, expenses will go down. However, this has very little to do with the ability to generate new products. It would be difficult but more effective to measure the number of new product ideas developed each week.

There are two things you need to know about a metric to understand it: evaluation and trend. The evaluation asks the question, "Is it good or bad?" and only has meaning when compared to a benchmark. Is a million dollar profit a good thing? Not if you were expected to generate two million dollars. The trend looks at the performance metric over time. Is it getting better or worse?

Ideally, the metric and its interpretation will be established at the time the goals are established. Creative people can always concoct a plausible excuse after the fact. There should be buy-in from stakeholders who will be affected by the plan as well as from the people who will be held accountable for achieving the objective.

Diagnostic vs. Outcome Measures

There are two possible explanations for why you might not achieve an objective. Either the strategy was flawed, or the execution was poor. Diagnostic measures and outcome measures are how we answer the questions: "Are we doing the right things?" and "Are we doing things right?" **Outcome** measures are an evaluative tool. They indicate whether or not you have achieved the objective. These metrics should be tied directly to the outcome you are trying to achieve. If the objective is to achieve 25% of sales from new products, the outcome measure would be the percentage of sales from new products. Anything 25% or higher indicates success, less than that represents failure.

Diagnostic measures indicate whether or not the plan is being executed properly. Diagnostic measures relate to the intermediate, tactical actions associated with the plan. These should only be metrics that are "actionable," meaning they suggest a course of action if they are above or below expectations. This is where contingency planning comes into play. Each diagnostic measure should highlight a critical point in the implementation of the plan. There should be contingencies in place should the result be less than expected or more than expected. This way you can minimize losses and maximize gains as the plan meets the real world.

If a tactic to achieve the new product sales objective is to hire a new product manager in the first six months of the year, the diagnostic measure might be whether or not the person was on board by July. The chain ratio method of forecasting (Chapter 21.5) is one way of identifying potential diagnostic measures.

Marketing Metrics

There are metrics to measure virtually every facet of marketing. Table 22.1 lists some commonly used marketing metrics and gives you a sense of their variety.[2] We'll take a closer look at sales, market share, and cost metrics.

Sales data is an important source of marketing metrics as sales are tied directly to financial performance. Sales volume can be either a diagnostic measure or an outcome measure. If the goal is to increase sales by 20%, then sales volume would be an outcome measure. Dollar volume relates to financial performance while unit volume relates to logistics and distribution. Sales can also be a diagnostic measure. If the goal is to increase profits by 20%, then sales is an important activity that leads to profits.

Market share measures our competitive position in the market place. Market share is the portion of the market you control while relative market share (your market share compared to that of your largest competitor) is a measure of your power in the market. Market share can be either an outcome measure or a diagnostic measure.

Cost is frequently used as a diagnostic measure. How much we are spending on a specific marketing activity has an impact on whether or not we will be able to successfully implement the plan. Comparing the actual cost of an activity to the actual cost is a common diagnostic measure. Cost should never be used as an outcome measure as it is too easy to achieve. Spending money is never a strategic goal in and of itself. Money is used as an investment to achieve some other business purpose.

Marketing Dashboard

There is a tremendous amount of information a marketing manager needs to be aware of, to absorb, and to analyze. The average enterprise company deals with 28

Table 22.1 Common Marketing Metrics

ACTIVITY	METRIC
General	Market Share Awareness Satisfaction Preference Customers Share of Voice Share of Wallet
Advertising	Impressions Reach Recall
Internet Advertising	Impressions Hits/Page Views Click-Through
Social Media	Hits/Page Views Number of Followers Media Coverage
Sales	Reach Responses Customer Retention
Distribution	Out-of-Stock Channel Relationships Product/Category Volume

Adapted from: Ofer Mintz and Imram S. Currim, "What Drives Managerial Use of Marketing and Financial Metrics and Does Metric Use Affect Performance of Marketing-Mix Activities?," *Journal of Marketing*, vol. 77, no. 2, American Marketing Association, 2013.

different marketing technology solutions.[3] As a way to focus attention quickly on areas that need attention, many marketing managers have adopted a **marketing dashboard**, or a collection of what the manager believes to be the key diagnostic and performance metrics, or key performance indicators (KPIs); organized in a way to highlight patterns of performance. The dashboard typically sits on the manager's desktop, uses graphics to make the metrics easier to follow, and is updated in real time.

Figure 22.2 is an example of a marketing dashboard from Klipfolio (klipfolio. com), a data analytics firm. This dashboard displays four key metrics. Total revenue is an outcome measure, while average revenue, sales leads progress through the sales funnel, and sources of leads are diagnostics. A quick glance at the dashboard shows a triangle (it would be red if we used color illustrations in this book) in front of total revenue, indicating that revenue at $775K is running behind last month. Looking at the diagnostic measures, leads are running a bit behind last month's pace, and most of the leads are coming from direct marketing. However, the big issue seems to be the inability to convert leads into sales as indicated by the exclamation points at the bottom of the sales funnel.

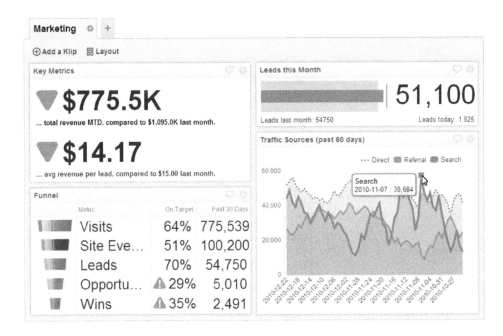

FIGURE 22.2   Marketing Dashboard, http://www.klipfolio.com/resources/dashboard-examples/marketing/current-performance. Copyright © by Klipfolio Inc. Reprinted with permission.

22.3 EVALUATING THE PLAN

At the end of the planning period, usually annually, the results of the previous year's activity are evaluated. The first question to answer is: "Did we achieve our goal?" Comparing the outcome measures to the objectives in the plan will tell you. If the outcome measure is higher than the plan, you have "made your numbers," and promotions and bonuses are in store. The celebration will continue for a short while, and then it is time to take another look at the numbers.

At second glance, the issue is not whether or not we achieved the goal, but how close to the planned outcome did we come? In this second analysis, it doesn't matter whether you were above or below the goal, it only matters by how much you missed it. A big difference either way suggests that planning and forecasting can be improved the next time around. After evaluating the outcome, it is time to dig into the diagnostic variables. Which activities were successful and which activities were not? The result of this second analysis feeds back into the situation analysis for the next iteration of the plan.

(ENDNOTES)

1. Nohria, Nitin, William Joyce, and Bruce Roberson, 2003, "What Really Works," *Harvard Business Review*, July, https://hbr.org/2003/07/what-really-works. Accessed October 5, 2015.

2. Source: Mintz, Ofer, and Imram S. Currim, 2013, "What Drives Managerial Use of Marketing and Financial Metrics and Does Metric Use Affect Performance of Marketing-Mix Activities?," *Journal of Marketing*, 77 (2), 17–40.

3. "Tomorrow's Marketer," Marketo and Forbes Luncheon, San Francisco, June 22, 2016.

MARKETING ETHICS

CH23

I n a 1970 article in the New York Times Magazine, Nobel Prize-winning economist Milton Friedman is said to have declared that the only purpose of a business is to return a profit to its shareholders. Acting in a way that is socially responsible would put a company at a competitive disadvantage.[1] This has been widely interpreted to mean that businesses are meant to make a profit by any means possible and has been the justification for every corporate scandal from the savings and loan crisis in the late '80s, to the Enron scandal at the turn of the century, to the subprime mortgage crisis leading to the Great Recession. What Milton Friedman really said was that managers of public corporations have a responsibility to conduct business in accordance with the stockholders' desires while conforming to the basic rules of society, both legal and embodied in ethical custom. Shareholders may care about how the profit was made, and they assume the business is behaving ethically. There is a growing body of research suggesting that ethical businesses may outperform their peers and have significant advantages in the market.

23.1 WHAT ARE ETHICS?

Ethics is commonly described as a set of principles prescribing a behavior code that explains what is good and right and what is bad and wrong. A typical definition of **business ethics** is the set of moral rules that govern how businesses operate, how business decisions are made, and how people are treated.[2] In this case, "moral rules" simply means the ability to determine right from wrong. Everybody knows the difference between right and wrong. Moral rules are heavily influenced by religion and culture. Laws are moral rules that are enforceable in court.

The problem is that there is no consensus on ethical principles in our diverse, pluralistic society. In addition, ethical principles are constantly shifting due to changing values, emerging technologies, and shifting political forces. Two traditional perspectives on personal ethical behavior are moral idealism and utilitarianism. Moral idealism takes the perspective that right is right and wrong is wrong. The important thing is your motive. Utilitarianism, or situational ethics, takes the perspective that the end justifies the means and whatever provides the greatest good for the greatest number of people. Business people tend to lean toward the utilitarian approach.

A more dynamic definition of ethics is that it is the process by which we clarify what constitutes human welfare and the kind of conflict necessary to promote it.[3] Rather than assuming a common understanding of right and wrong, this approach focuses on resolving differences.

The point is that there are three levels of "right" behavior: that which is right, that which is legal, and that which is profitable. Some people are able to "compartmentalize," or use different standards for different aspects of their lives. For example, a person may choose "that which is right" for personal relationships and "that which is legal" for business relationships. Unfortunately, there are always people who will choose "that which is profitable" even if they know it is wrong and against the law. We call these people criminals. You get to choose the level of rightness that works for you. We hope to make the case that choosing the highest standard is in your best interest.

Ethical Legal Framework

As implied from the previous discussion, there are two dimensions to consider when making business decisions: legal and ethical. Similar to ethical principles, legal principles are not as clear-cut as one might like. In the United States, there are multiple jurisdictions—federal, state, regional, and local—each of which has the authority to issue rules applying to their constituents. In addition, what is legal and what is illegal are constantly changing. New laws and court interpretations of old laws can change the rules overnight.

There are four stages of a business decision where an ethical evaluation might occur: goal setting, methods, motives, and consequences. With multiple stakeholders, any broad goals and objectives set by the company require a balancing of the interests of multiple constituencies. Assuming the goal is ethical, the methods used to achieve it can come under scrutiny. As the saying goes: "It's not the *what*, it's the *how*." The motives of the people making the decision can be suspect because they are somewhat hidden. Was there a personal motive behind the decision? And finally, what were the consequences of the decision? Did it achieve the goals in the manner expected? Were there unintended consequences?

The ethical legal framework is a tool to help evaluate the ethics of a decision. The assumption is that most business decisions are made privately to avoid tipping off competitors. After the decision is made, it is either announced publicly, or people can infer the decision based on the company's actions. At that point, the decision comes under public scrutiny, and this is where the ethics of the decision will be evaluated. The framework has two axes: ethical/unethical and legal/illegal (Figure 23.1).

The upper left quadrant represents issues that are both legal and ethical. A business operating in this quadrant will have a solid reputation as being an ethical player. The upper right quadrant represents issues that you consider to be ethical but are against the law. Many activists are working to bring awareness to laws that they believe are unethical in the hope that the laws will be changed. The recent Supreme Court decision striking down laws prohibiting same-sex marriage is an example of public pressure to change a law that was perceived to be unethical.

The lower left quadrant represents issues that are legal but are considered to be unethical. Businesses that operate in this area are frequently cited as examples of what is wrong with business today. Even though they do not necessarily believe that what they are doing is correct, they still do it. If there is an opportunity to make a profit, some businesses will engage in the activity because if they didn't, "somebody else would." In September 2015, Turing Pharmaceuticals acquired the rights for an off-patent drug, Daraprim. Because the market for the drug was so small, there was no economic incentive for other manufacturers to produce the drug, so Turing

FIGURE 23.1 Ethical Legal Framework (Adapted from: Verne E. Henderson, "The Ethical Side of Enterprise," *MIT Sloan Management Review*, vol. 23, no. 3, Massachusetts Institute of Technology, 1982.)

had an effective monopoly on the product and raised the price by 5,000%.[4] This is a perfectly legal practice. The decision was made in private; the uproar over the decision didn't occur until the decision came under public scrutiny.

Finally, the lower right quadrant represents issues that are illegal and unethical. However, if the activity is profitable, someone will probably do it. This is where criminals, who have no illusions about the legitimacy of what they are doing, operate. Very few businesses choose to operate in this area. However, those that do work in this area do so under the assumption that it isn't wrong unless you get caught. Take, for example, the scandal that happened when it was discovered that Volkswagen had installed software in its diesel cars to cheat on emissions tests.[5]

23.2 ETHICS IN BUSINESS

The good news is that most people tell the truth. Honesty is the norm in business, and for most businesspeople, "my word is my bond" holds true. This is what makes exchange possible. Could you imagine how complicated life would be if you needed to have a lawyer and the police with you every time you purchased a case of copier paper? However, not everyone behaves ethically all the time, so it is important to "trust, but verify."

In 1962, President Kennedy gave a speech proposing a **consumer bill of rights,** including the right to be safe, the right to be informed, the right to have choices, and the right to be heard. While these rights are not law, they have been the principle underlying legal thinking in the United States. From a global perspective, the United Nations' *Guidelines on Consumer Protection* outlines eight consumer rights: the right to the satisfaction of basic needs, the right to safety, the right to be informed, the right to choose, the right to be heard, the right to redress, the right to consumer education, and the right to a healthy environment.[6]

Good ethics is good business. A meta-analysis of 200 studies looking at environmental, social, and governance issues (ESG) in business found 88% of reviewed sources indicated companies with robust sustainability practices demonstrate better operational performance. 80% of reviewed studies showed sustainability practices have a positive impact on investment performance.[7]

Some of the ethical issues in business in general revolve around competition, company culture, and social responsibility.

Ethics of Competition

In general, the government favors things that increase competition and discourages things that limit competition or create monopolies. In addition to illegal pricing activity (Chapter 12.1), bribery and espionage are two areas where business behavior can be considered unethical.

Bribery

Bribery is the offering, giving, receiving, or soliciting of something of value for the purpose of influencing the action of an official in the discharge of his or her public or legal duties.[8] The Federal Corrupt Practices Act makes it illegal to bribe foreign officials. Domestic bribery is usually covered by laws at the state level; however, the Securities Exchange Commission (SEC) may intervene if it is apparent that a publicly traded company's success is due to undue influence rather than due to the quality of its products.

It is common business practice to give gifts and provide travel opportunities and entertainment in order to develop and maintain cordial relationships with current and potential customers. The difference between a bribe and a gift in demonstration of goodwill is if there is an expectation of a specific action either beforehand or afterward as a result of the gift. Many businesses put limits on the monetary amount of gifts they can receive from vendors as a way to minimize the possibility of undue influence because of the size of the gift.

Espionage

All businesses gather intelligence about their competitors. There is a fine line between business intelligence and espionage. **Espionage**, or spying, is the gathering of business intelligence through unethical or illegal means. According to the SCIP (Strategic and Competitive Intelligence Professionals), competitive intelligence is the process of legally and ethically gathering and analyzing information about competitors and the industries in which they operate in order to help your organization make better decisions and reach its goals. Corporate spying often implies illegal activities, such as bribing or hiring employees to divulge confidential information.[9]

For example, making use of a competitor's confidential information that has been discarded is probably unethical, and it's definitely unethical if the information was obtained illegally. Pretending to be a news reporter or a customer in order to obtain information from a competitor would also be unethical.

On the other hand, researching publicly available information such as SEC filings or patent filings is perfectly acceptable. Mystery shopping, or having people pretend to be shoppers in order to evaluate service delivery, is ethical as long as it is done in collaboration with the business and according to its ethical principles.

Corporate Culture

Corporate culture plays a significant role in business ethics. In companies where there are performance cultures, there may be a temptation to "bend the rules" in order to "make the numbers" or exceed the quarterly or annual performance targets (Chapter 22.2). In large organizations, this bending of the rules can lead to major ethical lapses. The small discrepancies at lower levels become larger and larger discrepancies as they are concentrated at higher levels of the organization.

The ethical behavior of a person in an organization is influenced by the behavior of others in the organization. If senior management is behaving unethically, there may be a perception that others in the organization are expected to act unethically. A key aspect of corporate culture is how dissent is handled. **Groupthink** is a term coined by Irving Janis (a research psychologist at Yale University and a professor emeritus at the University of California, Berkeley) to describe the flawed decisions that come out of highly insular groups. The pressure to conform can lead to self-deception, manufactured consent, and pressure to conform to group values. **Whistleblower** is a term for a person who exposes an organization's wrongdoing to the public or to the authorities. Because there is a risk of retaliation against someone who airs the company's dirty laundry, there are a variety of federal and state laws to protect and, in some cases, reward whistleblowers.

A **code of ethics,** or **code of conduct,** is a written statement of an organization's values, ethics, and standards of behavior. While many businesses have a written code of ethics, such a document only has meaning when people are rewarded (or at least not penalized) for following it. Enron Corporation, the center of a major accounting scandal that led to the eventual dissolution of the company, had a written code of ethics. In this case, the code of ethics wasn't worth the paper it was printed on.

From a management perspective, the consequences of an unethical business culture include lower employee performance, increased employee turnover, and more employee fraud. Those bothered by the unethical culture don't stay, leaving a higher concentration of unethical employees. After all, someone who is willing to act unethically *for* you could be willing to act unethically *against* you.[10]

The good news is that good ethics can be good business. In their book *Built to Last*, Jim Collins and Jerry Porras found that companies that faced a situation where they had to choose between short-term profitability and their code of ethics and chose to follow the code were significantly more profitable than other businesses in their industries.[11]

Social Responsibility

It is no longer appropriate (if it ever was) to have the goal of returning a profit to shareholders as the only consideration in running a business. Shareholders today expect businesses to generate profit in a way that ensures the long-term sustainability of the business. Social responsibility means that in addition to shareholders, companies need to consider the impact of business decisions on all stakeholders. Without customers, employees, vendors, distributors, and a stable political environment, the company will not be able to achieve its goals. Taking it one step further, for long-term profitability, companies need to consider the impact of business decisions on the physical environment and to the general public, regardless of whether or not they are currently customers.

In recognition of this trend toward social responsibility, more than 30 states have passed laws allowing the creation of benefit corporations. A benefit corporation is a for-profit organization with dual missions. In addition to making a profit, the benefit corporation is allowed to have environmental or social goals as part of the corporate charter.[12] This allows shareholders to make explicit their desire for social outcomes in addition to profit.

Environmental Stewardship

Environmental stewardship is the desire to protect or enhance the physical environment as a part of doing business. In most cases, environmental stewardship is simply good business. Making the most efficient use of resources reduces costs. In the book *Marketing 3.0*, Philip Kotler and associates propose that environmental stewardship leads to lower cost, better reputation, and more motivated employees.[13]

Some businesses seek to differentiate themselves through green marketing, or adopting environmentally friendly practices or products. Until recently, this has been a challenge, as customers have been unwilling to pay a premium for sustainable products. As a result, some companies engaged in "greenwashing," or putting more effort into promoting the idea of sustainability than in producing sustainable products. The good news is that consumer attitudes are changing. A 2014 Nielsen study found 55% of people worldwide are now willing to pay a premium for sustainable products. North America is a little behind at 42%, but this was a 7% increase from 2011.[14]

Promoting Diversity

One way businesses work for the good of the general public is by promoting diversity. Promoting diversity is the conscious act of including people of different ethnicity, culture, beliefs, etc., as employees and as customers. While the consequence may be for the general good, the practice is also good business. Today, we compete in a global marketplace. The world is diverse, and a homogeneous organization may not be competitive in the long term. This involves hiring people different from you as well as developing markets that may be foreign to you.

One of the biggest barriers to promoting diversity is "centrism." Egocentrism recognizes that we have difficulty looking at the world from another's point of view, and ethnocentrism is the tendency to evaluate other cultures based on the values of our own culture. Because of this, marketers seeking to truly promote diversity have to make a conscious effort to recognize the value offered by people who are different from us.

23.3 MARKETING ETHICS

Some of the ethical criticisms of marketing in general include a perception that marketers: (a) create artificial needs, (b) teach us to value people for what they own rather than for who they are, and (c) overpromise and underdeliver when it comes to products. Marketers might counter with: (a) we don't create artificial needs, we uncover ways for people to improve their lives; (b) it is human nature to establish one's relative position in society, and in a consumer culture, we do that through the products we consume; and (c) it is important to show products in their best light to help people see the benefit in using them. The truth probably lies in the middle. We don't create artificial needs, but we do encourage people to overconsume. We have choices in the products we offer for people to construct their social identity. We minimize the negative aspects of our products.

The point is that marketers are also customers. We play a significant role in shaping our culture, and we have to live in the culture that is created. Hopefully, we'll leave the world a better place than when we found it.

Amen.

Some of the specific ethical issues in marketing include unethical customers, privacy, unsafe products, marketing to vulnerable groups, pricing, and advertising.

Unethical Customers

Not all customers are ethical. While everyone would agree that robbing a liquor store at gunpoint is stealing, there are other forms of unethical consumption that may not be so clear-cut. For example, suppose a customer buys a dress, wears it to a party, and then returns it for a refund. Is that stealing? Or is the customer simply taking advantage of a generous customer service policy?

How about a person who buys a song from iTunes and then shares it with a bunch of friends in violation of the terms and conditions? Is that stealing? I once had a teenage friend offer to send me literally hundreds of songs he thought I might enjoy. When I asked if he had paid for any of them, he looked at me as if I was from Mars and said, "The company should pay *me* for helping them market their tunes." Because it is so easy to copy and distribute digital products over the web, many people don't bother to make the distinction between copyrighted and public domain material.

Some customers refuse to pay for a product or take so long to pay—even when they could afford to pay for the product if they chose to do so—that it creates a financial hardship for a business. This is why a customer's credit history can be important. In B2B marketing, a credit rating is an important consideration when deciding whether or not to enter into a relationship with a potential customer.

As marketers, we need to be prepared for a certain amount of unethical consumption. Customers rationalize the behavior by saying, "Everybody does it" or "It's only a small thing and it is such a big company." It all becomes part of the lifetime value of a customer. If, considering everything, the relationship is mutually beneficial, we accept some unethical consumption. If, considering everything, the customer is costing us money, we need to encourage an end to the relationship.

Unless the customer is stealing to the point where you choose to pursue criminal charges, it is important to end the relationship tactfully. People get embarrassed and defensive when they are called on behavior they know was wrong. The backlash from an angry former customer using social media to prove to the world that you were unfair is the kind of negative attention you want to avoid. If the parting is amicable, it leaves the door open for a possible mutually beneficial relationship sometime in the future.

> "One of the biggest changes, particularly for a service business, are these customer review sites like Yelp. It's good and bad. It gives the customer a voice and can warn consumers about shady companies. On the flip side, there are people who make a practice of blackmailing businesses to get free service when it's really not warranted by threatening to post negative or nasty reviews. We call these 'one-star assassins.'"
>
> **Marketing Professional**

Privacy

The tremendous amount of digital information available allows us to satisfy customer needs in ways that were not possible before. The downside of this avalanche of data is sensitivity about the privacy of the individuals to whom we are marketing. The permanence of online information and the ability to make inferences about personal characteristics and data security are of particular concern. Because digital storage is so inexpensive, information on the internet is essentially permanent.[15] Negative information never truly goes away and may surface at any time. This is especially important, as people's choices about what they choose to disclose will change over time. Pictures from a drunken revel as a teenager may surface years later as a prospective employer searches for background information about you.

The increasing availability of digital information as well as the ability to combine information from multiple sources allows marketers to make inferences about potentially sensitive information. For example, Target used data mining techniques to infer whether guests may be in the early stages of pregnancy. With this information, it was able to send coupons for baby products to new mothers in their second trimester.[16] Is this an invasion of privacy or a helpful service? Further complicating the issue is the "privacy paradox." There is a disconnect between what people say their privacy preferences are and their actual behavior. People who say political affiliation is a private matter may post their political affiliation on social media.[17]

Data security is an increasing concern in the digital world. The number of security breaches is increasing, with more than 780 incidents involving more than 85 million records in 2014.[18] The biggest concern with data security breaches is the potential for identity theft. Identity theft is the fastest-growing crime in the

United States, with more than 9.9 million victims losing $5 billion in 2014 alone.[19] However, the risk of disclosure of sensitive personal information is also of concern, as subscribers to Ashley Madison, a dating site for illicit affairs, found out when hackers posted account information of 30 million customers online.[20]

Two issues in early 2018 brought the issue of data privacy to the forefront. The first was a revelation that Cambridge Analytica, a marketing firm, had obtained private information from more than 50 million Facebook users and used the data to develop voter profiles used in the 2016 presidential campaign.[21] This caused people in the United States to recognize there were risks in allowing technology companies access to personal data. On a related note, the European Union enacted the General Data Protection Regulation (GDPR). This is a set of rules for both consumers and businesses governing how data should be handled.[22]

Mobile Data

This sensitivity over privacy has only increased with the widespread adoption of smartphones and mobile media. There were more than 180 million smartphone users in the United States in 2014.[23] People use mobile devices to read news, text, email, pay bills, make and receive phone calls, post status updates on social media, download and launch apps, and make purchases. Mobile devices are personal to the user, almost always on, and always with the user.

This facilitates unprecedented amounts of data collection. In addition to collecting all of the information described above, mobile devices provide precise information about location and time. In addition, this information is frequently shared with the manufacturer of the phone, the wireless provider, and app developers as well as third-party analytics and advertising companies.

The Federal Trade Commission (FTC) makes several recommendations for protecting consumer privacy in the mobile world. Platforms such as Apple, Google, or Microsoft should make disclosures about the information apps are accessing, provide oversight of apps, be transparent about the app review process, and offer DNT (Do Not Track) capability for mobile devices. App developers should have a privacy policy, provide real-time disclosure when accessing sensitive information, and coordinate with advertisers the information collected through the app. Advertising networks should communicate how they used data to the app developer so the developer can accurately inform users.[24]

Unsafe Products

As marketers, we have a responsibility not to sell unsafe products. However, it is impossible to make a product that is 100% safe—one that a customer would be willing to buy. A car that is 100% safe might weigh 5,000 pounds, go 10 miles an hour, and get lousy gas mileage, and even then, you could hurt yourself getting in and out of it. That means there is a trade-off between customer utility and safety for many products. This is especially true for products that are inherently dangerous, such as dynamite or cigarettes.

With that in mind, we have a responsibility to make products reasonably safe and to alert customers to the potential dangers of using our products. This is ethically sound as well as being good business. Injuries are not good for customer loyalty. The Consumer Product Safety Commission (CPSC; cpsc.gov), maintains a list of regulatory as well as voluntary product safety standards for many industries. In addition, many trade associations promote product safety standards for their particular industry. These should be a minimum starting point in developing safety standards for your products.

Product warnings should include instructions for proper use of the product and the risk of injury associated with proper use of the product. In addition, there should be warnings about common or known ways customers may misuse the product and the risk of injury through improper use of the product.

Marketing to Vulnerable Groups

In order for marketing to happen, there has to be a voluntary exchange between two people, each with something of value and a means of communication, and it has to be appropriate to deal with the other party (Chapter 1.1). The assumption is that both the marketer and the customer are playing on a level playing field. But what if the customer is incompetent? In that case, the marketer might be taking unfair advantage of the customer.

George Brenkert, professor of business ethics at Georgetown University, suggests there are five characteristics of competent customers: (1) they know they should shop around and are able to do so, (2) they are competent to determine differences in quality and the best price, (3) they are aware of their legal rights, (4) they have knowledge of the products and their characteristics, and (5) they have the resources to enter into market relations.[25] Any customer or customer group that fails to meet these five criteria should be considered vulnerable.

This definition of vulnerability covers the groups most often cited when discussing marketing to vulnerable groups (e.g., children or the elderly). It also helps identify customers who may be temporarily incompetent, such as a person grieving the death of a loved one or an accident victim.

In dealing with these groups, marketers shouldn't exploit these vulnerabilities. Rather, care should be taken to avoid exploiting these groups. At the very minimum, a marketer should work to compensate for any vulnerability, such as making the person aware of his or her legal rights or giving that person full information about the product and its characteristics. There may be a temptation to exploit these vulnerabilities for "good," such as using a fear appeal to encourage elderly people to take their medications or using television advertising to encourage children to exercise. Even if the intentions are noble, this would be unethical, as you are taking advantage of people who are the most vulnerable.

Pricing

As marketers, we are taught to charge "all the market will bear" for our products. Creating value for customers and capturing some of that value through the prices we charge are essential to a successful business. Normally, competitive forces work to keep prices in check. If our prices are too far out of line, customers will find a substitute product. However, there are situations where one party has undue power over the process and can use the advantage to capture more than his or her fair share. An example is when there is a shortage of building materials following a natural disaster, such as a hurricane; retailers who raise prices dramatically may be perceived as taking unfair advantage of the situation.

In retail, it is not uncommon for a manufacturer to pay **slotting fees** in order to gain distribution with a retailer. This fee covers the cost of adding the new product and is also a consequence of the power retailers have over manufacturers. This fee also serves to restrict customer choice to those products whose manufacturers are able to pay the slotting fee.

Advertising

As marketers, we want to show our products in their best light, and our advertising reflects this. However, false advertising or deceptive advertising is unethical. Any time you make a specific claim in your advertising—say, "nine out of ten dentists endorse our toothpaste"—you need to be able to substantiate that claim with scientific data. If you make a claim that a competitor believes is false or misleading, that competitor could file a complaint with the Federal Trade Commission (FTC), the agency responsible for enforcing truth-in-advertising laws.

Puffery is when an advertiser makes grossly exaggerated or nonspecific claims about the product. The courts have held that puffery is acceptable, as most competent consumers understand that this is simply exaggeration. Examples of puffery might include claiming, "This is the most awesome product ever to have been invented!!!" An obvious exaggeration. Or "Our brand of toothpaste is better." Better than what? A nonspecific claim.

(ENDNOTES)

1. Friedman, M. (1970, September 13). The social responsibility of business is to increase its profit. *New York Times Magazine.*

2. Retrieved from http://www.yourdictionary.com/business-ethics

3. Henderson, V. E. (1982). The ethical side of enterprise. *Sloan Management Review, 23* (3).

4. Retrieved from http://www.nytimes.com/2015/09/21/business/a-huge-overnight-increase-in-a-drugs-price-raises-protests.html?_r=0

5. Retrieved from http://www.latimes.com/business/autos/la-fi-hy-volkswagen-qa-html-20151007-htmlstory.html

6. Retrieved from http://unctad.org/en/Pages/DITC/CompetitionLaw/UN-Guidelines-on-Consumer-Protection.aspx

7. Clark, G. L., Feiner, A., & Viehs, M. (2015). *From the stockholder to the stakeholder: How sustainability can drive financial outperformance.* University of Oxford and Arabesque Partners. Retrieved from https://ssrn.com/abstract=2508281 or http://dx.doi.org/10.2139/ssrn.2508281

8. Retrieved from http://legal-dictionary.thefreedictionary.com/bribery

9. Retrieved from https://www.scip.org/CodeOfEthics.php

10. Cialdini, R. (2016). *Pre-suasion: A revolutionary way to influence and persuade.* New York: Simon & Schuster.

11. Collins, J., & Porras, J. I. (1994). *Built to last* (3rd ed.). New York: Harper Business.

12. Retrieved from http://benefitcorp.net/

13. Kotler, P., Kartajaya, H., & Setiawan, I. (2010) *Marketing 3.0: From products to customers to the human spirit.* Hoboken, NJ: John Wiley & Sons.

14. The Nielsen Company. *Nielsen Global Survey of Corporate Social Responsibility.* (Q1 2014). Retrieved from http://www.nielsen.com/us/en/insights/reports/2014/doing-well-by-doing-good.html

15. Mayer-Schoenberger, V. (2011). *Delete: The virtue of forgetting in the digital age.* Princeton NJ: Princeton University Press.

16. Retrieved from http://www.nytimes.com/2012/02/19/magazine/shopping-habits.html?pagewanted=1&_r=2&hp

17. Acquisti, A., Brandimarte, L., & Loewenstein, G. (2015). Privacy and human behavior in the age of information. *Science, 347,* 509–514.

18. Retrieved from http://www.idtheftcenter.org/Data-Breaches/the-year-of-the-data-breach-recap-2014-and-ten-years-of-data.html

19. Retrieved from https://postalinspectors.uspis.gov/investigations/mailfraud/fraudschemes/mailtheft/identitytheft.aspx

20. Retrieved from http://www.wired.com/2015/08/happened-hackers-posted-stolen-ashley-madison-data/

21. Confessore, R. (2018, April 5). Cambridge Analytica and Facebook: The scandal and the fallout so far. *New York Times.* Retrieved from https://www.nytimes.com/2018/04/04/us/politics/cambridge-analytica-scandal-fallout.html

22. Retrieved from https://eur-lex.europa.eu/legal-content/EN/LSU/?uri=uriserv:OJ.L_.2016.119.01.0001.01.ENG

23. Retrieved from http://www.comscore.com/Insights/Market-Rankings/comScore-Reports-December-2014-US-Smartphone-Subscriber-Market-Share

24. United Stated Federal Trade Commission. (2013, February). *Mobile privacy disclosures: Building trust through transparency.* FTC staff report. Retrieved from www.ftc.gov/os/2013/02/130201mobileprivacyreport.pdf

25. Brenkert, G. G. (1998). Marketing and the vulnerable. *The Ruffin Series of the Society for Business Ethics,* 7–20. Retrieved from http://philpapers.org/rec/BREMAT-2

BEGINNING YOUR PROFESSIONAL CAREER

APPENDIX

There is a difference between a job hunt and beginning a career. A job hunt is all about finding something that pays the bills. The higher the pay and the shorter the hours, the better the job. A career looks at the bigger picture. You will be holding more than one job over the course of your working life. The Bureau of Labor Statistics found that people who started their careers in 1979 held 11.7 jobs on average, most of them in the early stages of their working life.[1] With a career, each job hunt is a step on the path that will let you achieve your personal goals. While pay is important, the real attraction for any job is the opportunities it will create for you.

The key to happiness in your career is to find something you are passionate about and then figure out a way to get paid for it. The good news is that whatever your passion, you can probably find a way to get paid for it in marketing. Marketing careers cover everything from sales, to corporate marketing, to advertising and public relations, to logistics . . . and even research.

The bad news is that because marketing covers such a wide range of opportunities, telling an employer you are a marketer doesn't open many doors. Unlike other disciplines, there are no widely recognized marketing credentials comparable to the CPA (Certified Public Accountant) in accounting. There are a couple of organizations working to establish such a credential. The American Marketing Association (AMA) offers a Professional Certified Marketer (PCM®) credential, and the SMEI® (Sales & Marketing Executives International) offers a number of certificates in sales and marketing. However, these programs are in their early stages.

It is important to "speak the language" of the field you choose to enter. Each industry has its own jargon, and one way to tell an insider from an outsider is the words you use. You can pick up the language by following industry news as well as through networking.

A.1 WHAT EMPLOYERS ARE LOOKING FOR

A company only hires when it has a problem. Either the person currently employed isn't doing a very good job and needs to be replaced, or the business is growing so fast, it needs more people to keep up with the work.

Employers are looking for experienced people who can hit the ground running and be effective with minimal supervision. This is why work experience is so important in job hunting. The best evidence that you can do a job well is that you have already done that job.

A college degree represents the potential to do a job well, but it is no substitute for experience. From an employer's perspective, your grade point average isn't an indication of how smart you are; it shows that over the course of your college career you worked with 30 or so different supervisors (instructors), and the GPA is your cumulative performance rating. A strong GPA shows that you can do well in a variety of situations and under a number of different supervisors. Your academic record is important in helping land that first job to begin your career. After that, your "track record," or work experience, becomes the best evidence of your potential to be successful.

A 2010 study by the National Association of Colleges and Employers (NACE) identified 20 skills or qualities desired by employers.[2] They are: communication skills, strong work ethic, initiative, interpersonal skills (relates well to others), problem-solving skills, teamwork skills (works well with others), analytical skills, flexibility/adaptability, computer skills, detail oriented, leadership skills, technical skills, organizational skills, self-confidence, tactfulness, friendly/outgoing personality, creativity, strategic planning skills, entrepreneurial skills/risk taker, and sense of humor. In general, they are looking for a balance of "hard," and "soft" skills. Hard skills are the analytical and quantitative skills that business students expect to acquire in college. Soft skills are the interpersonal and communications skills that students expect to acquire from extracurricular activities and part-time work outside of the classroom.[3]

A survey of business students at San Francisco State University compared the top five job skills ranked by employers in the NACE study with the top five job skills ranked by 684 undergraduate business students (Table A.1).[4] While both employers and students agree that communication is the number one job skill, employers give more emphasis to the hard skills such as analytical and technical skills while students are more likely to emphasize the softer skills such as self-confidence. The point is, good soft skills help you demonstrate your competence with the hard skills.

Table A.1 Top Five Candidate Skills Ranked by Employers and Students

TOP FIVE CANDIDATE JOB SKILLS/QUALITIES			
EMPLOYER RANK ORDER		STUDENT RANK ORDER	
1	Communication skills	1	Communication skills
2	Analytical skills	2	Strong work ethic
3	Teamwork skills (works well with others)	3	Self-confidence
4	Technical skills	4	Problem-solving skills
5	Strong work ethic	5	Teamwork skills (works well with others)

A.2 JOB HUNTING TACTICS

If you think about it, a job search is a personal marketing program. You need to discover the particular needs of a potential employer and use the marketing mix to develop a need-satisfying offering that includes you as part of the solution. A job interview is a selling situation. The sales process described in Chapter 18.3 is an excellent approach to use while interviewing.

One of the sad realities for the job hunter is that an unemployed person looking for a job is not as attractive a candidate as a person working full time. The perception is that if you don't have a job, there must be something wrong with you otherwise someone else would have hired you. When I was a sales manager, every now and then an old acquaintance called to say, "Hi." Inevitably, the person had recently lost a job and was "networking." There was a tinge of desperation in the conversation. This is why people in a position to hire become defensive when they think people are looking for a job. They are constantly being contacted by people currently out of work and desperate for a job.

However, if you are a college student, you are not expected to be in a full time job. This gives you an opportunity to make connections with potential employers without seeming to be desperate. I call this "playing the college card." Here are some tactics you can use to get a head start on your career while still in school.

Preparation

The first step, and for many the hardest step, is to decide what you want to do after you graduate. College is a place to explore options, and many students may not feel that they have found their "passion" yet. That's OK. Just pick something. Choose whichever career seems most attractive to you right now. You can meet with your professors or connect with the school's career center if you need help making up your mind. Remember, odds are that you are going to change jobs more than ten times over the course of your career, so that first job isn't necessarily a life sentence.

Then, having decided on which career you want to pursue, you need to do some basic research. First, identify at least five companies that hire people for the career you want to pursue. Second, find the names of at least one person at each company who is well established in the career you are looking for. This is your starting point. You now have identified a target market for your career search.

Networking

You have probably heard the saying: "It's not *what* you know, it's *who* you know that counts." This refers to the importance of having a personal network. While you cannot afford to ignore any tactic that has a chance of landing that first job, the vast majority of placements are through personal referrals.

Networking is the process of interacting with people to exchange information and to develop contacts. Working to your advantage is the "generative" urge, where people in middle adulthood (ages 40 to 65) take an interest in giving back to society.[5] This means that people in the later stages of their careers are likely to be interested in passing along their experiences to the next generation. Having a college student asking for advice gives these people a chance to share their wisdom and also gives meaning to their success. The referral interview and focused classwork are two tactics which allow you to connect with the people on your list of companies.

You do not want to come off as looking for a job during this process. If it ever looks like you are asking for a job, the defenses go up.

Referral Interview

The referral interview is a classic job hunting technique. The goal is to set up an information interview with the people on your list. You are approaching a senior professional for career advice. You are not looking for a job, you are looking for advice.

Once you have an appointment with the person on your list, you prepare for the interview the same way you would for a job interview. At a minimum, you should know everything publicly available about the person and the company. Make sure your resume is up-to-date and have a copy with you for the interview.

When you meet with the person, treat it as an opportunity to get a better understanding of the career and industry you are considering. Let the person share what factors lead to success in the industry—specifically, ask the person to share some career highlights. It may be appropriate at some point to talk about what you can do while you are still in college to help prepare for a career. Are there classes you should be taking? What sorts of activities outside of the classroom might be helpful to launch your career? It may be appropriate to ask the person to look over your resume for advice on how to improve it. Remember, you are not asking for a job, you are asking for advice. This is an invaluable opportunity to learn what is happening from an insider's perspective.

At the end of the conversation, ask for a referral: "Now that you know a little about me, perhaps you could recommend someone else I should be speaking with." When you get a referral, ask if you can use the person's name when arranging a meeting. Keep asking; you may get several referrals from a single interview.

"It drives me absolutely bananas when I interview somebody and when I give them an opportunity to ask questions about the role they are there to interview for and they have no questions. Really? No questions? Like you've looked at our website and checked out the cool things we made for Burton and Google or MTV, and you have no questions about how that got made or how it got conceived, or how it went from idea to finished product? Nothing. 'No, I'm good.'

They don't even ask for the job or say that they're interested. It baffles my mind. And when the few times somebody says, 'I really want to work here, what's it gonna take?' I want to get up and give them a hug."

Ted Church

As you conduct more of these referral interviews, they will be easier to schedule because you will have learned a lot about what is happening in the industry and will be in a position to share this knowledge.

After the interview is over, be sure to send a handwritten thank you. A thank you is always appropriate, and in a digital world, a handwritten note really stands out. It shows you made a significant effort to say thanks.

The most challenging part is to get that first interview. Lots of people are using the referral interview technique. Because of this, the people you want to meet with may be getting many requests for interviews. This is where attending industry functions and networking events can help. Most professional associations encourage student involvement and can be a good way to make an initial contact.

It is important for you to do your homework for these interviews. You are the product, and if the product isn't good, nobody will buy. Ask good questions and really listen to the answers. The impression you make during the conversation will determine how willing the person is to make referrals for you.

Success Breeds Success

Look for people who have been successful in their careers when seeking career advice. People who have not been successful will be happy to share their experience with you, but they can't tell you what it takes to be successful. They can only tell you why they didn't succeed.

Focused Classwork

Another way to play the student card is through class projects. As a business student, you will undoubtedly be assigned projects where you are asked to look at an industry or to do some research about a company. If you already have your list of people and companies you would like to connect with, the choice is obvious. If you are working on a group project, volunteer to contact someone at the company if the group chooses your suggestion for the project. The other members of the group will be thrilled you are willing to make this effort.

Use the class project as a reason to meet with the people on your list. You are looking for information related to the project you are working on. This has two benefits. First, it gives you an opportunity to make contacts in your chosen field. Second, it means you will be doing primary research for your project. Your instructor can't help but be impressed that you actually met with the company as part of the project.

After the meeting, send a thank you. And, when the project report is completed, send the person a copy of the report along with a note acknowledging the person's contribution to the project.

If you do this for every project you have over the course of your college career, you will have the opportunity to make several contacts with people you have identified as important in your chosen field.

Using Your Network

At no time during the network-building activities, have you been asking for a job. You have been asking for advice and information. However, the people you've met with understand that someday you will graduate and will be looking for a job. By the time you are ready to graduate, you will have several people who have an interest in your career because they've contributed to your academic success.

As you get close to graduation, you can send a note or contact the people you've met explaining that you are going to graduate soon are grateful for their help in getting you to this point. This is the time to let them know you will be looking for a job. Ask them if they know of any companies with openings in your area. Notice, you still haven't asked for a job. You've asked for referrals. It may happen that you have impressed the people you met with, and one of them may have an opening. If not, they are probably aware of what is happening in the industry and may be able to point you in the right direction and possibly offer a recommendation.

A.3 DIGITAL FOOTPRINT

One of the first things any prospective employer will do is to "Google you," to see what they can find about you online—your digital footprint. This represents both an opportunity and a threat for a job seeker. The threat is that you have to assume everything you ever posted online is still out there if someone is willing to dig deep enough. There may have been photos or postings that seemed like a good idea at the time, but in retrospect, you ask yourself, "What was I thinking!" Run an internet search on your name and see what comes up. You may or may not be able to remove postings, but you should be aware of what is out there that employers will be seeing. Also, double check your privacy settings on social media to be clear about what is public.

The opportunity is that you have the ability to market yourself online. At the very minimum, you should be on LinkedIn® and connected with everyone you know. Are the people on your target list using Twitter® or keeping blogs? Follow them. Employers like LinkedIn because they can search for people with the desired profile even if the people aren't currently looking for a job. Your profile and postings are examples of the contribution you could make as an employee.

A resume and cover letter are very brief statements about what you can do. Online you can really demonstrate what you can do. Between LinkedIn, Facebook®, and YouTube™, you have unlimited space to create your online persona. Are you a good communicator? Post examples of you communicating. Are you creative? Post examples of your creativity online. Keep a blog, or comment on industry issues to show you are up-to-date with what is happening in the field. Want to get into advertising but don't have a portfolio? Go ahead and create some ads and post them online.

The point is, you don't have to wait for someone to give you the job for you to be able to do the work. Over time, the digital contributions add up and the footprint becomes bigger.

(ENDNOTES)

1. "Number of Jobs Held, Labor Market Activity, and Earnings Growth Among the Youngest Baby Boomers: Results from a Longitudinal Survey," Bureau of Labor Statistics USDL-15-0528, March 31, 2015, http://www.bls.gov/news.release/pdf/nlsoy.pdf. Accessed October 23, 2015.

2. NACE Research, "Job Outlook 2010," National Association of Colleges and Employers, November 2009.

3. Robertson, Bruce, "SF State College of Business Student Job Skills Study," September 13, 2010. For a copy email robertbc@sfsu.edu.

4. Robertson, Bruce, "SF State College of Business Student Job Skills Study," September 13, 2010. For a copy email robertbc@sfsu.edu.

5. http://www.simplypsychology.org/Erik-Erikson.html. Accessed October 26, 2015.

INDEX OF GLOSSARY TERMS

TERM	DEFINITION	FIRST APPEARANCE	ADDITIONAL APPEARANCES
A/B Testing	A common approach used for optimization. With a/b testing, you post at least two versions of your marketing message and let the audience tell you which is best.	19.1	
Actual Product	The form a product takes when a customer buys it.	7.1	
Ad Campaigns		**17.2**	
Ad Clutter	Refers to the ever increasing number of ads competing for our attention.	17.1	
Advertising	Paid messages placed in any of the mass media by an identified sponsor in order to persuade members of a particular target audience about products or ideas.	17.1	
Advertising Agencies	Intermediaries who provide advertising services to other businesses.	17.1	
Advertising Media		**17.3**	
Advertising Wearout	A principle recognizing an ad will lose its effectiveness after a number of exposures.	17.2	
Advertising Campaigns	A group of advertisements or related promotional activities conducted over a specified period of time in order to achieve a desired outcome.	17.2	
Advocacy Advertising	Advertising intended to communicate a viewpoint about a controversial issue.	17.1	
AIDA Model	The template for persuasive communication in four stages: attention, inderest, desire, action.	16.2	

TERM	DEFINITION	FIRST APPEARANCE	ADDITIONAL APPEARANCES
Association	A service marketing strategy of pairing an intangible product with something known or tangible the customer likes.	10.2	
Atmospherics	The lights, colors, noise, events, temperature and other sensory stimulation used to attract attention, to generate excitement, and to create a mood for a store.	2.3	15.5
Attitude	A learned predisposition to respond to an object or to a class of objects in a consistently favorable or unfavorable way	2.3	
Attribute	Features or qualities that are an inherent part of the whole.	1.1	2.2, 7.1
Augmented Product	Also Extended Product. The actual product enhanced by other elements of the marketing mix.	7.1	
Automated Marketing		**19.6**	
Awareness Set	The pool of known alternatives from which a consumer will make a purchase.	2.2	
B2B	Business to Business	3.2	
B2C	Business to Consumer	3.2	
Bait and Switch	A pricing tactic where one product is advertised at a very low price with the intention of switching customers to a different, higher priced product.	12.1	
Bases for Segmentation		**5.2**	
Basic Communication Model		**16.2**	
Benefit	The utility a customer receives from a product.	1.1	5.2, 7.1
Biased	An inclination that inhibits a person from making an impartial decision. Not to be confused with an unfair prejudice, another meaning for the term.	2.2	
Big Data and Marketing Analytics		**4.3**	
Brand	A name, term, design, symbol, or any other feature that identifies one sellere's good or service from those of other sellers.	9.1	
Brand Competition	Direct compteition between brands in the same product category.	19.2	

TERM	DEFINITION	FIRST APPEARANCE	ADDITIONAL APPEARANCES
Cannibalization	Lost sales of an existing product due to the introduction of a new product.	8.4	9.4
Captive Pricing	A pricing strategy for when two products have to be used in conjunction with each other. One product is priced low, while the other product, usually something that has to be purchased frequently, is priced high.	12.3	
Causal Research	Research conducted to determine if one thing causes another.	4.4	
Channel	Also Communication Channel. A medium for transmitting information.	16.2	
Channel Captain	A member of a channel of distribution that coordinates the activities of the rest of the channel.	13.6	
Channel Conflict	Conflict that occurs when one member of a channel of distrribution perceives another member of the channel is keeping it from achieving its goals.	13.6	
Channel Flows		**13.2**	
Channel Flows	The set of functions associated with moving the product from producer to consumer.	13.2	
Channel Relationships		**13.6**	
Channel Richness	The number of different cues that can be encoded in a channel of communication.	16.2	
Channel Strategy		**13.4**	
Channel Structure		**13.5**	
Characteristics of Business Markets		**3.2**	
Characteristics of Services		**10.2**	
Classifying Products		**8.3**	
Classifying Retailers		**15.3**	
Click-Through Rate	A measure of online advertising effectiveness. The percentage of people exposed to an online ad that clicked on it.	17.2	
Code of Ethics	Also Code of Conduct. A written statement of an organization's values, ethics, and standards of behavior.	22.2	

TERM	DEFINITION	FIRST APPEARANCE	ADDITIONAL APPEARANCES
Cognitive Dissonance	Also Buyer's Remorse. The psychological process of reconciling the reality with imagined alternatives after making a major purchase. Having decided on one alternative, the alteratives not chosen become salient.	2.2	
Cognitive Miserliness	We expend the least amount of mental effort in solving problems. The result is the first acceptable solution rather than the best solution.	2.2	
Cohort Marketing	A market segmentation strategy based on generational cohorts.	5.2	
Collaterals	Materials introduced later in an advertising campaing to support the message.	17.2	
Commission	A payment made to a salesperson according to a fixed formula, usually as a percentage of sales.	18.2	
Comparative Advertising	Advertising that seeks to generate interest in a particular brand from among competing products.	17.1	
Competition-Based Pricing		**12.5**	
Complementary Products	A product whose use is related to the use of an associated product.	11.2	
Consideration Set	The alternatives evaluated by a consumer when making a purchase.	2.2	
Consultative Selling	Also Adaptive Selling, Need Satisfaction Selling. A sales approach where the salesperson acts as an expert consultant, working with the customer to develop the best solution to the customer's problem, even if the best solution doesn't involve the salesperson's product.	18.1	
Consumer	A person who purchases a product for personal use.	2.1	
Consumer Bill of Rights	Four principles underlying consumer regulation in the United States: the right to be safe, the right to be informed, the right to have choices, and the right to be heard.	22.2	

TERM	DEFINITION	FIRST APPEARANCE	ADDITIONAL APPEARANCES
Consumer Buying Process		**2.2**	
Consumer Buying Process	A five-stage process people use when making purchase decisions. The stages are: (1) Problem recognition, (2) Identify alternatives, (3) Evaluate alternatives, (4) Decision, (5) Post-purchase behavior.	2.2	
Consumer Goods	Products that will be used by the purchaser in their present form.	8.3	
Consumer Packaged Goods	Products that are consumed regularly, get used up, and need to be replaced frequently.	8.1	9.2
Continuous Innovation	Small, incremental changes to an existing product.	7.2	
Continuous Schedule	An advertising schedule that runs ads continuously over the course of a campaign.	17.2	
Content Marketing		**18.5**	
Content Marketing	A strategic marketing approach focused on creating and distributing valuable, relevant, and consistent content to attract and retain a clearly defined audience and, ultimately, to drive profitable customer action.	18.5	
Controlling the Plan		**21.2**	
Convenience Products		**8.3**	
Convenience Sample	[i] http://contentmarketing institute.com/what-is-content-marketing/. Accessed September 23, 2015.	4.4	
Conversion	The point at which the subject of a marketing message performs the desired action.	19.2	
Co-operative Chains		**15.3**	
Core Benefit	The basic need a product satisfies for a customer.	7.1	
Cost	The combination of fixed and variable expenses.	11.3	
Cost-Based Pricing		**12.4**	
Cost-Plus Pricing	A pricing strategy where the profit margin is negotiated when the final cost of the product is not known.	12.4	
CPM	Cost per thousand impressions.	17.2	

331

TERM	DEFINITION	FIRST APPEARANCE	ADDITIONAL APPEARANCES
Development Gap	The challenge of a new product making the transition from early users to a mass market.	8.1	
Diagnostic Measures	Metrics used to determine whether or not a plan is being executed properly.	21.2	
Diffusion of Innovations		**7.5**	
Diffusion of Innovations	A theory that looks at how large populations over time in five stages. The stages are: innovators, early adopters, early majority, late majority, and laggards.	7.5	
Digital Footprint		**A.3**	
Digital Marketing		**19.1**	
Digital Marketing	Any technology-mediated marketing activity. This includes marketing using digital channels of communication such as social media, internet, and mobile devices; e-commerce; as well as computer-assisted marketing activity such as automated marketing, programmatic advertising, and marketing analytics		
Direct Channel	A marketing channel consisting of a producer and a consumer.	13.5	
Direct Marketing	A direct selling approach where customers are exposed to products through an impersonal medium such as an email, a catalog, or a television show, and then purchase the merchandise online, by telephone, or by mail.	15.4	
Direct Selling	Selling directly to the customer through an in-person explanation or demonstration, frequently at the customer's home or place of business.	15.4	
Discontinuous Innovation	A radically different new product.	7.2	
Discretionary Income	Money left over after taxes and necessities have been paid, available for luxuries or savings.	19.2	
Disposable Income	Money left over after taxes have been paid and available for necessities such as rent, utilities, medicine, and food.	19.2	

TERM	DEFINITION	FIRST APPEARANCE	ADDITIONAL APPEARANCES
Diversification Strategy	An approach to increasing sales that involves selling new products to new customers.	20.3	
Documentation	A service marketing strategy using evidence of past performance or third party certification as an assurance of quality.	10.2	
Dynamic Pricing	Also Yield Management Pricing. A highly flexible pricing structure that fluctuates depending on various demand factors in an attempt to maximize revenue from available capacity.	10.2	12.3, 12.6
Dynamically Continuous Innovation	A significant modification of an existing product. May require educating consumers about the new product.	7.2	
Elastic Price	High sensitivity to price changes. A small change in price leads to a larger change in quantity demanded.	11.2	
Environmental Scanning		**19.2**	
Espionage	Also Spying. The gathering of business intelligence through unethical or illegal means.	22.2	
E-tailing	The part of e-commerce that involves selling goods to consumers over the internet.	15.4	
Ethics in Business		**22.2**	
Evaluating the Plan		**21.3**	
Every Day Low Pricing (EDLP)	A retail pricing tactic where prices are fixed and do not go on sale.	12.6	
Evolution of Retailing		**15.2**	
Exchange	The giving or taking of one thing for another.	1.1	
Exclusive Distribution	A distribution strategy where a producer limits distribution to a single outlet in a market area.	13.4	
Experiential Attributes	Characteristics of a product a customer an only evaluate after consuming the product.	10.4	

333

TERM	DEFINITION	FIRST APPEARANCE	ADDITIONAL APPEARANCES
Experiment	A test to determine cause and effect. A formal experiment requires a theoretical framework, a dependent variable, an independent variable, a control group, and a probability sample.	4.4	
Exploratory Research	Research conducted to clarify the research question when the alternatives are not clear.	4.4	
Exposures	The number of times each member of a target audience is exposed to an ad.	17.2	
Express Warranty	A clear statement (usually in writing) that describes the minimum standard of performance for a product and what the manufacturer will do if the product fails to meet the standard.	9.6	
Extensive Problem Solving	Making purchase decisions with significant cognitive effort. May involve time and effort at each stage of the consumer buying process.	2.2	
External Micro-Environment		**19.3**	
External Search	Effort is made to acquire information not readily available in memory.	2.2	
Factors That Influence Buying		**2.3**	
Fad	A product with a very short life cycle.	8.2	
Familiarity Effect	People develop a preference for things that are familiar to them.	2.3	
Family Branding	Also Umbrella Branding. Using a single brand to cover a range or related products.	9.4	
Family Life Cycle	A market segmentation strategy based on family living situation such as marital status and children. The family living situation will change over time as people age and children leave the nest.	5.2	
Fashion	An accepted and popular style.	8.2	
Fashions and Fads		**8.2**	
Feature	An attribute used to distinguish one product from another.	1.1	7.1

335

TERM	DEFINITION	FIRST APPEARANCE	ADDITIONAL APPEARANCES
Heuristic	Mental shortcuts, or rules of thumb, that reduce the cognitive effort needed to make a decision.	2.2	
Hierarchy of Goals		**20.2**	
High-Low Pricing	A retail pricing tactic where overall prices are high, and many items are put on sale.	12.6	
High-Pressure Selling	A sales approach where the salesperson attempts to control the sales interaction and pressures the customer to make an immediate purchase.	18.1	
Horizontal Conflict	Channel conflict that occurs among members at the same level of a channel of distribution.	13.6	
Horizontal Price Fixing	An agreement between competitors in the same industry to fix prices.	12.1	
How to Create a Brand		**9.2**	
How to Establish a Market Position		**6.2**	
How to Protect a Brand		**9.3**	
Hypermarket	A gigantic retail concept including a discout store, supermarket, and warehouse under one roof.	15.2	
Identity Group	People used to define a person's sense of identity. Identity groups can be membership groups, aspirational groups, or dissociative groups.	2.3	
Implementing the Plan		**21.1**	
Implied Warranty	The assumption that a product will perform as represented. Implied warranties are binding on any product unless specifically limited in a written warranty.	9.6	
Indirect Channel	A marketing channel consisting of a producer, a consumer, and one or more intermediaries.	13.5	
Industrial Customers	Businesses that buy things in order to produce finished goods and components for other businesses to use.	3.1	

TERM	DEFINITION	FIRST APPEARANCE	ADDITIONAL APPEARANCES
Involvement	Also Ego Involvement. The degree to which an individual's value system is engaged while malking a purchase.	2.2	
Job Hunting Tactics		**A.2**	
Label	Information attached to or on a product for the purpose of naming it and describing its use, its dangers, its ingredients, its manufacturer, etc.	9.5	
Legal Issues in Pricing		**12.1**	
Levels of the Product	A conceptual tool that considers a product in three levels: the core product, the actual product, and the augmented product.	7.1	
Lifetime Value of a Customer	The anticipated profit from a long-term customer relationship.	1.1	
Limited Problem Solving	Making purchase decisions with minimal cognitive effort. May skip stages of the consumer buying process.	2.2	
Limited Service Wholesaler	A wholesaler that provides backup inventory and may provide other services as determined by the needs of the marketing channel.	14.3	
Limited Warranty	A warranty that specifically excludes things that will be covered by the warranty.	9.6	
Line Extension	Adding an additional item to an existing product line.	9.4	
Logistics	The part of distribution that deals with the flow of physical goods an related information through the value chain.	14.1	
Logistics Functions		**14.2**	
Loss Leader	A retail pricing tactic where a frequently purchased item is offered at a very low price, sometimes below cost, in order to generate traffic to the store.	12.6	
Make-Goods	Free ad space or air time to compensate an advertisor for lower than expected audiences and missed or incorrect ads.	17.2	
Managing Services		**10.3**	
Market	All of the potential customers for a product; potential demand.	1.1	

338

TERM	DEFINITION	FIRST APPEARANCE	ADDITIONAL APPEARANCES
Market Basket Analysis	Also Affinity Analysis. A data mining technique to identify products likely to be purchased together.	4.2	
Market Development Strategy	An approach to increasing sales that involves finding new customers for existing products.	20.3	
Market Research	The systematic gathering, recording, and analyzing of data with respect to a specific customer group in a specific geographic area.	4.4	
Market Research Process		**4.4**	
Market Segment	A group of potential customers similar to each other and different from others with respect to the product, reachable, and economically viable.	5.1	
Market Share	The portion of a market captured by a single entity, usually expressed as a percentage.	20.5	21.2
Marketing	The activity, set of institutions, and processes for creating, communicating, and exchanging offerings that have value for customers, clients, and society at large	1.1	
Marketing Analytics	The practice of measuring, managing and analyzing marketing performance to maximize its effectiveness.	4.3	
Marketing Automation	Software that emphasizes marketing-related activities such as lead generation, segmentation, lead nurturing, lead scoring, relationship marketing, customer retention, and return on marketing investment.	18.5	
Marketing Channel	Also Channel of Distribution. All of the organizations and activities associated with moving the finished product from producer to consumer.	13.1	
Marketing Channels and the Value Chain		**13.1**	
Marketing Dashboard	A collection of key diagniostic and performance metrics organized in a way to highlight performance and monitored in real time.	4.2	21.2

TERM	DEFINITION	FIRST APPEARANCE	ADDITIONAL APPEARANCES
Marketing Ethics		**23.3**	
Marketing Information System		**4.2**	
Marketing Information System	A three-resource system to support marketing decision making. The three resources are information from within and without the organization, technology to manage the information, and people using the information to make decisions.	4.2	
Marketing Myopia		**19.1**	
Media Relations	Activities involved in working with the media to generate publicity for a product, service, or organization.	17.4	
Merchandise Mix	The breadth and length of the product lines carried by a retailer.	15.3	
Merchant Wholesalers	Wholesalers that take title to goods and re-sell them to retailers or to other businesses.	14.3	
Metric	A quantifiable measure used to track, monitor, and to assess the success or failure of a business practice.	21.2	
Milking a Product	A decline-stage strategy where no effort is made to stimulate demand for a product beyond residual sales.	8.1	
Mission	A formal statement that describes the overall purpose of the organization, and identifies its customers, products, processes, and values.	20.2	
Modified Rebuy	A modification of the reorder of a previous business purchase.	3.3	
Multibrand Strategy	Creating multiple individual brands in the same product category.	9.4	
Multi-Level Marketing	A direct selling approach where in addition to making presentations to customers, the salesperson recruits others to serve as distributors.	15.4	
NAICS	North American Industry Classification System, a system used to organize statistical information by industry group.	3.1	

340

TERM	DEFINITION	FIRST APPEARANCE	ADDITIONAL APPEARANCES
Nature of Demand		**11.2**	
Need	The difference between an actual state and a desired state. A perceived lack of something. In practice, the terms, "need" and "want" are used interchangeably.	1.1	2.1
Need for Innovation		**7.2**	
Networking	The process of interacting with people to exchange information and to develop contacts.	A.3	
New Product Adoption		**7.4**	
New Product Adoption Process	The six stages consumers go through when incorporating a new product into their purchase patterns. The stages are: awareness, interest, evaluation, trial, adoption, and confirmation.	7.4	
New Product Development		**7.3**	
New Product Development Process	A seven-step process for developing new products. Steps include: new product strategy, idea generation, screening and evaluation, business analysis, technical development, market testing, and commercialization.	7.3	
New Product Pricing		**12.2**	
New Task Buying	Also New Buy. A first-time business purchase, it may involve extensive problem solving.	3.3	
Non-Store Retailing		**15.4**	
Not-for-Profit Marketing		**10.5**	
Not-for-Profit Organization	Also Non-Profit. An organization created to provide a public or mutual benefit other than the pursuit or accumulation of profits for owners or investors.	10.5	
Objectives	Also Goals. Long-term accomplishments the organization wants to achieve.	20.2	
Omni-Channel Marketing		**19.2**	
Omni-Channel marketing	Creating a seamless customer experience regardless of which channel or device a customer uses to interact with the brand.	13.5	15.4, 19.2
Opinion Leaders	Those we look to for cues or advice.	2.3	

341

TERM	DEFINITION	FIRST APPEARANCE	ADDITIONAL APPEARANCES
Optimization	A process that involves using customer feedback to make continuous incremental improvements to improve the effectiveness of your marketing activity	19.1	
Organic Search	The unpaid results of an online search.	19.4	
Outcome Measures	Metrics used to indicate whether or not an objective has been met.	21.2	
Outsourcing	An arrangement where another company provides goods or services previously created in-house.	3.3	
Package	The container used to protect, promote, transport, and/or identify a product.	9.5	
Packaging		**9.5**	
Paid Search	A form of search engine marketing that involves creating clickable ads and paying to have them displayed in the sponsored listings when a person searches for a specific term.		
Party Selling	A direct selling approach where a host invites a group of friends to a social gathering for a product demonstration.	15.4	
Pay-Per-Click	An online search advertising practice where an advertiser is only charged for an ad if the customer clicks on it.	17.3	
Penetration Pricing	A new product pricing strategy that sets initial prices low to gain market share and discourage competitors from entering the market.	8.1	12.2
Penetration Strategy	An approach to increasing sales that involves selling more existing products to existing customers.	20.3	
Perceived Risk	A customer's perception of what is at stake when making a purchase decision.	2.1	2.2
Perceptual Map	A visual tool that graphically displays customer perceptions of the relative position of competitors based on key attributes of a product.	6.2	

TERM	DEFINITION	FIRST APPEARANCE	ADDITIONAL APPEARANCES
Price Discrimination	The practice of charging different customers different prices for the same product.	12.1	
Price Elasticity	The degree to which demand is influenced by changes in price.	11.2	
Price Lining	Offering multiple products at different price points in the same product category.	9.4	12.3
Price Rationing	A strategy to maximize the efficiency of a service provider by using price to encourage customers to choose the level of service they desire.	10.2	
Price Signalling	A price setting mechanism used in highly concentrated industries where one company will announce a price change effective at a future date.	11.2	12.1
Pricing Framework		**11.5**	
Primary Data	Information collected by the researcher.	4.4	
Primary Demand	First-time buyers for a new product category.	8.1	17.1
Probability Sample	A sample where every member of the population has a known chance of being included.	4.4	
Product	A bundle of tangible abnd intangible attributes that provide value to customers in exchange for money (or something else of value).	7.1	
Product Competition	Industry-level competition including indirect competition from alternative products in the same industry.	19.2	
Product Development Strategy	An approach to increasing sales that involves introducing new products to existing customers.	20.3	
Product Life Cycle		**8.1**	
Product Life Cycle	A theory that assumes product categories have a limited life and go through four stages of development: introductory, growth, maturity, and decline.	8.1	
Product Line	A group of items that have some characteristics, customers, or uses in common.	8.4	

| --- | --- | --- | --- |
Product Line Length	Also Product Line Depth. The number of individual items in a product line.	8.4	
Product Mix		**8.4**	
Product Mix	All of the products an organization offers for sale.	8.4	
Product Mix Width	Also Product Mix Breadth. The number of different lines in an organization's product mix.	8.4	
Product Placement	Also Embedded Advertising. The practice of using name brand products as props in entertainment vehicles such as film or television.	17.6	
Product Quality		**8.5**	
Profit	Revenue minus costs.	11.3	
Promotion	Also Marketing Communication. All of the communication to support the marketing program.	16.1	
Promotional Mix		**16.3**	
Promotional Mix	The tools marketers use to communicate with customers: advertising, personal selling, public relations, and sales promotion.	16.3	
Prospecting	The process of identifying and qualifying potential customers.	18.3	
Psuedo-research	Information collected to support a decision that has already been made.	4.1	
Psychographic Segmentation	A market segmentation strategy based on personality, lifestyle, attitudes, or values.	5.2	
Public Relations		**17.4**	
Public Relations	A strategic communication process that builds mutually beneficial relationships between organizations and their publics.	17.4	
Publicity	Any activity that results in unpaid mass communication.	17.4	
Puffery	Making an exaggerated or non-specific claim about a product in advertising.	22.3	
Pull Strategy	Communicating directly with the customer to generate demand for a product.	16.3	

TERM	DEFINITION	FIRST APPEARANCE	ADDITIONAL APPEARANCES
Pulsing	An advertising schedule where ads are run continuously over the course of a campaign, but the frequency of the ads will vary over time.	17.2	
Push Strategy	Working with members of the channel of distribtion make the product available to the customer.	16.3	
Quasi-Experiment	An experiment that lacks one of more of the conditions for a formal experiment.	4.4	
Reach	The percentage of the target audience covered by an advertising vehicle.	17.2	
Recall	A measure of advertising effectiveness where members of the target audience are contacted after an ad has run and asked if they remember seeing the advertisement.	17.2	
Reference Group	An actual or imaginary individual or group that has a significant effect on a person's evaluations, aspiriations, and behavior.	2.3	
Reference Pricing	A pricing tactic where a retailer sets the actual price below a competitor's price or a manufacturer's suggested price.	12.1	
Relationship Marketing	A longer-term perspective where each individual transaction is consdered in the context of a relationship between the buyer and seller.	1.1	
Relative Market Share	The ratio of a company's market share compared to that of its largest competitor.	20.5	
Repositioning		**6.3**	
Resellers	Businesses that buy things in order to resell them at a profit.	3.1	
Retail Life Cycle	A theory that suggests retail concepts go through a life cycle similar to the product life cycle with four stages: introductory (early growth), growth (accelerated growth), maturity and decline.	15.2	
Retail Positioning		**15.5**	

Retail Price Tactics		**12.6**	
Retailing	The process of selling goods and services to individuals or households for their personal use.	15.1	
Retargeting	An internet advertising strategy that tracks peoples' internet activity and targets them for ad based on prior online activity.	19.4	
Revenue	The amount of money you take in.	11.3	
Risk Aversion Principle	People weigh the negative consequences of a decision more heavily than the positive consequences.	2.3	
Sales Force Automation (SFA)	Software that automates such activities as inventory control, sales processing, tracking of customer interactions, sales forecasts, and performance monitoring.	18.5	
Sales Forecasting		**20.5**	
Sales Management		**18.4**	
Sales Process	A systematic approach to selling involving six stages: prospecting, pre-approach, presentation, close, and follow-up.	18.3	
Sales Promotion		**17.6**	
Sales Promotion	Short-term marketing programs to stimulate trial, increase demand, or imprive product availability.	17.6	
Salesforce Survey Forecast	A forecasting technique that involves asking salespeople to estimate future sales.	20.5	
Scrambled Merchandising	A retail strategy where the merchandise mix includes products unrelated to the retailer's primary lines.	15.3	
Search Attributes	Characteristics of a product a customer can evaluate before making a purchase.	10.4	
Search Engine Marketing		19.4	
Search Engine Optimization (SEO)	Designing a website so that the site will appear toward the top of the unpaid or "organic" results to an online query.	17.3	
Secondary Data	Information that already exists.	4.4	

347

INDEX: INDEX OF GLOSSARY TERMS

TERM	DEFINITION	FIRST APPEARANCE	ADDITIONAL APPEARANCES
Second-mover strategy	A market entry strategy that waits until a new product has been proven to be successful before entering the market.	8.1	
Secret Shopper	An agent trained to understand service standards who, unknown to the staff, poses as a customer in order to evaluate service quality.	10.4	
Selective Attention	Filtering irrelevant information in order to focus on what is important.	2.3	
Selective Distribution	A distribution strategy where a producer limits distribution to a small number of outlets in a market area.	13.4	
Selective Interpretation	Also Confirmation Bias. The tendency to interpret new information in a way that confirms existing beliefs.	2.3	
Selective Retention	The tendency to only remember things consistent with existing beliefs.	2.3	
Selling as a Career		**18.2**	
Service	A product that consists primarily of intangible attributes.	10.1	
Service Quality		**10.4**	
Shopping Products	Products consumers are willing to spend significant time and effort in order to purchase.	8.3	
Shotgun Selling	A sales approach that involves contacting as many people as possible in the hope that some will want to buy the product.	18.1	
Situation Analysis	The Study of past and present data to identify trends, forces, and conditions with the potential to influence the performance of the business and the choice of appropriate strategies.	20.3	
Skimming	A new product pricing strategy that sets initial prices high and gradually lowers them as competition intensifies.	8.1	12.2

349

INDEX: INDEX OF GLOSSARY TERMS

TERM	DEFINITION	FIRST APPEARANCE	ADDITIONAL APPEARANCES
Standard Markup Pricing	A pricing strategy that considers the total cost of a product as well as a desired profit margin. Usually expressed as a percentage markup over cost of goods sold.	12.4	
Stereotyping	Assigning a characteristic to a group based on race, nationality, etc., that has been perpetuated in a society.	5.2	
Store Layout	The interior arrangement or aisles, shelves, and merchandise groupings throughout a store.	15.5	
Straight Rebuy	A reorder of a previous business purchase with no modifications.	3.3	
Strategic Planning	The process of determining what an organization is, who it serves, what it does, and why it does what it does, with a focus on the future.	20.1	
Strategic Planning		**20.1**	
Strategy	A broad initiative or action undertaken to help achieve an organization's objectives.	20.2	20.3
Strict Liability	Legal responsibility for damages or injury, even if the seller was not negligent or at fault.	9.6	
Style	A distinctive mode of presentation or performance.	8.2	
Subculture	A group of individuals within a larger cultural setting that shares unique values, ideas, and attitudes.	2.3	
Substitute Products	Two products that can be used for the same purpose.	11.2	
Successful Person	Someone who has read Marketing Fundamentals for Future Professionals.		
Supply Network	All of the organizations and activities associated with moving raw materials and components from their point of origin to the producer.	13.1	
SWOT Analysis	Also TOWS. An approach to evaluating internal and external factors in terms of whether they are positive or negative.	20.3	

TERM	DEFINITION	FIRST APPEARANCE	ADDITIONAL APPEARANCES
Transaction	An exchange between people. A transaction requires five conditions to be met: (1) Two or more parties, (2) Each side has something of value to offer, (3) A means of communication, (4) Voluntary participation, (5) It must be appropriate to deal with the other party.	1.1	
Trial Pricing	A new product pricing tactic where a temporary low introductory price is used to encourage customers to try the product.	12.2	
Trigger	An external stimulus that causes an individual to realize there is an unmet need.	2.2	
Uniform Commercial Code (UCC)	A series of recommendations for states to consider as they develop their business regulations.	19.2	
Unique Selling Proposition	An advertising appeal which focuses on a uniquely differentiating characteristic of a product that is important to customers and a strength when compared to competing products.	17.2	
Unsought Products	Products a customer either doesn't know about, or knows about and prefers not to consider.	8.3	
Using Market Research		**4.5**	
Utility	The usefulness or benefit the customer receives from using the product. There are many types of utility including form, place, time, possession, information, and image utility.	1.1	
Value	A function of the benefits received from using a product less the cost of acquiring the product.	1.1	11.1
Value Chain	All of the activities involved with taking raw material and turning it into a finished product in the hands of the customer.	13.1	
Variability	A characteristic of a service recognizing the lack of consistency when different people perform a service.	10.2	

353

INDEX: INDEX OF GLOSSARY TERMS

TERM	DEFINITION	FIRST APPEARANCE	ADDITIONAL APPEARANCES
What Is a Brand?		9.1	
What Is a Business Customer?		3.1	
What Is a Customer?		2.1	
What Is a Decision?		4.1	
What Is Digital Marketing?		19.1	
What Is Environmental Scanning?		20.2	
What Is a Price?		11.1	
What Is a Product?		7.1	
What Is a Segment?		5.1	
What Is a Service?		10.1	
What Is Advertising?		17.1	
What Is Logistics?		14.1	
What Is Marketing?		1.1	
What Is Promotion?		16.1	
What Is Retailing?		15.1	
Wheel of Retailing	A hypothesis that proposes new retail operations start out at the low end of the price spectrum and gradually move upscale.	15.2	
Whistleblower	A person who exposes an organization's wrongdoing to the public or to the authorities.	22.2	
Wholesalers	Firms that handle the flow of goods from the producer to the retailer.	14.3	
Wholesalers		14.3	
Why Is Positioning Important?		6.1	
Yield Management Pricing	Also Dynamic Pricing. A highly flexible pricing structure that fluctuates depending on various demand factors in an attempt to maximize revenue from available capacity.	12.3	10.2

CPSIA information can be obtained
at www.ICGtesting.com
Printed in the USA
FSHW022053271221
87214FS